PLAY BETTER GOLF

PLAY BETTER GOLF

An illustrated guide to lower scores

by JACK NICKLAUS

with Ken Bowden
Illustrated by Jim McQueen

PLAY BETTER GOLF: The Swing From A-Z
    Copyright © 1980 by Jack Nicklaus
PLAY BETTER GOLF, Volume II: The Short Game and Scoring
    Copyright © 1981 by Jack Nicklaus
PLAY BETTER GOLF, Volume III: Short Cuts to Lower Scores
    Copyright © 1983 by Jack Nicklaus

Published in 1988 by
Galahad Books, a division of LDAP, Inc.
166 Fifth Avenue
New York, NY 10010

By arrangement with Pocket Books, a division of Simon &
Schuster, Inc.

Library of Congress Catalog Card Number: 88-80332
ISBN: 0-88365-725-2

Printed in the United States of America

CONTENTS

PART ONE

THE SWING FROM A-Z

Introduction

Will this book *really* help you play better golf?

Well, to improve at this marvelous but maddening game you must first know what you are doing wrong and then how to make it right. Unless you've got enough time and energy to work things out purely by trial and error, that requires information. The best way to get that information is from a skilled teacher in one-on-one lessons—as I was fortunate to be able to do as a youngster. If that's impractical or unappealing, the next best way is via the printed page—especially when each piece of information is self-contained, to the point and well illustrated, as I hope we've achieved here.

Within these pages I've tried to present all I know about the tee-to-green golf swing as clearly, crisply and logically as possible. That's the most exciting part of golf, and the most demanding. Improving at it even a little bit will give you great inner satisfaction, as well as lower scores. (That's why I'm still in the game.) In the following sections of this book we will deal in similar style and scope with the art of scoring, which includes the short game, and then with faults, cures and trouble shots.

One word of warning. If you choose to read the book first time around from cover to cover, you'll quickly realize that it contains a large amount of information. Don't try to put everything into effect at once, or even to absorb it all at one reading. Be selective in relation to your own present golfing capabilities and problems, and try always to work on one thing at a time, preferably in a properly ordered sequence. Remember that improving a golf swing or mastering a particular type of shot always takes time and patience, as well as mental know-how and physical effort.

Hopefully, you'll also find the book easy to use for quick refreshers and reminders on specific points, as well as for self-correction.

Finally, a word of appreciation. All the articles herein were originally created for distribution to newspapers worldwide by King Features Syndicate of New York, and I would like to thank my friends at King for their fine efforts in that direction.

Jack Nicklaus

CHAPTER ONE

Some Fundamentals

1

Thinking Your Way to a Better Game

Learn and Stick to Fundamentals

IF YOU **REALLY** WANT TO PLAY BETTER GOLF, LEARN THE FUNDAMENTALS OF THE GAME, THEN STICK TO THEM THROUGH THICK AND THIN.

RESIST TRYING **BAND-AID** REMEDIES ANY TIME YOU HIT A BAD PATCH — THEY NEVER LAST.

START WITH GRIP AND SET-UP, THEN WORK THROUGH THE REST OF THE BASICS — IN YOUR GENERAL GOLF THINKING, YOUR PLAY, AND ESPECIALLY DURING YOUR **PRACTICE**.

IF YOU DON'T KNOW WHAT THE FUNDAMENTALS ARE, GO SEE A GOOD TEACHING PRO.

Review Your Game Honestly

TAKE THE TIME EVERY ONCE IN A WHILE, IF YOU'RE SERIOUS ABOUT GOLF, TO SIT DOWN AND HONESTLY REVIEW YOUR GAME.

IDENTIFYING YOUR WEAKNESSES IS OBVIOUSLY THE VITAL FIRST STEP IN DESIGNING ANY MEANINGFUL IMPROVEMENT PROGRAM.

I DO THIS AT LEAST ONCE A YEAR, BREAKING MY GAME DOWN INTO DRIVING, APPROACHING, RECOVERY PLAY, PUTTING, COURSE-MANAGEMENT AND SELF-MANAGEMENT. HAVING DETERMINED WHERE MY PROBLEMS LIE, I THEN DESIGN AN ACTION PLAN TO TRY TO SOLVE THEM — OFTEN BEGINNING WITH A LESSON FROM MY LIFE-LONG TEACHER, **JACK GROUT**. A SIMILAR APPROACH MIGHT BRING YOU A LOT MORE SATISFACTION FROM GOLF.

Keep it Simple

Develop Key Swing Thoughts

Don't Be Too Proud to Take Lessons

Be Prepared to Practice

HOW WELL YOU PLAY GOLF ISN'T ENTIRELY A MATTER OF HOW MUCH YOU PRACTICE, BUT THE TWO ARE CLOSELY RELATED.

ONE THING IS FOR SURE: THERE'S NEVER BEEN A GREAT PLAYER WHO DID NOT HIT HUNDREDS OF THOUSANDS OF PRACTICE SHOTS, AT LEAST WHILE HE OR SHE WAS LEARNING THE GAME.

NO TIME OR OPPORTUNITY TO PRACTICE? WELL, WHERE THERE'S A WILL THERE'S A WAY. AS A YOUNGSTER, I'D EVEN PRACTICE IN THE SNOW, CLEARING A SPOT OR HITTING OFF COMPACTED SNOW IF I COULDN'T GET TO GROUND LEVEL. NOT MANY AMATEURS WOULD GO THAT FAR, I ADMIT, BUT THERE'S NOTHING TO STOP YOU AT LEAST SWINGING A CLUB FOR FIVE OR SO MINUTES A DAY WHEN YOU CAN'T GET OUT TO THE COURSE.

Never Hit a "Quit" Shot

PEOPLE OFTEN COMMENT ON MY ABILITY TO CONCENTRATE AND COMPETE HARD EVEN WHEN NOT PLAYING MY BEST.

ONE FACTOR BEHIND THESE ASSETS IS A LIFELONG HABIT OF NEVER HITTING SHOTS CARELESSLY, HALF-HEARTEDLY, OR BAD-TEMPEREDLY.

PERHAPS THE SAME HABIT WOULD HELP YOUR GAME — AND YOUR MENTAL APPROACH. RESOLVE TO GIVE EVERY SINGLE STROKE YOU PLAY YOUR **ABSOLUTE** BEST TRY, IN PRACTICE AS WELL AS IN PLAY.

IN OTHER WORDS, NEVER HIT A "QUIT" SHOT.

2

Ten Basics of Good Technique

Swing the Same with Every Club

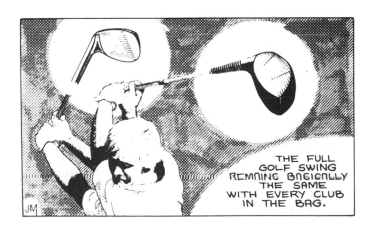

THE FULL GOLF SWING REMAINS BASICALLY THE SAME WITH EVERY CLUB IN THE BAG.

YOU'LL AUTOMATICALLY STAND CLOSER TO THE BALL THE SHORTER THE CLUB YOU'RE PLAYING, AND THUS SWING PROGRESSIVELY MORE UPRIGHT.

BUT THERE SHOULD BE NO CONSCIOUS CHANGE IN YOUR OVERALL SWING PATTERN ON ALL NORMAL SHOTS.

Strive for a Full Arc

ONE REASON FULL SWINGERS GENERALLY LAST LONGER THAN SHORT SWINGERS IS THAT THEY CAN STILL MAKE A GOOD, BIG - ARC EVEN AS AGE INEVITABLY REDUCES MUSCULAR AGILITY.

ANOTHER REASON IS THAT THE LONGER THE SWING — SO LONG AS IT IS CONTROLLED — THE MORE ROOM YOU HAVE TO ACHIEVE PROPER TIMING AND RHYTHM.

THAT'S WHY I ENCOURAGE MY BOYS TO SWING AS FULLY AS POSSIBLE AS SOON AS POSSIBLE. I ALSO ENCOURAGE THEM TO HIT THE BALL HARD NOW, AND WORRY ABOUT CONTROL LATER.

Never Try for "Topspin"

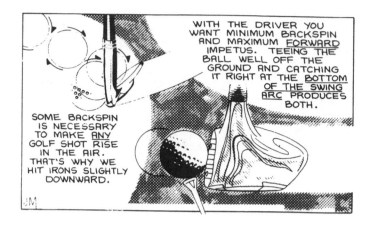

Focus Strongly on the Ball

Develop a Preferred Shot "Shape"

Beware of Overexperimenting

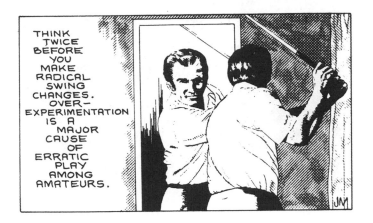

THINK TWICE BEFORE YOU MAKE RADICAL SWING CHANGES. OVER-EXPERIMENTATION IS A MAJOR CAUSE OF ERRATIC PLAY AMONG AMATEURS.

IF YOUR SHOTS START GOING BADLY ASTRAY, DON'T SEARCH FOR DESPERATE SOLUTIONS BY TRYING SOMETHING DIFFERENT ON EVERY SWING — ESPECIALLY NOT ON THE GOLF COURSE ITSELF. RETIRE TO THE PRACTICE TEE AND METHODI-CALLY CHECK YOUR OWN PERSONAL BASICS, ONE BY ONE, ONE AT A TIME.

IF THIS DOESN'T OFFER A SOLUTION, TAKE A LESSON FROM A PRO WHO KNOWS YOUR GAME.

Don't Be Too "Position" Conscious

IN SEEKING IMPROVEMENT BY ANALYZING THE GOLF SWING, AND PARTICULARLY YOUR OWN FORM, BEWARE OF BECOMING TOO "POSITION" CONSCIOUS.

REMEMBER THAT YOU SWING **THROUGH**, NOT TO THE VARIOUS POSITIONS THAT REPRESENT GOOD FORM, AND THAT TO BE EFFECTIVE YOUR ACTIONS MUST BE A CONTINUOUS AND RHYTHMICAL FLOW OF MOVEMENT. ABOVE ALL, THINK AND FEEL **SWING**, ESPECIALLY IN THE CLUBHEAD.

Always Fully "Wind Your Spring"

I BELIEVE THE FARTHER A GOLFER CAN SWING THE CLUB BACK AND STILL RETAIN CONTROL OVER IT, THE MORE POWER-FULLY HE'LL PLAY THE GAME — AND THE LONGER HE'LL GO ON PLAYING WELL. **SAM SNEAD**'S THE PERFECT EXAMPLE OF THAT.

HOWEVER, NOT EVERYONE HAS THE PHYSIQUE TO SWING BACK AS FULLY AS SAM. IF YOU DON'T, FORGET THE ACTUAL LENGTH OF YOUR BACKSWING ARC AND WORK INSTEAD ON **MAXIMUM COILING** OF YOUR UPPER HALF AGAINST THE RESISTANCE OF YOUR LOWER HALF.

EVEN IF THE CLUB ONLY GETS HALF AS FAR BACK AS SAM'S, YOU'LL STILL GIVE THE BALL A FINE RIDE IF YOU "WIND THE SPRING" AS HARD AS YOU CAN.

Use All Your Resources

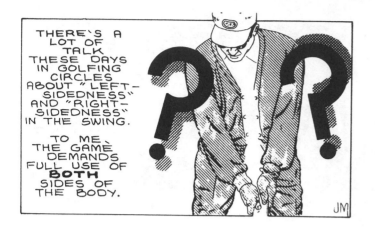

THERE'S A LOT OF TALK THESE DAYS IN GOLFING CIRCLES ABOUT "LEFT-SIDEDNESS" AND "RIGHT-SIDEDNESS" IN THE SWING.

TO ME, THE GAME DEMANDS FULL USE OF **BOTH** SIDES OF THE BODY.

I DON'T BELIEVE A GOLFER CAN USE HIS RIGHT SIDE TOO MUCH SO LONG AS HIS LEFT SIDE **LEADS AND CONTROLS** THE SWING. FOR EXAMPLE, ONCE MY LEFT SIDE HAS INITIATED THE DOWNSWING, WHEN DRIVING I HIT JUST ABOUT AS HARD AS I CAN WITH MY RIGHT SIDE GOING THROUGH THE BALL.

PLAYING WITH ONLY HALF THE BODY, I FEEL, WOULD PRODUCE ONLY HALF THE DISTANCE I NEED ON TEE SHOTS.

Never Forget to Hit The Ball

DON'T GET SO BOUND UP IN SWING THEORY AND "POSITIONS" THAT YOU FORGET TO **HIT** THE BALL WITH THE CLUBHEAD.

YOU MUST RELEASE THE CLUBHEAD TO HIT THE BALL FAR AND TRUE. WAY TO DO THAT IS START DOWN WITH YOUR LEGS OFF A GOOD, TORQUE-PACKED BACKSWING. THEN **LET GO** FULLY AND FREELY WITH YOUR ARMS, WRISTS AND HANDS.

3

Golf's "Geometry"

Don't Try to Play a Dead Straight Game

YOU'LL RARELY SEE A PRO TRY TO HIT THE BALL DEAD STRAIGHT. REASON IS THAT THE ABSO-LUTELY STRAIGHT SHOT IS SO DIFFICULT AS TO BE ALMOST A FLUKE.

HERE'S WHAT YOU MUST DO AT IMPACT TO ACHIEVE THAT FLUKE:
1. YOUR CLUBHEAD MUST MOVE DIRECTLY ALONG YOUR TARGET LINE.
2. YOUR CLUBFACE MUST BE PERFECTLY SQUARE TO YOUR TARGET.
3. YOU MUST HIT THE BALL ABSOLUTELY ON THE CENTER OF THE CLUBFACE.

... AND ALL THAT WITH THE CLUBHEAD TRAVELING AT AROUND 100 M.P.H.! BECAUSE OF THE IMPOSSIBILITY OF ALWAYS REPEATING THOSE IDEALS, MOST TOUR PROS FAVOR EITHER A DELIBERATE **FADE** OR **DRAW** — THE BEST OF THEM BEING CAPABLE OF EITHER 'SHAPE' AT ANY TIME. THAT SHOULD BE YOUR APPROACH, TOO.

Know What Causes Slices, Hooks...

GOOD GOLF STARTS WITH KNOWING WHAT CAUSES YOUR SHOTS TO CURVE.

SLICING COMES FROM IMPACTING THE BALL WITH YOUR CLUBFACE LOOKING RIGHT OF THE DIRECTION IN WHICH YOUR CLUBHEAD IS TRAVELING.

A FADE — MY BASIC SHOT — COMES FROM THE SAME INTERACTION, ONLY THE ANGLE BETWEEN CLUBFACE AND SWING PATH IS **SMALLER**.

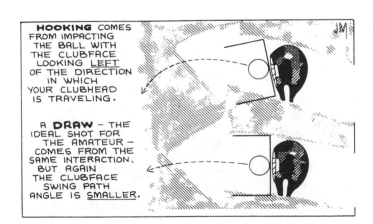

HOOKING COMES FROM IMPACTING THE BALL WITH THE CLUBFACE LOOKING LEFT OF THE DIRECTION IN WHICH YOUR CLUBHEAD IS TRAVELING.

A **DRAW** — THE IDEAL SHOT FOR THE AMATEUR — COMES FROM THE SAME INTERACTION, BUT AGAIN THE CLUBFACE SWING PATH ANGLE IS SMALLER.

...and Pulls and Pushes

LET'S STAY WITH GOLF'S CAUSE AND EFFECT FACTORS.

YOUR CLUBFACE ALIGNMENT MATCHES YOUR SWING PATH WHEN YOU **PULL**. TROUBLE IS YOU'RE SWINGING OUT-TO-IN ACROSS THE TARGET LINE.

YOUR CLUBFACE ALIGNMENT ALSO MATCHES YOUR SWING PATH WHEN YOU **PUSH**. TROUBLE HERE IS SWINGING IN-TO-OUT ACROSS THE LINE.

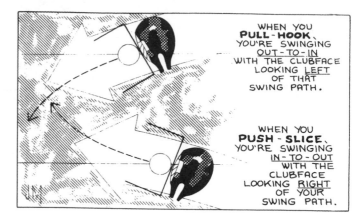

WHEN YOU **PULL-HOOK**, YOU'RE SWINGING OUT-TO-IN WITH THE CLUBFACE LOOKING LEFT OF THAT SWING PATH.

WHEN YOU **PUSH-SLICE**, YOU'RE SWINGING IN-TO-OUT WITH THE CLUBFACE LOOKING RIGHT OF YOUR SWING PATH.

Understand These Spin Effects

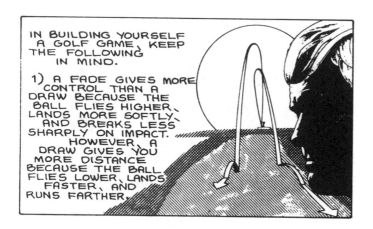

IN BUILDING YOURSELF A GOLF GAME, KEEP THE FOLLOWING IN MIND.

1) A FADE GIVES MORE CONTROL THAN A DRAW BECAUSE THE BALL FLIES HIGHER, LANDS MORE SOFTLY, AND BREAKS LESS SHARPLY ON IMPACT. HOWEVER, A DRAW GIVES YOU MORE DISTANCE BECAUSE THE BALL FLIES LOWER, LANDS FASTER, AND RUNS FARTHER.

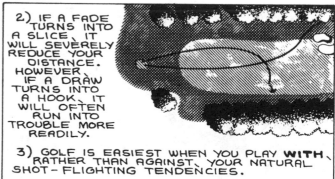

2) IF A FADE TURNS INTO A SLICE, IT WILL SEVERELY REDUCE YOUR DISTANCE. HOWEVER, IF A DRAW TURNS INTO A HOOK, IT WILL OFTEN RUN INTO TROUBLE MORE READILY.

3) GOLF IS EASIEST WHEN YOU PLAY **WITH**, RATHER THAN AGAINST, YOUR NATURAL SHOT-FLIGHTING TENDENCIES.

Fit Your Plane to Your Build

DON'T LET ALL THE TALK AND LITERATURE ABOUT "FLAT" AND "UPRIGHT" SWING PLANES THROW YOU OUT OF YOUR OWN NATURAL SHAPE OF SWING. ACTUALLY, THE DIFFERENCE BETWEEN SO-CALLED FLAT AND UPRIGHT PLANES AMONG GOOD PLAYERS IS GENERALLY ONLY A FEW DEGREES.

IF YOU'RE TALL, YOU'LL NATURALLY STAND FAIRLY CLOSE TO THE BALL AND THUS NATURALLY SWING ON A FAIRLY UPRIGHT PLANE. IF YOU'RE SHORTER, STANDING FARTHER FROM THE BALL WILL NATURALLY CREATE A SOMEWHAT FLATTER PLANE. GO WITH WHAT'S NATURAL, AND DON'T EXAGGERATE.

Have These Angles Checked Out

SHOULD YOU TRY TO SWING ON AN UPRIGHT OR A FLAT PLANE?

THE SHORT ANSWER IS: DO WHAT COMES MOST NATURALLY, BUT DON'T EXAGGERATE ONE WAY OR THE OTHER.

BEYOND THAT, IT DEPENDS WHAT KIND OF GOLF SHOTS YOU PRIMARILY WANT TO HIT. GENERALLY, THE MORE UPRIGHT YOUR SWING, THE HIGHER YOU WILL HIT THE BALL AND THE MORE EASILY YOU WILL BE ABLE TO FADE IT. CONVERSELY, THE FLATTER YOU SWING, THE LOWER YOU'LL HIT THE BALL AND THE MORE EASILY YOU WILL BE ABLE TO DRAW IT.

Know the Proper Clubhead Path

MANY GOLFERS GET BACKACHE AND BAD SCORES THROUGH A FUNDAMENTAL MISCONCEPTION OF THE PATH THE CLUBHEAD SHOULD FOLLOW THROUGH IMPACT.

THE CORRECT PATH IS FROM INSIDE THE TARGET LINE, TO MOMENTARILY ALONG IT, TO INSIDE AGAIN.

TRYING TO FORCE THE CLUBHEAD TO GO FROM INSIDE TO OUTSIDE THROUGH IMPACT, OR FOLLOW THE TARGET LINE FOR ANY APPRECIABLE DISTANCE, IS A SURE WAY TO HURT BOTH YOURSELF AND YOUR SCORE.

Swing Shaft to Parallel at Top

WHEN THE CLUB POINTS LEFT OF THE TARGET LINE AT THE TOP OF THE BACKSWING, IT WILL GENERALLY SWING ACROSS THAT LINE FROM OUT TO IN AT IMPACT.

CONVERSELY, WHEN THE CLUB POINTS RIGHT OF THE TARGET LINE AT THE TOP, IT WILL USUALLY BE MOVING FROM IN TO OUT AT IMPACT.

THAT'S WHY I ALWAYS STRIVE NOT TO "CROSS THE LINE" AT THE TOP. WHEN THE CLUB SHAFT PARALLELS THE TARGET LINE THERE, ITS NATURALLY POSITIONED TO SWING ON LINE THROUGH IMPACT.

IN A PROPER GOLF SWING, THE CLUBFACE APPEARS TO OPEN AS THE CLUB MOVES AWAY FROM THE BALL, AND APPEARS TO CLOSE AS IT TRACKS THE BALL INTO THE FOLLOW-THROUGH.

ACTUALLY, IT DOES NEITHER UNLESS YOU MANIPULATE IT IN SOME WAY WITH YOUR HANDS AND ARMS.

TO PROVE THE POINT, SWING BACK TO WAIST HEIGHT, THEN TURN SO THAT YOUR BODY FACES DIRECTLY DOWN THE CLUBSHAFT. DO THE SAME AFTER SWINGING TO WAIST HEIGHT IN THE FOLLOW-THROUGH.

IN BOTH CASES, YOU'LL FIND THE CLUBFACE IS IN THE SAME **SQUARE** RELATIONSHIP TO YOUR HANDS AND BODY AS IT WAS AT ADDRESS.

4

Your
Equipment

Let a Pro Help You Pick Clubs

BUYING NEW CLUBS? UNLESS YOU'RE A GOOD ENOUGH GOLFER TO KNOW FROM EXPERIENCE EXACTLY WHAT YOU WANT, GET THE HELP OF A GOOD TEACHING PRO WHO KNOWS YOUR GAME IN DETERMINING THEIR PLAYABILITY CHARACTERISTICS.

PROPERLY MATCHING YOUR TOOLS TO YOUR TRAITS AND TALENTS — ESPECIALLY IN THE AREAS OF WEIGHT AND SHAFT FLEX — COULD DEFINITELY SAVE YOU A SHOT OR TWO. THAT'S WHY, IF YOU HAVE A FAVORITE CLUB, IT'S A GOOD IDEA TO KNOW ITS SPECIFICATIONS AND USE THOSE AS A GUIDE WHENEVER YOU'RE RE-EQUIPPING YOURSELF.

Understand the Technology

MANY GOLFERS TALK OF SWINGWEIGHT WITHOUT REALLY UNDERSTANDING WHAT IT MEANS.

ESSENTIALLY, SWINGWEIGHT IS A CONCEPT RELATING THE WEIGHT OF THE GRIP END OF A GOLF CLUB TO ITS HEAD WEIGHT.

JM

BASICALLY, THE HIGHER THE SWINGWEIGHT DESIGNATION THE HEAVIER THE CLUBHEAD WILL FEEL IN RELATION TO THE GRIP END AS YOU SWING. USE THIS CONCEPT AS A GUIDE IN SELECTING CLUBS, BUT DON'T STOP THERE. DEADWEIGHT AND SHAFT FLEXIBILITY ARE ALSO IMPORTANT FACTORS, AND YOU SHOULD OBTAIN PROFESSIONAL HELP IN MATCHING ALL THREE TO YOUR OWN PHYSIQUE AND SWING STYLE.

Match Your Set to Your Ability

THE RULES ALLOW YOU 14 CLUBS. SELECT THEM TO MATCH YOUR PERSONAL ABILITIES, NOT SOME THEORETICAL IDEAL. FOR EXAMPLE, I CARRY A DRIVER, 3-WOOD, IRONS 1 THROUGH 9, PITCHING WEDGE, MODERATELY-FLANGED SAND-WEDGE, AND PUTTER. THAT'S A MIX PERHAPS SUITABLE FOR ANYONE WHO SHOOTS 75 OR BETTER.

IF YOU SCORE MORE THAN A FEW SHOTS HIGHER THAN THAT, HOWEVER, YOU NEED AN "EASIER" SET — SUCH AS, FOR EXAMPLE, DRIVER, 3-, 4-, AND 5- (OR 6-) WOODS, IRONS 3 THROUGH 9, PITCHING WEDGE, DEEP-FLANGED SAND-WEDGE, AND PUTTER.

DON'T LET EGO PREVENT YOU FROM CARRYING CLUBS THAT YOU CAN ACTUALLY PLAY, RATHER THAN ONES THAT SIMPLY LOOK GOOD IN THE BAG.

Experiment to Find Ideal "Specs"

SELECT YOUR CLUBS TO MATCH YOUR PHYSIQUE. BASICALLY, THE HEAVIER A CLUB, THE STRONGER YOU HAVE TO BE TO CONTROL IT AND GENERATE MAXIMUM 'HEAD SPEED.

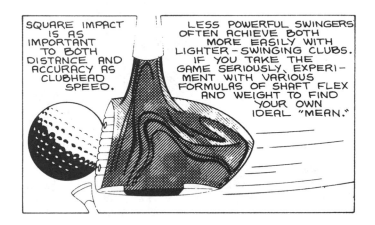

SQUARE IMPACT IS AS IMPORTANT TO BOTH DISTANCE AND ACCURACY AS CLUBHEAD SPEED.

LESS POWERFUL SWINGERS OFTEN ACHIEVE BOTH MORE EASILY WITH LIGHTER-SWINGING CLUBS. IF YOU TAKE THE GAME SERIOUSLY, EXPERIMENT WITH VARIOUS FORMULAS OF SHAFT FLEX AND WEIGHT TO FIND YOUR OWN IDEAL "MEAN."

Take Your Height into Account

DOES A TALL GOLFER NEED LONGER-THAN-STANDARD CLUBS?

IT MIGHT BE WORTH EXPERIMENTING, BUT THE DANGER IS THAT LONGER CLUBS CAN CAUSE A TALL PLAYER TO LOSE CONTROL BY LENGTHENING HIS ALREADY LARGE SWING ARC. PROFESSIONAL COUNSEL IS ADVISABLE.

SHORT GOLFERS, ON THE OTHER HAND, CAN SOME-TIMES GAIN VALUABLE DISTANCE FROM THE BIGGER ARC THAT RESULTS FROM LONGER-THAN-STANDARD CLUBS .... ONCE THEY ARE ABLE TO CONTROL THE EXTRA LENGTH.

GARY PLAYER IS A CASE IN POINT — HIS CLUBS ARE AN INCH LONGER THAN STANDARD.

AGAIN, TALK TO YOUR PRO BEFORE YOU DECIDE.

Consider Lighter Clubs

ALTHOUGH I'M NOT REALLY FAMILIAR WITH THE SPECIAL PROBLEMS OF SENIOR MEN AND LADY GOLFERS, I'VE OFTEN FELT BOTH MIGHT ENJOY THE GAME MORE BY USING LIGHTER-THAN-NORMAL CLUBS.

VELOCITY HAVING TWICE THE VALUE OF MASS IN TERMS OF DISTANCE, IT SEEMS LOGICAL THAT BOTH GROUPS COULD HIT THE BALL FARTHER WITH CLUBS THEY COULD SWING FASTER.

ALSO, THE LIGHTER THE CLUBS, THE LESS THEY'RE GOING TO TAKE OUT OF YOU PHYSICALLY, WHICH CAN BE IMPORTANT TOWARD THE END OF A ROUND.

18
350 YDS
PAR 4

Know the Importance of "Lie"

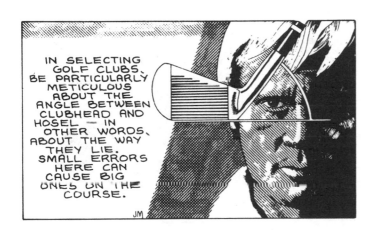

IN SELECTING GOLF CLUBS, BE PARTICULARLY METICULOUS ABOUT THE ANGLE BETWEEN CLUBHEAD AND HOSEL — IN OTHER WORDS, ABOUT THE WAY THEY LIE. SMALL ERRORS HERE CAN CAUSE BIG ONES ON THE COURSE.

JM

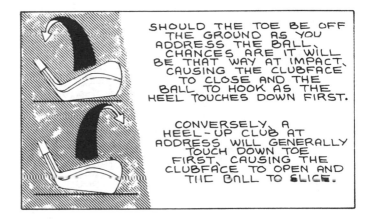

SHOULD THE TOE BE OFF THE GROUND AS YOU ADDRESS THE BALL, CHANCES ARE IT WILL BE THAT WAY AT IMPACT, CAUSING THE CLUBFACE TO CLOSE AND THE BALL TO HOOK AS THE HEEL TOUCHES DOWN FIRST.

CONVERSELY, A HEEL-UP CLUB AT ADDRESS WILL GENERALLY TOUCH DOWN TOE FIRST, CAUSING THE CLUBFACE TO OPEN AND THE BALL TO SLICE.

Go for Good Quality

YOU CAN'T "BUY" A GOLF GAME IN THE CLUBS YOU CHOOSE. BUT YOU CAN SAVE YOURSELF SHOTS BY SEEKING OUT GOOD-QUALITY EQUIPMENT... AND ESPECIALLY THE FINE WORKMANSHIP THAT PRODUCES COMPATABILITY OF EACH CLUB TO ALL THE OTHERS IN A SET.

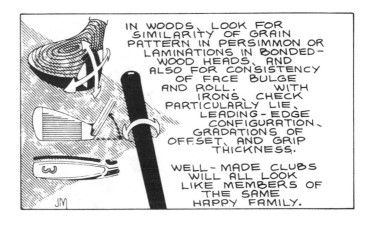

IN WOODS, LOOK FOR SIMILARITY OF GRAIN PATTERN IN PERSIMMON OR LAMINATIONS IN BONDED-WOOD HEADS, AND ALSO FOR CONSISTENCY OF FACE BULGE AND ROLL. WITH IRONS, CHECK PARTICULARLY LIE, LEADING-EDGE CONFIGURATION, GRADATIONS OF OFFSET, AND GRIP THICKNESS.

WELL-MADE CLUBS WILL ALL LOOK LIKE MEMBERS OF THE SAME HAPPY FAMILY.

JM

Join the Pros—Use a Glove

YOU HAVE NOTICED PERHAPS THAT ALMOST EVERY GOLFER ON THE PGA TOUR WEARS A GLOVE ON HIS LEADING HAND (WHICH IS USUALLY THE LEFT, OF COURSE).

THERE ARE TWO REASONS.

THE FIRST IS THAT A GLOVE ON THIS PRIMARY SWING—CONTROLLING HAND IS THE GREATEST AID TO SECURE GRIPPING ALLOWED UNDER THE GAME'S RULES.

THE SECOND REASON IS THAT A GLOVE HELPS GREATLY IN AVOIDING THE BLISTERS AND CALLUSES THAT CAN RESULT FROM EXTENSIVE PRACTICE.

Try to "Custom-Fit" Your Driver

BECAUSE THE CLUB IS SO IMPORTANT IN PLACING THE BALL IN PLAY, TOUR GOLFERS GO TO GREAT LENGTHS TO "CUSTOM FIT" THEIR DRIVERS TO THEIR INDIVIDUAL SWING STYLES. YOU MIGHT BENEFIT FROM SOME EXPERIMENT IN THIS DIRECTION IF YOU'RE A SERIOUS AND REASONABLY CAPABLE GOLFER.

IF DISTANCE IS YOUR BIGGEST PROBLEM, EXPERIMENT WITH SOFTER SHAFTS, MORE FACE LOFT, AND PERHAPS LIGHTER CLUBS.

IF DIRECTION IS YOUR MAIN DIFFICULTY, TRY STIFFER SHAFTS AND/OR DIFFERENT CLUB FACINGS—SAY A DEGREE OR SO CLOSED IF YOU HABITUALLY SLICE, OR A DEGREE OR SO OPEN IF YOU HOOK.

Play the Ball You Can Really Handle

DON'T LET EGO DETERMINE THE COMPRESSION OF GOLF BALL YOU USE. A VERY POWERFUL SWING IS NECESSARY TO GET MAXIMUM DISTANCE FROM A HIGH COMPRESSION (100) BALL.

EVEN SOME OF THE TOUR PLAYERS PREFER A SLIGHTLY SOFTER BALL, ESPECIALLY IN COLD WEATHER.

MOST AMATEURS SEEM TO DO BEST WITH MEDIUM COMPRESSION (90) BALLS. THE VERY EASY SWINGER MIGHT FIND HE OR SHE DOES BETTER YET WITH EVEN LESS COMPRESSION—SAY 70 TO 80. EXPERIMENT TO FIND YOUR OWN IDEAL "AMMUNITION."

CHAPTER TWO

The Swing Step-by-Step

5

Building a
Sound Grip

Meet These Three Goals

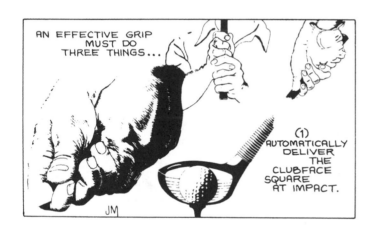

Place Your Hands Naturally

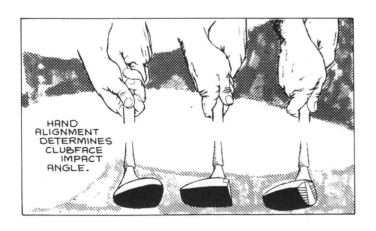

Hold the Club like This

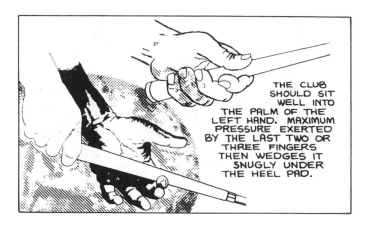

THE CLUB SHOULD SIT WELL INTO THE PALM OF THE LEFT HAND. MAXIMUM PRESSURE EXERTED BY THE LAST TWO OR THREE FINGERS THEN WEDGES IT SNUGLY UNDER THE HEEL PAD.

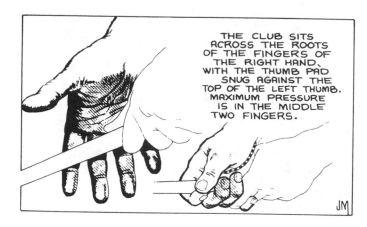

THE CLUB SITS ACROSS THE ROOTS OF THE FINGERS OF THE RIGHT HAND, WITH THE THUMB PAD SNUG AGAINST THE TOP OF THE LEFT THUMB. MAXIMUM PRESSURE IS IN THE MIDDLE TWO FINGERS.

Set Your Hands in Parallel

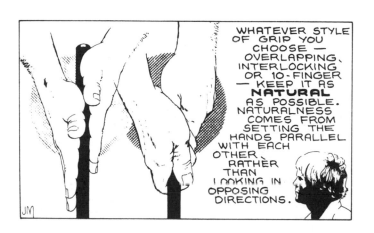

WHATEVER STYLE OF GRIP YOU CHOOSE — OVERLAPPING, INTERLOCKING OR 10-FINGER — KEEP IT AS **NATURAL** AS POSSIBLE. NATURALNESS COMES FROM SETTING THE HANDS PARALLEL WITH EACH OTHER, RATHER THAN LOOKING IN OPPOSING DIRECTIONS.

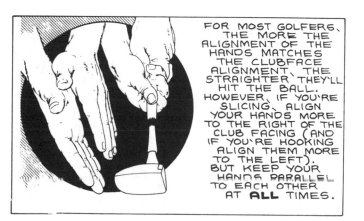

FOR MOST GOLFERS, THE MORE THE ALIGNMENT OF THE HANDS MATCHES THE CLUBFACE ALIGNMENT, THE STRAIGHTER THEY'LL HIT THE BALL. HOWEVER, IF YOU'RE SLICING, ALIGN YOUR HANDS MORE TO THE RIGHT OF THE CLUB FACING (AND IF YOU'RE HOOKING ALIGN THEM MORE TO THE LEFT). BUT KEEP YOUR HANDS PARALLEL TO EACH OTHER AT **ALL** TIMES.

Meld Your Hands Together

EFFICIENT WRIST HINGING AND RESISTANCE TO IMPACT SHOCK COME FROM LINKING THE HANDS AS A UNIT. HAVING SMALL HANDS, I FAVOR THE INTERLOCKING GRIP.

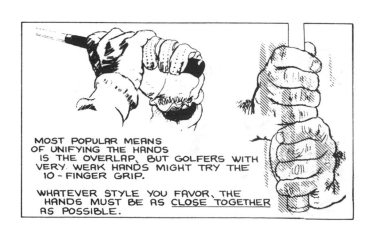

MOST POPULAR MEANS OF UNIFYING THE HANDS IS THE OVERLAP, BUT GOLFERS WITH VERY WEAK HANDS MIGHT TRY THE 10-FINGER GRIP.

WHATEVER STYLE YOU FAVOR, THE HANDS MUST BE AS CLOSE TOGETHER AS POSSIBLE.

Wedge Shaft into Left Palm

HOWEVER YOU GRIP — OVERLAP, INTERLOCK OR 10-FINGER STYLE — YOUR LEADING HAND NEEDS TO HANG ON VERY FIRMLY, FIRST TO GUIDE THE CLUB THROUGHOUT THE SWING, AND SECOND TO PROVIDE A BUTTRESS AGAINST THE HITTING ACTION OF THE TRAILING HAND.

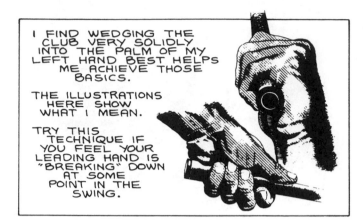

I FIND WEDGING THE CLUB VERY SOLIDLY INTO THE PALM OF MY LEFT HAND BEST HELPS ME ACHIEVE THOSE BASICS.

THE ILLUSTRATIONS HERE SHOW WHAT I MEAN.

TRY THIS TECHNIQUE IF YOU FEEL YOUR LEADING HAND IS "BREAKING" DOWN AT SOME POINT IN THE SWING.

Beware of Too "Strong" a Grip

MOST PEOPLE STARTING GOLF TEND TO TAKE A VERY "STRONG" GRIP ON THE CLUB, BECAUSE THEY INSTINCTIVELY FEEL THIS WILL GIVE THEM MORE POWER.

UNFORTUNATELY, IT DOESN'T ALWAYS WORK THAT WAY.

THE BETTER PLAYER DEVELOPS POWER WITH HIS **ENTIRE SWING**, NOT WITH JUST HIS HANDS AND WRISTS.

TOO STRONG A GRIP ACTUALLY INHIBITS THE FULL CLUBHEAD RELEASE NECESSARY FOR GOOD DISTANCE, SO WORK ON DEVELOPING A MORE "NEUTRAL" HOLD ON THE CLUB AS YOUR SWING SKILLS DEVELOP.

Maintain Consistent Pressure

TOO TIGHT A GRIP CAN DESTROY TEMPO AND RHYTHM BY FORCING YOU TO SWING JERKILY — ESPECIALLY DURING THE TAKEAWAY.

HOLD THE CLUB LIGHTLY AT ADDRESS, FIRM UP YOUR HANDS SLIGHTLY JUST BEFORE YOU START BACK, THEN MAINTAIN THE SAME PRESSURE THROUGHOUT THE BACKSWING.

BIG THING TO AVOID IS GRABBING HARDER WITH EITHER HAND ONCE THE CLUB'S IN MOTION.

Test Your Grip like This

HERE'S A TEST OF YOUR ABILITY TO HANG ONTO THE CLUB THROUGHOUT THE SWING WITHOUT CHANGING YOUR HAND POSITION -- A MAJOR SOURCE OF INCONSISTENCY.

PLACE THREE OR MORE BALLS IN A LINE AND TRY TO HIT THEM ALL WITHOUT REGRIPPING THE CLUB. IF YOU CAN'T, YOUR HANDS HAVE SLIPPED AT SOME POINT IN THE SWING. CHECK FOR LOOSENESS PARTICULARLY DURING THE TAKEAWAY AND AT THE TOP OF THE BACKSWING.

How to Aim Accurately

Select a Specific Target

THE MORE SPECIFICALLY YOU SIGHT AND MENTALLY FOCUS ON A TARGET IN SETTING UP TO PLAY ANY SHOT, THE BETTER YOUR CHANCE OF HITTING WHERE YOU INTEND.

FOR THAT REASON, I ALWAYS TARGET TO A SPECIFIC POINT, RATHER THAN A VAGUE GREEN AREA, ON ALL APPROACH SHOTS. USUALLY THAT POINT IS THE PIN, BUT IF IT'S HIDDEN OR I CAN'T SHOOT DIRECTLY AT IT FOR SOME REASON, THEN I'LL SELECT A MOUND OR A TREE IN THE BACK-GROUND. MAKE A SPECIAL POINT OF DOING THIS WHENEVER YOUR APPROACH PLAY BECOMES LESS SHARP THAN YOU'D LIKE.

Use This 3-Point Aiming System

INCORRECT AIM AND ALIGNMENT LIES BEHIND PROBABLY 80 PER CENT OF GOLF'S MISDIRECTED SHOTS, ESPECIALLY AMONG HIGH HANDICAPPERS. HERE'S A ROUTINE THAT WILL HELP SOLVE THAT PROBLEM FOR YOU.

1. SELECT YOUR TARGET LINE FROM BEHIND THE BALL, AND USE A MARK ON THE GROUND A FEW FEET AHEAD OF IT AS A REFERENCE POINT. 2. SET THE CLUBFACE BEHIND THE BALL LOOKING SQUARELY AT YOUR MARK AND THUS DOWN YOUR TARGET LINE, BEFORE YOU FINALIZE YOUR GRIP AND STANCE. 3. ALIGN YOUR BODY PARALLEL TO THE TARGET LINE — PARTICULARLY YOUR SHOULDERS.

Check Those Shoulders...

REASON IS THAT THE CLUBHEAD PATH AT IMPACT USUALLY MATCHES THE ALIGNMENT OF THE SHOULDERS AT THAT MOMENT, AND THE ANGLE OF THE SHOULDERS AT IMPACT USUALLY MATCHES THEIR ANGLE AT ADDRESS. THUS IF YOU START WITH AN OPEN OR CLOSED SHOULDER LINE, YOU ALMOST GUARANTEE AN OUT-TO-IN OR IN-TO-OUT SWING PATH.

PLACING YOUR FEET PARALLEL TO THE TARGET LINE AT ADDRESS WILL HELP YOU SWING THE CLUB ALONG THAT LINE THROUGH IMPACT, BUT SETTING YOUR **SHOULDERS** SQUARE TO THE LINE WILL HELP YOU DO SO EVEN MORE.

...and the Clubface

MOST GOLFERS INSTINCTIVELY LINE THEMSELVES UP PARALLEL TO WHERE THE CLUBFACE LOOKS AT ADDRESS.

MOST GOLFERS ALSO INSTINCTIVELY DELIVER THE CLUBHEAD TO THE BALL ON A PATH PARALLEL TO THEIR SHOULDER ALIGNMENT AT ADDRESS.

SO A SQUARE CLUBFACE AT ADDRESS ESTABLISHES YOUR BEST CHANCE OF SWINGING ALONG THE TARGET LINE AT IMPACT.

Never Neglect Your Alignment

CHECK YOUR ADDRESS ALIGNMENT FIRST ANY TIME YOU BEGIN TO MIS-DIRECT MORE SHOTS THAN NORMAL.

FAULTY AIMING CAUSES MORE BOGEYS THAN ANY OTHER SINGLE ERROR AMONG EXPERIENCED PLAYERS.

AND IT'S EASY TO SLIP INTO UNKNOWINGLY.

YOU'LL NOTICE AT TOUR EVENTS THAT THE PLAYERS ARE CONSTANTLY CHECKING THEIR OWN AND EACH OTHERS' SET-UPS.

HAVE A PRO OR A PAL CHECK YOURS PERIODICALLY, OR DO IT YOURSELF IN PRACTICE BY ALIGNING TO A CLUB LAID ON THE GROUND. REMEMBER, THE GREATEST SWING IN THE WORLD WON'T SCORE IF IT'S MIS-AIMED.

7

Posture, Stance and Ball Position

Don't Exaggerate Your Posture

KEY TO GOOD POSTURE IS TO _AVOID EXAGGERATION_.

FORCE ANYTHING AT ADDRESS AND INSTINCTIVELY IT WILL COME APART DURING YOUR SWING.

YOUR BASIC POSTURAL ADDRESS OBJECTIVE IS SIMPLY TO **MIRROR** YOUR IDEAL IMPACT POSITION. YOU'LL DO THAT MOST EFFECTIVELY BY BEING AS _NATURAL_ AS POSSIBLE WITHIN GOOD SET-UP FUNDAMENTALS.

Set Shaft and Left Arm in Line

BY SETTING-UP WITH YOUR LEFT ARM AND CLUBSHAFT IN A _STRAIGHT LINE_ FROM LEFT SHOULDER TO BALL, YOU'LL AUTOMATICALLY POSITION YOUR HANDS _SLIGHTLY AHEAD OF THE CLUBHEAD_ — WHICH IS WHERE THEY SHOULD BE THROUGH IMPACT.

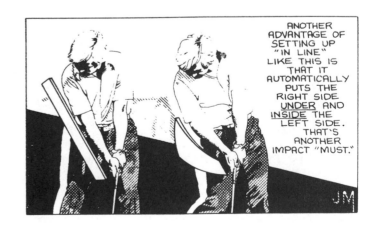

ANOTHER ADVANTAGE OF SETTING UP "IN LINE" LIKE THIS IS THAT IT AUTOMATICALLY PUTS THE RIGHT SIDE _UNDER_ AND _INSIDE_ THE LEFT SIDE. THAT'S ANOTHER IMPACT "MUST."

Flex Your Knees Slightly

A SLIGHT FLEX IN BOTH KNEES IS CRITICAL TO GOOD LEG ACTION, SO BUILD IT INTO YOUR ADDRESS POSTURE.

BUT DON'T OVER-BEND YOUR KNEES, BECAUSE THAT LEADS TO SLOPPY LEG ACTION ON THE THROUGH-SWING.

SEEK THE FEELING OF FIRM RESILIENCE WITH JUST A LITTLE "GIVE" AT THE KNEES.

Let Your Arms Hang Freely

RIGIDITY OR EXCESS MUSCULAR STRESS IN ANY PART OF THE BODY AT ADDRESS IS A SURE SWING INHIBITOR, BUT PARTICULARLY IN THE ARMS.

THEY MUST BE "LOOSE" ENOUGH TO BE ABLE TO SWING FREELY IN RESPONSE TO YOUR SHOULDER, HIP AND LEG ACTION.

TO ENSURE THAT THEY ARE, LET THEM HANG FREELY FROM YOUR SHOULDERS IN A RELAXED AND NATURAL POSITION AS YOU SET UP TO THE BALL. AVOID ANY POSTURE THAT CREATES A FEELING OF TENSION, PARTICULARLY IN YOUR FOREARMS. IF THIS MEANS EASING YOUR GRIP PRESSURE A LITTLE, DO SO — IT WILL NATURALLY FIRM UP AS THE SWING PROCEEDS.

Be as Natural as You Can

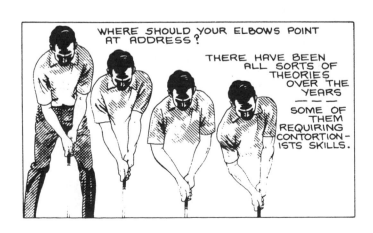

WHERE SHOULD YOUR ELBOWS POINT AT ADDRESS?

THERE HAVE BEEN ALL SORTS OF THEORIES OVER THE YEARS — SOME OF THEM REQUIRING CONTORTION-ISTS SKILLS.

MY RECOMMENDATION IS THAT YOU TRY TO PLAY GOLF AS NATURALLY AS POSSIBLE, WHICH MEANS IN THIS RESPECT NOT CONSCIOUSLY TWIST-ING OR TURNING YOUR ELBOWS IN ANY PARTICULAR DIRECTION. UNFORCED IN ANY DIRECTION, THEY'LL PROBABLY BE IN THE SAME ALIGN-MENT AT ADDRESS AS WHEN YOUR ARMS HANG NATUR-ALLY AT YOUR SIDES, WHICH IS JUST FINE.

Strike a Balance in Stance Width

THE WIDTH OF YOUR STANCE HAS QUITE AN INFLUENCE ON THE QUALITY OF YOUR SWING.

IF IT'S TOO **WIDE**, TURNING FREELY AND FULLY BECOMES DIFFICULT.

IF IT'S TOO **NARROW**, YOU'LL LACK STABILITY AND BALANCE.

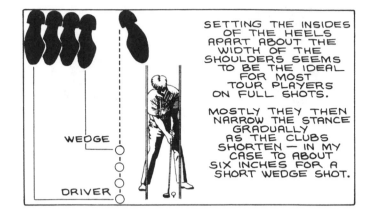

SETTING THE INSIDES OF THE HEELS APART ABOUT THE WIDTH OF THE SHOULDERS SEEMS TO BE THE IDEAL FOR MOST TOUR PLAYERS ON FULL SHOTS.

MOSTLY THEY THEN NARROW THE STANCE GRADUALLY AS THE CLUBS SHORTEN — IN MY CASE TO ABOUT SIX INCHES FOR A SHORT WEDGE SHOT.

WEDGE

DRIVER

Distribute Your Weight Evenly

SOME MODERN INSTRUCTORS SUGGEST SETTING MOST OF THE WEIGHT ON THE REAR FOOT AT ADDRESS, TO PRE-ESTABLISH THE WEIGHT TRANSFER AND ENSURE GOOD LEG ACTION INTO THE DOWNSWING.

I PREFER TO ACHIEVE THAT EFFECT BY DIVIDING MY WEIGHT EVENLY AT ADDRESS, THEN BRACING MYSELF BY **PUSHING** SLIGHTLY TOWARDS THE TARGET FROM THE INSIDE OF MY RIGHT FOOT.

THIS WAY THERE'S LESS CHANCE OF SWAYING THE UPPER BODY THAN WHEN MOST OF THE WEIGHT IS CONSCIOUSLY SET ON THE BACK FOOT.

Angle Feet to Suit Swing Style

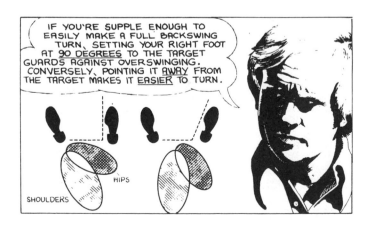

IF YOU'RE SUPPLE ENOUGH TO EASILY MAKE A FULL BACKSWING TURN, SETTING YOUR RIGHT FOOT AT 90 DEGREES TO THE TARGET GUARDS AGAINST OVERSWINGING. CONVERSELY, POINTING IT AWAY FROM THE TARGET MAKES IT EASIER TO TURN.

SHOULDERS

HIPS

ANGLING THE LEFT FOOT TOWARDS THE TARGET — AS I DO — ENCOURAGES FAST DOWNSWING HIP CLEARANCE.

BUT DON'T OVERDO THIS IF YOU HAVE A TENDENCY TO "SPIN OUT" WITH YOUR HIPS OR "COME OVER" THE BALL WITH YOUR SHOULDERS.

Distance Yourself from Ball like This

TO FIND YOUR PROPER DISTANCE FROM THE BALL WITH ANY CLUB, STAND UPRIGHT BUT RELAXED, THEN FLEX YOUR KNEES SLIGHTLY AND SLUMP YOUR SHOULDERS DOWNWARD.

NOW BEND FROM THE WAIST UNTIL YOU CAN SET THE CLUB COMFORTABLY BEHIND THE BALL WITH YOUR ARMS HANGING ALMOST STRAIGHT DOWN.

YOUR LEFT ARM AND THE CLUB SHOULD DIP SLIGHTLY BENEATH AN IMAGINARY LINE RUNNING FROM YOUR LEFT SHOULDER TO THE BALL.

Position Ball at Bottom of Swing Arc

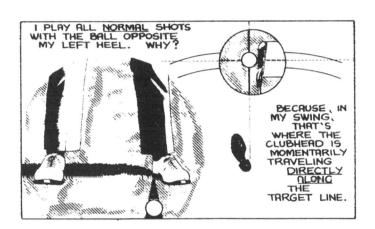

I PLAY ALL NORMAL SHOTS WITH THE BALL OPPOSITE MY LEFT HEEL. WHY?

BECAUSE, IN MY SWING, THAT'S WHERE THE CLUBHEAD IS MOMENTARILY TRAVELING DIRECTLY ALONG THE TARGET LINE.

IF I HAD THE BALL BACK, THE CLUBHEAD WOULD STILL BE COMING FROM INSIDE, AND I'D PUSH OR HOOK DEPENDING ON CLUBFACE ALIGNMENT.

IF I HAD THE BALL FORWARD, THE CLUBHEAD WOULD BE COMING FROM OUTSIDE, AND I'D PULL OR SLICE THE BALL.

EXPERIMENT TO FIND YOUR IDEAL BALL POSITION.

Center Clubface Behind Ball

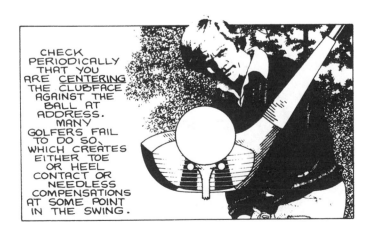

CHECK PERIODICALLY THAT YOU ARE CENTERING THE CLUBFACE AGAINST THE BALL AT ADDRESS. MANY GOLFERS FAIL TO DO SO, WHICH CREATES EITHER TOE OR HEEL CONTACT OR NEEDLESS COMPENSATIONS AT SOME POINT IN THE SWING.

IF YOU FAIL TO MEET THE BALL SQUARELY AFTER HAVING ADDRESSED IT CORRECTLY, THERE IS A FLAW IN EITHER YOUR SET-UP OR YOUR SWING.

MOST OFTEN YOU'LL FIND THAT YOU'RE STANDING EITHER TOO FAR FROM OR TOO CLOSE TO THE BALL.

31

Starting
Back

Stay in Motion to Avoid "Freezing"

STARTING BACK 1

A LOT OF JERKY SWINGS, AND VISITS TO THE WOODS, ARE THE RESULT OF "FREEZING" OVER THE BALL AT ADDRESS.

ALL GOOD GOLFERS STAY IN MOTION IN SOME PART OF THE BODY AS THEY GET READY TO SWING.

MOST POPULAR TENSION-PREVENTER IS THE WAGGLE, BUT I ALSO LIKE TO KEEP MY LEGS LOOSE BY SHIFTING MY WEIGHT SLIGHTLY FROM FOOT TO FOOT AS I GET SET TO SWING.

Find Yourself a Swing "Trigger"

STARTING BACK 2

EVERY GOLFER NEEDS AN EFFECTIVE SWING "TRIGGER," AND THERE ARE PLENTY TO CHOOSE FROM. FOR EXAMPLE, **GARY PLAYER** "KICKS IN" HIS RIGHT KNEE --

-- WHEREAS **JULIUS BOROS** GETS GOING OFF THE FINAL SHUFFLING OF HIS FEET INTO POSITION.

MOST POPULAR "TRIGGER" ON THE TOUR — AND THE ONE I FAVOR — IS THE FORWARD PRESS: A SLIGHT INCLINATION OF THE HANDS TOWARDS THE TARGET, FROM WHICH YOU "REBOUND" INTO THE TAKEAWAY.

Begin as *Deliberately* as You Can

STARTING BACK 3

YOU CAN'T START A GOLF CLUB BACK TOO SLOWLY, PROVIDED YOU SWING RATHER THAN TAKE OR LIFT IT AWAY FROM THE BALL.

I TRY ON EVERY SHOT TO SWING INTO MOTION VERY DELIBERATELY — JUST FAST ENOUGH TO AVOID JERKINESS.

OBVIOUSLY THE MOTION SPEEDS UP AS THE BACKSWING PROGRESSES.

BUT THE SLOWER YOU CAN KEEP THOSE FIRST TWO OR THREE FEET, THE BETTER YOU'LL PLAY — ESPECIALLY WHEN YOU WANT DISTANCE.

Let Club Path Follow Body Turn

STARTING BACK 4

JACK, SHOULD I START THE CLUB BACK INSIDE OR ALONG THE TARGET LINE?

MOST TOUR PLAYERS — INCLUDING ME — START THE CLUB BACK ALONG THE TARGET LINE.

BUT IT ACTUALLY STAYS ON THAT LINE ONLY FOR A FOOT OR TWO, IF THAT.

THE CLUB NATURALLY SWINGS INSIDE THE LINE IN RESPONSE TO THE SHOULDER TURN. HOW SOON AND HOW MUCH DEPENDS ON YOUR BUILD, YOUR DISTANCE FROM THE BALL, AND THE LENGTH OF THE CLUB.

Start Back in "One Piece"

STARTING BACK 5

I FAVOR A "ONE-PIECE" TAKEAWAY, WHICH MEANS KEEPING ALL MOVING PARTS OF THE BODY IN STEP WITH EACH OTHER DURING THE INITIAL BACKSWING MOTION.

A ONE-PIECE START-BACK SETS UP A WIDE SWING ARC, FORCES THE BODY TO TURN, PREVENTS "PICKING UP" THE CLUB WITH THE HANDS AND ARMS ONLY, AND PROMOTES A SMOOTH AND WELL-PACED OVERALL SWING TEMPO.

Watch Out for Those Wrists!

STARTING BACK 6

OVER-ACTIVE HANDS AND WRISTS AT THE START OF THE SWING ARE RESPONSIBLE FOR A LOT OF GOLF'S FOUL BALLS.

MY LEFT ARM AND CLUB SHAFT RETAIN THE STRAIGHT-LINE RELATIONSHIP THEY FORM AT ADDRESS UNTIL MY HANDS REACH ABOUT HIP HEIGHT.

THEN THE WEIGHT OF THE RISING CLUBHEAD NATURALLY BEGINS TO COCK THE WRISTS WITHOUT ANY CONSCIOUS EFFORT ON MY PART.

Feel Left Shoulder Pushing Club Back

STARTING BACK 7

JACK, WHAT'S YOUR MAIN FEELING DURING THE EARLY PART OF THE BACKSWING?

THAT THE LEFT ARM AND CLUB ARE BEING PUSHED BACK BY MY LEFT SHOULDER AS IT BEGINS TO TURN DOWN AND AROUND UNDER MY CHIN.

A HELPFUL FEELING IS THAT YOUR LEFT ARM'S SWINGING MOTION NEVER GETS AHEAD OF YOUR LEFT SHOULDER'S PUSHING MOTION EARLY IN THE BACKSWING. THIS WILL ENCOURAGE YOU TO TURN FULLY, RATHER THAN JUST LIFTING THE CLUB WITH YOUR ARMS.

Don't Manipulate the Clubface

STARTING BACK 8

A SURE WAY TO GET ALL PRETZELED UP AT GOLF IS TO TRY TO FORCE THE CLUBFACE TO STAY "SQUARE" TO THE TARGET TOO LONG INTO THE BACK-SWING.

AS THE SHOULDERS TURN, THE CLUB-FACE WILL APPEAR TO "OPEN"— LOOK INCREASINGLY RIGHT OF TARGET. BUT WHEN YOU GO BACK IN "ONE PIECE," WITHOUT INDEPENDENT HAND/ARM MANIPULATION, IT WILL STILL BE CORRECTLY SQUARE TO THE ARC THE CLUB IS DESCRIBING.

9

To the
Top

Know Your Options

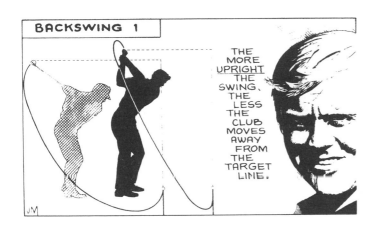

BACKSWING 1

THE MORE UPRIGHT THE SWING, THE LESS THE CLUB MOVES AWAY FROM THE TARGET LINE.

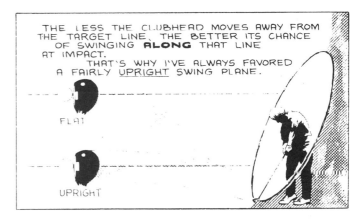

THE LESS THE CLUBHEAD MOVES AWAY FROM THE TARGET LINE, THE BETTER ITS CHANCE OF SWINGING **ALONG** THAT LINE AT IMPACT.

THAT'S WHY I'VE ALWAYS FAVORED A FAIRLY UPRIGHT SWING PLANE.

FLAT

UPRIGHT

Coil Shoulders, Swing Hands High

DANGER OF BECOMING TOO UPRIGHT IS THAT THE CLUB WON'T STAY AT GROUND LEVEL LONG ENOUGH THROUGH IMPACT TO MEET THE BALL SOLIDLY.

BACKSWING 2

WAY TO AVOID THAT IS TO COMBINE A **FULL COILING** OF YOUR UPPER BODY WITH THE UPWARD SWINGING OF YOUR ARMS.

ATTEMPTING TO SWING UPRIGHT WITHOUT FULLY TURNING AND TILTING THE SHOULDERS RESULTS IN LIFTING THE CLUB TO THE TOP -- AND A WEAK CHOPPING ACTION AT IMPACT.

Extend Arms but Stay "Centered"

BACK-SWING 3

FIRST ESSENTIAL FOR A WIDE ARC IS MAXIMUM EXTENSION OF YOUR ARMS AWAY FROM YOU AS THEY SWING BACK AND UP, WITHOUT SWAYING YOUR BODY.

A WIDE SWING ARC IS ESSENTIAL TO GENERATE MAXIMUM CLUBHEAD SPEED THROUGH MAXIMUM LEVERAGE.

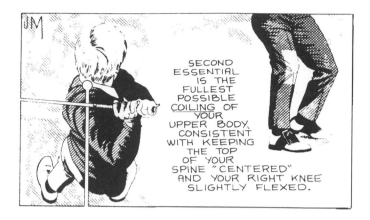

SECOND ESSENTIAL IS THE FULLEST POSSIBLE COILING OF YOUR UPPER BODY, CONSISTENT WITH KEEPING THE TOP OF YOUR SPINE "CENTERED" AND YOUR RIGHT KNEE SLIGHTLY FLEXED.

Play from the Insides of Your Feet

BACKSWING 4

MANY GOLFERS' POOR SWINGS ORIGINATE IN WEAK FOOT AND ANKLE ACTION.

BASICALLY, THE MORE YOU CAN SWING FROM THE INSIDES OF YOUR FEET, AND THE MORE OF YOUR FEET YOU CAN KEEP ON THE GROUND, THE BETTER YOU'LL PLAY.

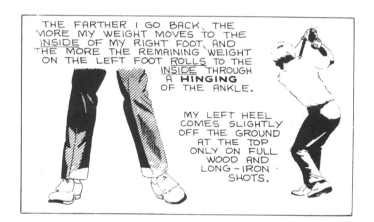

THE FARTHER I GO BACK, THE MORE MY WEIGHT MOVES TO THE INSIDE OF MY RIGHT FOOT, AND THE MORE THE REMAINING WEIGHT ON THE LEFT FOOT ROLLS TO THE INSIDE THROUGH A HINGING OF THE ANKLE.

MY LEFT HEEL COMES SLIGHTLY OFF THE GROUND AT THE TOP ONLY ON FULL WOOD AND LONG-IRON SHOTS.

Anchor Swing with Flexed Right Knee

BACKSWING 5

YOUR RIGHT KNEE IS YOUR BACKSWING "ANCHOR."

KEEPING IT FLEXED AND RESILIENT IS THE KEY TO A STRONG WIND-UP AND PROPER DOWNSWING INITIATION.

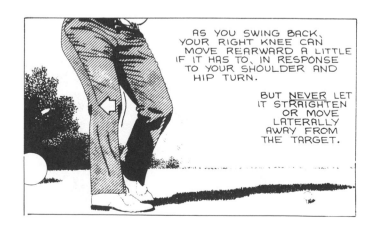

AS YOU SWING BACK, YOUR RIGHT KNEE CAN MOVE REARWARD A LITTLE IF IT HAS TO, IN RESPONSE TO YOUR SHOULDER AND HIP TURN.

BUT NEVER LET IT STRAIGHTEN OR MOVE LATERALLY AWAY FROM THE TARGET.

Let Left Knee Move Behind Ball

BACKSWING 6

TURNING FULLY IN THE SHOULDERS AND HIPS REQUIRES THAT YOUR LEFT KNEE FLEX <u>INWARD</u>, TOWARDS THE BALL, AS THE BACKSWING PROGRESSES.

BEWARE SIMPLY BENDING THE LEFT KNEE <u>FORWARD</u> BY LIFTING YOUR LEFT HEEL HIGH OFF THE GROUND.

PROPER LEG WORK CALLS FOR THE KNEE TO BE <u>PULLED</u> TOWARDS THE BALL BY THE FORCE OF YOUR BODY WIND-UP.

Beware Too Much Heel Lift

BACKSWING 7

LIFTING THE LEFT HEEL HIGH OFF THE GROUND IS A DANGEROUS MOVE, FOR TWO REASONS.

FIRST, THE RAISING ACTION MAY CAUSE AN INVOLUNTARY LIFTING OF THE ENTIRE BODY, WHICH WILL OBVIOUSLY DISTORT YOUR SWING ARC.

SECOND, THE HIGHER YOUR LEFT HEEL RISES, THE MORE DIFFICULT IT IS TO GET IT FIRMLY BACK TO EARTH AS THE INITIATING MOVE OF THE DOWNSWING — A FREQUENT CAUSE OF "THROWING" THE CLUB WITH THE HANDS AND SHOULDERS.

Don't Restrict Hip Turn . . .

BACKSWING 8

THERE'S A SCHOOL OF THOUGHT THAT SAYS THE HIPS SHOULD TURN VERY SLIGHTLY, IF AT ALL, ON THE BACKSWING.

I DON'T SUBSCRIBE TO IT, BECAUSE IF I DON'T LET MY HIPS TURN I CAN'T TURN MY SHOULDERS -- AND IF I DON'T TURN MY SHOULDERS I CAN'T GENERATE <u>LEVERAGE</u>.

THUS, GOING BACK, I ALLOW MY HIPS TO TURN <u>AS FAR</u> <u>AROUND AS THEY'LL GO</u> WITHOUT FORCING MY RIGHT LEG TO STRAIGHTEN OR COLLAPSE, OR MY WEIGHT TO MOVE TO THE OUTSIDE OF MY RIGHT FOOT.

YOU SHOULD, TOO.

...Let Shoulders Wind Up Hips

BACKSWING 9

MODERN GOLFERS ALLOW THEIR HIPS TO TURN GOING BACK IN RESPONSE TO THE PULL OF THE SHOULDER TURN, NOT AS A CONSCIOUS OR INDEPENDENT ACT.

IN MY CASE, THE HIPS ONLY BEGIN TO BE TURNED BY THE SHOULDER WIND-UP AFTER THE CLUB REACHES ABOUT HIP-HIGH.

BE SURE TO MAKE THE HIPS FOLLOWERS, NOT LEADERS, IN YOUR WIND-UP.

Make Your Spine Your Swing "Hub"

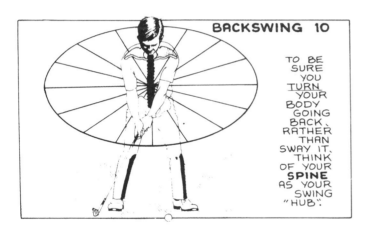

BACKSWING 10

TO BE SURE YOU TURN YOUR BODY GOING BACK, RATHER THAN SWAY IT, THINK OF YOUR **SPINE** AS YOUR SWING "HUB".

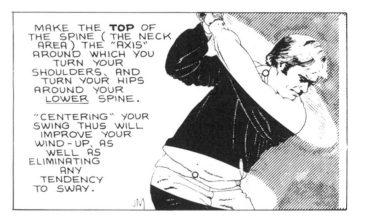

MAKE THE **TOP** OF THE SPINE (THE NECK AREA) THE "AXIS" AROUND WHICH YOU TURN YOUR SHOULDERS, AND TURN YOUR HIPS AROUND YOUR LOWER SPINE.

"CENTERING" YOUR SWING THUS WILL IMPROVE YOUR WIND-UP, AS WELL AS ELIMINATING ANY TENDENCY TO SWAY.

Coil Your Shoulders as Fully as You Can

BACKSWING 11

FLAILING AT THE BALL WITH THE HANDS AND ARMS, INSTEAD OF **LEVERING** THE CLUB THROUGH IT VIA A FULL UPPER-BODY TURN, IS ONE OF GOLF'S COMMONEST FAULTS.

CURE IS TO TURN YOUR SHOULDERS AS FAR AROUND AS THEY'LL GO SHORT OF FORCING YOUR RIGHT KNEE TO STIFFEN, YOUR WEIGHT TO MOVE TO THE OUTSIDE OF YOUR RIGHT FOOT, OR YOUR LEFT HEEL TO RISE MORE THAN ABOUT AN INCH OFF THE GROUND.

Practice These 3 "Feels"

HERE ARE THREE PRACTICE-TEE THOUGHTS TO HELP YOU MAXIMIZE YOUR UPPER-BODY TURN.

FOR THE FIRST THIRD OF THE BACKSWING, DEVELOP THE FEELING THAT YOUR SHOULDERS ARE **PUSHING** YOUR ARMS BACK AND UP.

BACKSWING 12

AS THE CLUB GETS HIP-HIGH, AND FOR THE NEXT THIRD OF THE BACKSWING, SWITCH TO A FEELING OF YOUR UP-SWINGING ARMS **PULLING** YOUR SHOULDERS AROUND.

DURING THE FINAL PART OF THE BACKSWING, CONCENTRATE ON THRUSTING YOUR HANDS AS HIGH AS THEY'LL GO BEHIND YOUR HEAD — REALLY "REACH FOR THE CLOUDS."

Keep Left Arm Straight but Not Stiff

BACKSWING 13

GOLFERS OF OLD PLAYED WELL WITH BENT LEFT ARMS, BUT YOU DON'T SEE MANY ON TOUR TODAY.

REASON IS THE DIFFICULTY OF CONSISTENTLY REPRODUCING THE PROPER SWING PATH THROUGH IMPACT WHEN THE ARC-CONTROLLING ARM BENDS GOING BACK AND THEN STRAIGHTENS COMING DOWN.

A STRAIGHT-BUT-NOT-STIFF LEFT ARM IS MOST TOUR PROS' GOAL, INCLUDING ME.

KEY TO ATTAINING IT IS A FIRM LEFT-HAND GRIP, AND A ONE-PIECE MOVEMENT AWAY FROM THE BALL FROM THE LEFT SHOULDER TO THE CLUBHEAD.

Never Loosen Your Grip

BACKSWING 14

LOOSENING THE GRIP AT THE TOP OF THE BACKSWING IS A SURE ROUTE TO DISASTER.

MANY GOLFERS DO IT INVOLUNTARILY IN TRYING TO SWING LONGER WITHOUT MAKING A FULLER BODY TURN.

CHECK THIS POINT IF YOU ARE SPRAYING SHOTS.

CURE LIES IN ESTABLISHING A SECURE GRIP AT ADDRESS, AND SUSTAINING IT BY USING THE BODY TURN AS WELL AS THE HAND-AND-ARM SWING TO GET THE CLUB FULLY BACK.

Try to Swing "In Line"

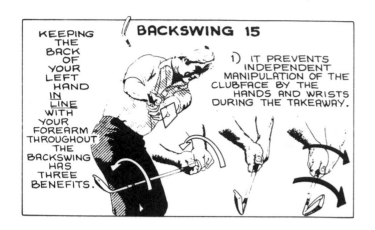

BACKSWING 15

KEEPING THE BACK OF YOUR LEFT HAND IN LINE WITH YOUR FOREARM THROUGHOUT THE BACKSWING HAS THREE BENEFITS.

1) IT PREVENTS INDEPENDENT MANIPULATION OF THE CLUBFACE BY THE HANDS AND WRISTS DURING THE TAKEAWAY.

2) IT KEEPS THE WRISTS FIRM, AND ENSURES THAT THEY COCK AT THE CORRECT ANGLE IN RESPONSE TO THE SWINGING WEIGHT OF THE CLUBHEAD.

3) IT KEEPS THE CLUBFACE CORRECTLY SQUARE TO THE ARC THE CLUB IS DESCRIBING THROUGHOUT THE SWING.

Don't Rush from the Top

BACKSWING 16

SHOULD YOU "PAUSE" AT THE TOP? A FEW FINE GOLFERS HAVE — NOTABLY TWO-TIME U.S. OPEN CHAMPION **CARY MIDDLECOFF.**

I HAVE NO DISCERNIBLE PAUSE, BECAUSE MY LOWER BODY ACTUALLY BEGINS THE DOWNSWING JUST AS MY UPPER BODY IS COMPLETING THE BACKSWING.

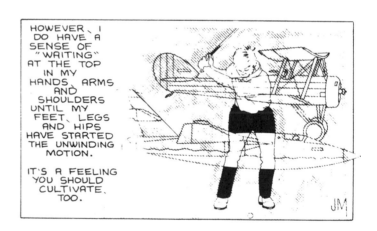

HOWEVER, I DO HAVE A SENSE OF "WAITING" AT THE TOP IN MY HANDS, ARMS AND SHOULDERS UNTIL MY FEET, LEGS AND HIPS HAVE STARTED THE UNWINDING MOTION.

IT'S A FEELING YOU SHOULD CULTIVATE, TOO.

Swing as "Long" as You Can

HOW FAR SHOULD I SWING BACK JACK?

BACK-SWING 17

AS FAR AS YOU CAN WITHOUT STIFFENING YOUR RIGHT KNEE, FORCING YOUR WEIGHT TO THE OUTSIDE OF YOUR RIGHT FOOT, LIFTING YOUR LEFT HEEL HIGH, BENDING YOUR LEFT ARM, OR LOOSENING YOUR GRIP.

WITHIN THOSE CONDITIONS, THE LONGER YOUR SWING THE BETTER YOU'LL PLAY -- AND THE LONGER YOU'LL GO ON PLAYING WELL.

YOU DON'T SEE MANY SENIOR CHAMPIONS WITH SHORT SWINGS — AS WITNESS **SAM SNEAD.**

10

Down and Through

Look for Downswing Fault in Backswing

THROUGH - SWING 1

BECAUSE IT HAPPENS TOO FAST TO BE CONSCIOUSLY DIRECTED, THE DOWNSWING MUST BE LARGELY A REFLEXIVE ACTION.

1 SECONDS

SO, IF YOU'RE FAULTY COMING DOWN, THE FIRST PLACE TO LOOK FOR THE PROBLEM IS IN HOW YOU GO BACK.

BUILD A GOOD BACKSWING AND YOU'LL AUTOMATICALLY DEVELOP A GOOD THROUGH - SWING PATTERN.

Reverse "Halves" Coming Down

THROUGH - SWING 2

HERE'S THE BASIC FACTOR TO ALWAYS REMEMBER ABOUT GOLF'S BACKWARD AND FORWARD MOTIONS.

GOING BACK, YOUR LOWER BODY WORKS IN RESPONSE TO THE COILING OF YOUR UPPER BODY. EXACTLY THE REVERSE MUST HAPPEN COMING DOWN — YOUR UPPER BODY MUST RESPOND ONLY TO THE UNCOILING OF YOUR LOWER BODY.

THAT'S FUNDAMENTAL WHATEVER YOUR PERSONAL SWING STYLE.

Maximize Your Leverage

VERY FEW GOLFERS (GOOD ONES) ACTUALLY PAUSE — HALT ALL MOTION — AT THE TOP OF THE BACKSWING.

WHAT HAPPENS IS THAT THE LOWER BODY STARTS THE DOWNSWING JUST BEFORE THE UPPER BODY COMPLETES THE BACKSWING.

THAT WAY YOU ACHIEVE BOTH MAXIMUM LEVERAGE AND A SMOOTH TRANSITION FROM BACKWARD TO FORWARD MOTION.

Swing Down from Feet Up

MOST GOLFERS WOULD IMPROVE IMMENSELY BY LEARNING TO START DOWN WITH THEIR FEET RATHER THAN THEIR HANDS.

GET THE FEELING OF YOUR LEFT HEEL REPLANTING SOLIDLY AS YOU PUSH HARD OFF THE INSIDE OF YOUR RIGHT FOOT.

DO THAT BEFORE ANYTHING UP TOP UNWINDS AND YOU'RE 90 PER CENT OF THE WAY TO PROPER LOWER-BODY ACTION.

Never Hurry Your Shoulders

HERE'S A TIP TO HELP YOU INITIATE THE DOWNSWING MOTION WITH YOUR FEET AND LEGS RATHER THAN YOUR UPPER BODY.

AS YOU START BACK TO THE BALL, TRY TO KEEP THE UPWARD MOVEMENT OF YOUR LEFT SHOULDER AS SLOW AS POSSIBLE.

THE SLOWER THIS HAPPENS, THE MORE TIME YOUR LEGS HAVE TO MOVE TARGETWARDS BEFORE YOUR SHOULDERS UNWIND.

Flex—and Use—Those Knees

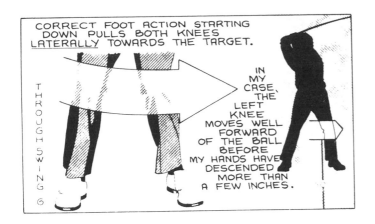

CORRECT FOOT ACTION STARTING DOWN PULLS BOTH KNEES LATERALLY TOWARDS THE TARGET.

THROUGH SWING 6

IN MY CASE, THE LEFT KNEE MOVES WELL FORWARD OF THE BALL BEFORE MY HANDS HAVE DESCENDED MORE THAN A FEW INCHES.

KEY TO ACHIEVING AND SUSTAINING THIS STRONG LEG ACTION IS TO KEEP BOTH KNEES FLEXED THROUGH IMPACT.

STIFFENING THE LEFT LEG TOO FAST IS A FREQUENT CAUSE OF SPINNING THE SHOULDERS OVER THE BALL.

S-t-r-e-t-c-h That Left Side

THROUGH - SWING 7

MANY GOLFERS HAVE A PROBLEM COMBINING A FLEXED LEFT KNEE THROUGH IMPACT WITH A FIRM LEFT SIDE.

FEELING TO STRIVE FOR IS ONE OF STRETCHING FROM YOUR LEFT FOOT TO YOUR LEFT SHOULDER WITHOUT STRAIGHTENING YOUR LEFT LEG — OR RAISING YOUR HEAD — UNTIL THE BALL HAS BEEN STRUCK.

THE BETTER SHAPE YOUR LEGS ARE IN, THE EASIER THIS BECOMES.

Don't Think About Wrist Action

THROUGH SWING 8

A GOOD TRANSITION FROM BACKSWING TO DOWNSWING ELIMINATES ANY NEED FOR DELIBERATE WRIST-COCKING.

NEARING THE TOP, THE SWINGING WEIGHT OF THE CLUBHEAD WILL NATURALLY BEGIN TO HINGE YOUR WRISTS.

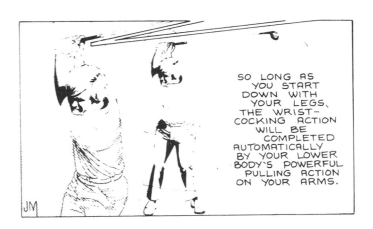

SO LONG AS YOU START DOWN WITH YOUR LEGS, THE WRIST-COCKING ACTION WILL BE COMPLETED AUTOMATICALLY BY YOUR LOWER BODY'S POWERFUL PULLING ACTION ON YOUR ARMS.

Keep Legs Moving Ahead of Arms

THROUGH - SWING 9

MANY TEACHERS FAVOR STARTING THE THROUGH - SWING WITH A DOWNWARD PULLING OF THE LEFT ARM — A "TOLLING THE BELL" ACTION.

THAT'S FINE SO LONG AS YOUR LEGS WORK IN HARNESS WITH YOUR ARM SWING.

IF YOUR LEGS DON'T MOVE JUST A LITTLE AHEAD OF YOUR ARMS, CHANCES ARE YOUR ARMS WILL PULL YOUR SHOULDERS FORWARD 'OVER' THE BALL.

Avoid These 3 Errors

THROUGH - SWING 10

RAISING THE BODY UP AS THE CLUB SWINGS DOWN CAUSES MANY HORROR SHOTS. IT COMES MAINLY FROM THE FOLLOWING:

1. CROUCHING OVER THE BALL AT ADDRESS, USUALLY WITH STIFF LEGS.

2. THROWING THE CLUB FROM THE TOP WITH THE HANDS AND WRISTS.

3. FAILING TO START DOWN WITH THE FEET AND KNEES, WHICH KEEPS THE WEIGHT ON THE RIGHT SIDE AND STIFFENS THE LEGS.

Let Hips Follow Knees . . .

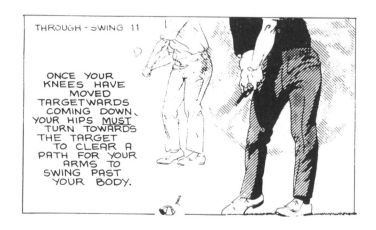

THROUGH - SWING 11

ONCE YOUR KNEES HAVE MOVED TARGETWARDS COMING DOWN, YOUR HIPS MUST TURN TOWARDS THE TARGET TO CLEAR A PATH FOR YOUR ARMS TO SWING PAST YOUR BODY.

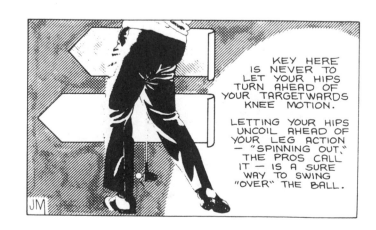

KEY HERE IS NEVER TO LET YOUR HIPS TURN AHEAD OF YOUR TARGETWARDS KNEE MOTION.

LETTING YOUR HIPS UNCOIL AHEAD OF YOUR LEG ACTION — "SPINNING OUT," THE PROS CALL IT — IS A SURE WAY TO SWING "OVER" THE BALL.

. . . but Keep Lower-Body Action <u>Smooth</u>

THROUGH SWING 12

IN TRYING TO IMPROVE YOUR LOWER-BODY ACTION, BE CAREFUL NOT TO OVER-DO YOUR LEG/HIP MOTION TO THE POINT WHERE YOU LURCH YOUR ENTIRE BODY FORWARD.

JM

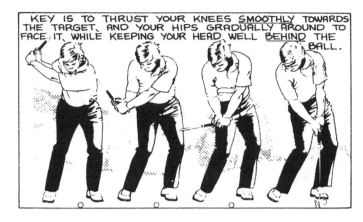

KEY IS TO THRUST YOUR KNEES <u>SMOOTHLY</u> TOWARDS THE TARGET, AND YOUR HIPS GRADUALLY AROUND TO FACE IT, WHILE KEEPING YOUR HEAD WELL <u>BEHIND</u> THE BALL.

Prefer "Left-Side" Thoughts

THROUGH-SWING 13

I BASICALLY CONTROL THE SWING WITH MY <u>LEFT SIDE</u>, BUT IF THINGS AREN'T GOING WELL I'LL TRY EMPHASIZING RIGHT-SIDE ACTION.

FOR EXAMPLE, MY PREFERRED THOUGHT COMING DOWN IS "MOVE THE LEFT SHOULDER UP AND THE LEFT HIP AROUND."

BUT IF THAT DOESN'T SEEM TO BE WORKING, I'LL TRY "MOVE THE <u>RIGHT</u> SHOULDER <u>DOWN</u> AND THE RIGHT HIP AROUND."

BALANCING OUT SWING "FEELS" THIS MIGHT HELP YOU PLAY BETTER.

JM

Work Lower Body—Then Release!

THROUGH-SWING 14

JOE, YOU'RE LETTING ALL THAT STUFF ABOUT HITTING "LATE" WITH THE HANDS AND WRISTS PREVENT YOU FROM RELEASING THE CLUBHEAD THROUGH THE BALL!

JM

AS LONG AS YOU START DOWN WITH YOUR LOWER BODY AND KEEP IT MOVING AHEAD OF YOUR UPPER HALF, YOU CAN'T HIT TOO "EARLY" WITH YOUR HANDS AND WRISTS.

SO GET THOSE LEGS GOING, AND THEN LET THAT CLUBHEAD <u>FLY</u>!

Meld Hip and Hand/Wrist Action

THROUGH - SWING 15

IF YOUR BASIC SWING PATTERN IS SOUND BUT YOU START TO SLICE SHOTS, CHANCES ARE YOUR HIP ACTION IS GETTING AHEAD OF YOUR HAND/WRIST ACTION.

EITHER SLOWING DOWN YOUR HIP UNWIND OR SPEEDING UP YOUR CLUBHEAD RELEASE SHOULD STRAIGHTEN YOU OUT.

IF THE PROBLEM'S A HOOK, CHANCES ARE THAT YOUR HANDS/WRISTS ARE RELEASING THE CLUB BEFORE YOU'VE ACHIEVED SUFFICIENT HIP CLEARANCE.

ANSWER HERE IS TO EITHER SPEED UP YOUR HIP ACTION OR HOLD BACK A LITTLE ON YOUR CLUBHEAD RELEASE.

Check for This Sign of "Spinning"

THROUGH - SWING 16

RISING UP ON THE RIGHT TOE WELL BEFORE IMPACT IS A SURE SIGN OF SPINNING THE UPPER BODY "OVER AND AROUND" INSTEAD OF SWINGING "UNDER AND THROUGH."

ONE WAY TO CURE THIS UGLY MOVE IS TO PRACTICE HITTING SHOTS WHILE KEEPING THE RIGHT HEEL ANCHORED AND THE RIGHT KNEE FACING THE BALL.

IT'LL BE A WHOLE NEW FEEL, SO START WITH THE SHORT IRONS AND WORK UP.

Let Right Arm Straighten

THROUGH SWING 17

IN MOST GOOD GOLF SWINGS THE RIGHT ELBOW STAYS SLIGHTLY BENT AND POINTING TOWARDS THE RIGHT SIDE, RIGHT UP UNTIL IMPACT.

ONCE THE BALL IS STRUCK, HOWEVER, A QUICKLY STRAIGHTENING AND EXTENDING RIGHT ARM IS A SIGN OF FULL CLUBHEAD RELEASE. FEELING I LIKE AT THAT POINT IS OF ALMOST BEING ABLE TO REACH OUT AND RETRIEVE THE FLYING BALL WITH MY RIGHT HAND.

Chase Ball with Clubface

GREATER ARM EXTENSION THROUGH THE BALL WOULD HELP MANY GOLFERS WITH DIRECTIONAL PROBLEMS.

FEELING I OFTEN SEEK WHEN I NEED MAXIMUM ACCURACY IS THAT OF KEEPING THE CLUBFACE ON THE BALL AS LONG AS POSSIBLE AFTER IMPACT.

FIRM WRISTS AND STAYING WELL DOWN AND BACK ON THE SHOT ARE ESSENTIAL TO PROMOTE IT.

Think "Acceleration"

SCIENTISTS SAY IT'S IMPOSSIBLE TO ACTUALLY KEEP ON ACCELERATING THE CLUBHEAD THROUGH THE BALL — THAT IT ALWAYS REACHES MAXIMUM SPEED BEFORE IMPACT.

THROUGH - SWING 19

NEVERTHELESS, I THINK IT PAYS TO HAVE THE FEELING OF TRYING TO ACCELERATE THROUGH THE BALL AND BEYOND. DANGER IS THAT, IF YOU DO NOT THINK ACCELERATION, YOU'LL PROBABLY DECELERATE BEFORE IMPACT.

ACCELERATION!

Strive for a Fine Follow-through

THROUGH SWING 20

BIG DOWN-SWING FAULT OF HIGH HANDICAP GOLFERS IS HITTING AT THE BALL INSTEAD OF SWINGING THE CLUBHEAD FREELY THROUGH IT.

ONE WAY TO OVERCOME THIS IS TO PRACTICE WHILE IMAGINING THE BALL SIMPLY ISN'T THERE.

IF THAT DOESN'T WORK, FOCUSING MENTALLY ON ACHIEVING A SPECIFIC FOLLOW-THROUGH PATTERN OR "FEEL" WILL REDUCE YOUR BALL CONSCIOUSNESS.

11

Tempo, Rhythm
and Timing

Understand What "Timing" Is

TIMING IS A WORD FOR THE WAY ALL YOUR SWING MOTIONS MELD TOGETHER.

WHEN THE MELD PRODUCES MAXIMUM SQUARENESS OF CLUBFACE AND CLUBHEAD SPEED AT IMPACT, YOUR TIMING IS PERFECT.

SLOW

SMOOTH

GOOD TIMING REQUIRES GOOD SWING FORM, SO WHEN YOUR TIMING GOES OFF LOOK BACK INTO THE FUNDAMENTALS OF YOUR ACTION — PARTICULARLY YOUR TAKEAWAY TEMPO AND TRANSITION FROM BACKSWING TO THROUGH-SWING.

Swing Rhythmically Within Natural Tempo

YOUR TEMPO, OR SPEED OF SWING, IS LARGELY DETERMINED BY YOUR PERSONALITY.

DELIBERATE PEOPLE NATURALLY TEND TO SWING SLOWLY, HYPERACTIVE PEOPLE QUICKLY.

RATHER THAN TAMPER WITH WHAT COMES NATURALLY, STRIVE TO SWING RHYTHMICALLY WHATEVER YOUR PACE.

RHYTHM IS THE QUALITY WITH WHICH YOU MELD ALL THE MOVING PARTS OF THE SWING, AND THE SMOOTHER IT IS THE BETTER YOUR TIMING WILL BE.

Use Bigger Muscles for Smoother Action

A SLOWER SWING ISN'T NECESSARILY GOING TO IMPROVE YOUR GAME, BUT A **SMOOTHER TEMPO** ALMOST ALWAYS WILL.

IT'S MY EXPERIENCE THAT THE BIGGER THE MUSCLES YOU USE TO PROPEL THE CLUB, THE MORE FLUIDLY AND SMOOTHLY YOU CAN SWING IT.

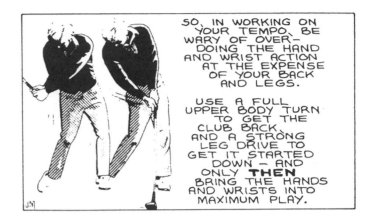

SO, IN WORKING ON YOUR TEMPO, BE WARY OF OVER-DOING THE HAND AND WRIST ACTION AT THE EXPENSE OF YOUR BACK AND LEGS.

USE A FULL UPPER BODY TURN TO GET THE CLUB BACK, AND A STRONG LEG DRIVE TO GET IT STARTED DOWN — AND ONLY **THEN** BRING THE HANDS AND WRISTS INTO MAXIMUM PLAY.

Work on Rhythm When Timing Is Off

BEWARE OF TRYING TO CHANGE YOUR OVERALL SPEED OF SWING, BECAUSE THIS ALMOST CERTAINLY IS A PRODUCT OF YOUR PERSONALITY, AND AS SUCH PRETTY DIFFICULT TO CHANGE EFFECTIVELY.

INSTEAD, WHEN YOU FEEL YOUR TIMING IS "OFF," CONCENTRATE ON THE **RHYTHM** OF YOUR ACTION RATHER THAN ITS OVERALL PACE.

WHETHER YOU NATURALLY SWING FAST OR SLOW, STRIVE FOR **SMOOTHNESS** OF MOTION FROM TAKEAWAY TO COMPLETION OF FOLLOW-THROUGH.

ALSO, THINKING OF SWINGING THE CLUBHEAD **THROUGH** THE BALL, NOT **AT IT**, IS OFTEN HELPFUL IN IMPROVING TIMING.

Try for Same Tempo with All Clubs

BEGINNERS AT GOLF OFTEN SEEM TO THINK THEY NEED A DIFFERENT SWING FOR EVERY CLUB IN THE BAG. THAT ISN'T TRUE — AND ESPECIALLY NOT IN TERMS OF TEMPO.

HIGH-SPEED FILMS OF ME HAVE SHOWN THAT, WHEN PLAYING WELL, MY SWING POSITIONS ARE THE SAME WHETHER SWINGING A ONE-IRON OR AN 8-IRON.... WHICH MEANS MY TEMPO IS PRETTY MUCH IDENTICAL.

THAT'S A GOAL I THINK EVERY GOLFER SHOULD STRIVE FOR.

Make Driver Swing Your Tempo Model

OBVIOUSLY THE SHORTER THE CLUB, THE SHORTER THE ELAPSED TIME OF THE SWING.

BUT YOU SHOULDN'T FEEL THAT YOU SWING A WEDGE ANY FASTER THAN YOU SWING A DRIVER.

WHEN I'M PLAYING WELL, I FEEL THAT THE PACE OF MY SWING IS EXACTLY THE SAME WITH EVERY CLUB IN THE BAG — EVEN THE PUTTER. AND THE IDEAL PACE IN MY CASE IS THE DRIVER SWING — THE SLOWEST.

JM

Try This to Smooth Out Takeaway

I'M ONE OF A SMALL NUMBER OF TOUR PLAYERS WHO NEVER GROUND THE CLUB AT ADDRESS.

THE TECHNIQUE BEGAN IN MY CASE AS A GUARD AGAINST ACCIDENTALLY MOVING THE BALL OR STUBBING THE CLUB STARTING BACK, BUT ITS BIGGEST VALUE HAS LONG BEEN ITS SMOOTHING EFFECT ON MY TAKEAWAY.

IT TAKES A WHILE TO GET USED TO STARTING BACK FROM AN UNGROUNDED POSITION, BUT IT'S A CERTAIN WAY TO SMOOTH OUT A JERKY TAKEAWAY, AND A BIG HELP IN BUILDING A ONE-PIECE BACKSWING.

BEGIN WITH THE SHORT IRONS AND WORK UP IF YOU DECIDE TO GIVE IT A TRY.

SMOOTH

Beware of a Dead Halt at Top

IS "PAUSE AT THE TOP" A GOOD THOUGHT?

NOT, IN MY VIEW, IF IT CAUSES YOU TO LITERALLY COME TO A DEAD STOP BEFORE YOU START DOWN AGAIN, BECAUSE THAT'S A SURE WAY TO WRECK YOUR TEMPO AND MOMENTUM — NOT TO MENTION YOUR BALANCE.

A BETTER THOUGHT TO ME WOULD BE "WAIT FOR THE LEGS TO WORK BEFORE THE HANDS START DOWN," OR "CHANGE DIRECTIONS SMOOTHLY," OR — MY FAVORITE — "START DOWN AT THE SAME SPEED YOU STARTED BACK."

IN OTHER WORDS, ANYTHING THAT PROMOTES GOOD TIMING — WHICH A DEAD HALT DOESN'T, IN MY VIEW.

12

Power!

Never Hit for Distance Only

IS DISTANCE AS BIG A GOLFING ASSET AS MOST PLAYERS SEEM TO THINK IT IS ??

ONLY IF YOU CAN HIT LONG **AND STRAIGHT** — AND ONLY THEN IF YOU USE LENGTH INTELLIGENTLY.

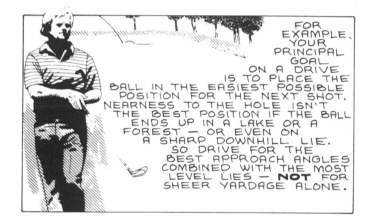

FOR EXAMPLE, YOUR PRINCIPAL GOAL ON A DRIVE IS TO PLACE THE BALL IN THE EASIEST POSSIBLE POSITION FOR THE NEXT SHOT. NEARNESS TO THE HOLE ISN'T THE BEST POSITION IF THE BALL ENDS UP IN A LAKE OR A FOREST — OR EVEN ON A SHARP DOWNHILL LIE. SO DRIVE FOR THE BEST APPROACH ANGLES COMBINED WITH THE MOST LEVEL LIES — **NOT** FOR SHEER YARDAGE ALONE.

Beware the "Steering" Tendency

AS A KID I WAS TAUGHT BY JACK GROUT TO HIT HARD FIRST AND DEVELOP ACCURACY LATER.

MANY GOLFERS LACK DISTANCE BECAUSE THEY'VE HABITUALIZED "BABYING" OR "STEERING" THE BALL STRAIGHT.

INCREASED BODY TURN AND ARM EXTENSION WILL LET YOU TAKE A BIGGER CUT AT IT.

BUT TRY FIRST ON A DRIVING RANGE. AND KEEP YOUR HEAD STILL AND YOUR TEMPO **SMOOTH.**

Stay a Little Within Yourself

THERE'S NO DOUBT SOME OF THE GAME'S LONGEST HITTERS SWING FLAT OUT ON MANY OF THEIR DRIVES. PERHAPS THAT'S WHY A NUMBER OF THEM ALSO SPEND SO MUCH TIME IN THE TALL GRASS!

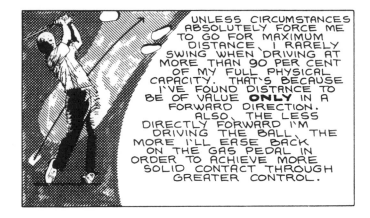

UNLESS CIRCUMSTANCES ABSOLUTELY FORCE ME TO GO FOR MAXIMUM DISTANCE, I RARELY SWING WHEN DRIVING AT MORE THAN 90 PER CENT OF MY FULL PHYSICAL CAPACITY. THAT'S BECAUSE I'VE FOUND DISTANCE TO BE OF VALUE **ONLY** IN A FORWARD DIRECTION. ALSO, THE LESS DIRECTLY FORWARD I'M DRIVING THE BALL, THE MORE I'LL EASE BACK ON THE GAS PEDAL IN ORDER TO ACHIEVE MORE SOLID CONTACT THROUGH GREATER CONTROL.

Work on a Square Hit

THE WOMEN PROFESSIONALS ARE LIVING PROOF THAT STRENGTH ALONE DOESN'T PRODUCE DISTANCE IN GOLF.

QUITE A NUMBER OF THE **LPGA** PROFESSIONALS DRIVE THE BALL FARTHER THAN MOST MALE CLUB GOLFERS.

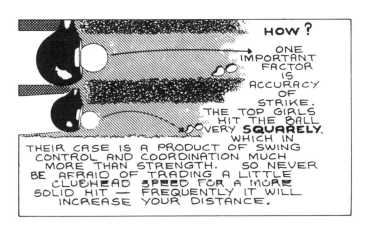

HOW? ONE IMPORTANT FACTOR IS ACCURACY OF STRIKE. THE TOP GIRLS HIT THE BALL VERY **SQUARELY**, WHICH IN THEIR CASE IS A PRODUCT OF SWING CONTROL AND COORDINATION MUCH MORE THAN STRENGTH. SO NEVER BE AFRAID OF TRADING A LITTLE CLUBHEAD SPEED FOR A MORE SOLID HIT — FREQUENTLY IT WILL INCREASE YOUR DISTANCE.

Determine Your Best Route

THERE ARE BASICALLY TWO WAYS TO GET DISTANCE! ONE IS VIA A LONG, HIGH, FLOATING CARRY --- WHICH IS THE WAY I FAVOR BECAUSE IT OFFERS THE GREATEST CONTROL. BUT IT TAKES A CERTAIN AMOUNT OF STRENGTH AND AN UPRIGHT SWING PLANE.

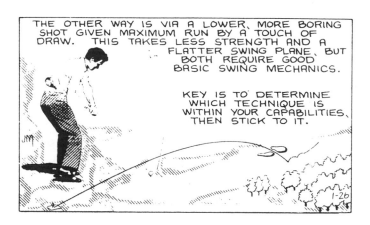

THE OTHER WAY IS VIA A LOWER, MORE BORING SHOT GIVEN MAXIMUM RUN BY A TOUCH OF DRAW. THIS TAKES LESS STRENGTH AND A FLATTER SWING PLANE, BUT BOTH REQUIRE GOOD BASIC SWING MECHANICS.

KEY IS TO DETERMINE WHICH TECHNIQUE IS WITHIN YOUR CAPABILITIES, THEN STICK TO IT.

Don't Cramp Your Style

TOO MANY GOLFERS CRAMP OR OVER-FLATTEN THEIR SWINGS BY TRYING TO AVOID A "FLYING" RIGHT ELBOW.

YOU CAN'T GET FULL ARM EXTENSION — AND THUS MAXIMUM DISTANCE-PRODUCING LEVERAGE — IF YOU OVER-CONSTRICT YOUR RIGHT ELBOW.

MY RIGHT ARM MOVES WELL AWAY FROM AND BEHIND MY BODY ON THE BACKSWING, BUT IT'S NOT "FLYING."

TO DO THAT IT WOULD HAVE TO POINT OUTWARD — BEHIND ME — WHEREAS IT ACTUALLY POINTS TOWARD THE GROUND.

SO, LONG AS YOURS DOES THE SAME, IT WON'T BE "FLYING" EITHER.

Try a Fuller Hip Turn

LOSING DISTANCE AS THOSE BIRTHDAYS KEEP COMING ALONG FASTER AND FASTER??

TRY LETTING YOUR HIPS TURN A LITTLE MORE FULLY GOING BACK IN RESPONSE TO YOUR ARM SWING AND SHOULDER WIND-UP.

IT'S TRUE THAT MANY OF THE YOUNGER OR MORE FLEXIBLE TOUR PLAYERS DON'T TURN THEIR HIPS MUCH -- BUT IT'S ALSO TRUE THAT **BOBBY JONES** WON HIS 13 MAJORS TURNING HIS HIPS ALMOST AS MUCH AS HIS SHOULDERS.

IN MY VIEW, A LOT OF HIP TURN IS BETTER THAN NONE — ESPECIALLY FOR SENIORS AND STOCKY PLAYERS.

Move Faster from the Hips Down

MOST AMATEURS WHEN TRYING FOR EXTRA DISTANCE INSTINCTIVELY TRY TO HIT HARDER WITH THEIR HANDS AND ARMS FROM THE TOP OF THE BACKSWING. IT'S A SURE WAY TO BOTH DIMINISH CLUBHEAD SPEED AND DISTORT CLUBFACE ALIGNMENT.

MY PRIMARY THOUGHT IN GOING FOR A BIG ONE IS A FASTER HIP UNWIND THROUGHOUT THE DOWNSWING.

SO LONG AS YOU CAN KEEP THE ACTION SMOOTH AND FLUID, THE FASTER YOU UNCOIL YOUR HIPS THE GREATER THE LEVERAGE YOU CREATE, AND THUS THE FASTER YOU'LL WHIP THE CLUBHEAD THROUGH THE BALL.

Tee Ball So You Can Meet It Flush

CHECK THE HEIGHT YOU TEE THE BALL IF YOUR DRIVES ARE STOPPING SHORTER THAN YOU'D LIKE.

TEEING THE BALL LOW ENCOURAGES HITTING DOWN ON IT, WHICH INCREASES BACKSPIN, WHICH <u>DECREASES</u> ROLL.

TEEING THE BALL SO THAT ITS CENTER IS ABOUT EVEN WITH THE TOP EDGE OF THE DRIVER WILL ENCOURAGE YOU TO <u>SWEEP</u> THE CLUBHEAD THROUGH ON A MORE LEVEL PATH AT IMPACT. THAT'LL GIVE YOU BOTH MAXIMUM CARRY <u>AND</u> ROLL.

Extend That Arc!

no. 7
572 YDS
PAR 5

USUAL RESULT OF AN ATTEMPT TO DRIVE FARTHER IS A VICE — LIKE GRIP, AN EXCESSIVE PIVOT, A SWAYING HEAD, A BENT LEFT ARM, AND A SHOULDER-SPINNING LUNGE AT THE BALL COMING DOWN.

NEXT TIME YOU NEED A BIG ONE, FORGET TRYING TO 'FORCE' THE SHOT.

INSTEAD, STAY WITH YOUR BASIC SWING MOVES AND TEMPO, BUT SIMPLY TRY TO <u>EXTEND THE ARC</u> BY GETTING YOUR ARMS HIGHER AT THE TOP. DON'T START DOWN UNTIL YOU'VE FELT YOUR HANDS REACH **ABOVE** YOUR SHOULDERS.

Try This Stance Adjustment . . .

CONSIDER YOUR RIGHT FOOT PLACEMENT IF YOU'RE HAVING TROUBLE MAKING A GOOD, FULL BODY TURN.

CURRENT PRO TOUR FASHION IS TO SET THE REAR FOOT AT 90 DEGREES TO THE TARGET LINE, BUT THAT'S TOO RESTRICTIVE FOR MANY SENIOR AND LESS SUPPLE GOLFERS.

THE FARTHER THE RIGHT FOOT POINTS AWAY FROM THE TARGET, THE FARTHER THE HIPS CAN BE ROTATED, AND THE FARTHER THE HIPS CAN BE ROTATED, THE MORE FULLY THE SHOULDERS CAN BE COILED.

SO POINT YOUR FOOT FOR POWER, NOT FOR APPEARANCES.

...or This One

WHEN I'M REALLY GOING FOR A BIG HIT, I MAKE A SLIGHT STANCE ADJUSTMENT THAT HELPS ME SPEED UP MY LEG THRUST AND HIP CLEARANCE.

15TH HOLE
PAR 5 520 YDS.
AUGUSTA NATIONAL

BY TURNING MY LEFT FOOT TARGETWARDS A LITTLE MORE, I GIVE MYSELF A RUNNING START ON SHIFTING MY HIPS OUT OF THE WAY FASTER ON THE FORWARD SWING.

IF YOU TRY THIS, BE SURE TO START DOWN WITH YOUR LEGS — OTHERWISE YOU RISK SPINNING OUT WITH YOUR SHOULDERS.

Set Right Hand to "Sling" Club

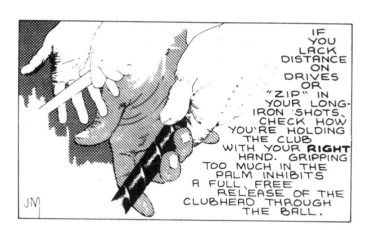

IF YOU LACK DISTANCE ON DRIVES OR "ZIP" IN YOUR LONG-IRON SHOTS, CHECK HOW YOU'RE HOLDING THE CLUB WITH YOUR **RIGHT** HAND. GRIPPING TOO MUCH IN THE PALM INHIBITS A FULL, FREE RELEASE OF THE CLUBHEAD THROUGH THE BALL.

TRY TO THROW A BALL HELD IN THE PALM OF YOUR HAND AND YOU WON'T MOVE IT VERY FAR.

GRIP THE BALL TOWARDS THE END OF YOUR FINGERS AND YOU CAN REALLY SLING IT.

LONG-HITTING AT GOLF REQUIRES THE SAME SORT OF SLINGING ACTION THROUGH IMPACT.

Let Clubhead Release Fully

FOR THE CLUB-HEAD TO BE FULLY RELEASED, THE RIGHT HAND AND WRIST MUST ROLL OVER THE LEFT SOMETIME BEYOND IMPACT.

BLOCKING OR OVER-DELAYING THAT ACTION IN AN EFFORT TO HOLD THE CLUBFACE SQUARE TO THE TARGET TOO LONG IS ONE REASON MANY GOLFERS LACK REAL "ZIP" IN THEIR SHOTS.

THE KEY IS TO LET THE FOREARMS ROTATE NATURALLY INTO THE FOLLOW-THROUGH, **WITHOUT** (A) THE LEFT WRIST BREAKING DOWN BY CUPPING INWARD (B).

A.
B.

THREE

Special Factors
and Situations

13

The Lower-Body Action

Allow Your Weight to Shift

THE MORE YOU CAN KEEP THE WEIGHT ON THE **INSIDES** OF YOUR FEET DURING THE SWING, THE MORE "CENTERED" YOUR BODY WILL BE AND THE LESS CHANCE YOU'LL HAVE OF SWAYING OFF THE BALL.

AT THE TOP I FEEL I HAVE ABOUT 80 PER CENT OF MY WEIGHT ON THE INSIDE OF MY RIGHT FOOT AND THE REST ON THE INSIDE OF MY LEFT.

AT **IMPACT**, THESE PROPORTIONS ARE REVERSED, WITH ALMOST ALL THE WEIGHT EVENTUALLY GOING OVER TO THE OUTSIDE EDGE OF THE LEFT FOOT AS THE FOLLOW-THROUGH PROGRESSES.

Practice "Rolling" with Heels Down

THE MORE YOU CAN ROLL RATHER THAN "DANCE" ON YOUR FEET, THE BETTER GOLF YOU'LL PLAY.

SOME OF THE BEST PRACTICE I EVER SPENT AS A YOUNGSTER WAS HITTING SHOTS WITHOUT ALLOWING MY HEELS TO LEAVE THE GROUND.

GOING BACK, ROLLING THE LEFT ANKLE AWAY FROM THE TARGET MOVES THE WEIGHT ONTO THE **INSIDE** OF THE RIGHT FOOT. COMING DOWN, ROLLING THE RIGHT ANKLE **TOWARDS** THE TARGET MOVES THE WEIGHT SOLIDLY BACK ONTO THE LEFT FOOT.

PRACTICE THESE MOTIONS WITH A MEDIUM-IRON AND A FAIRLY NARROW STANCE IF YOU WANT TO IMPROVE YOUR LEG ACTION. YOU'LL FIND YOUR BALANCE IMPROVING, TOO.

Don't Deliberately Lift Left Heel

WHETHER YOUR LEFT HEEL LIFTS ON A FULL SWING DEPENDS ON YOUR SUPPLENESS. IF IT _HAS_ TO COME OFF THE GROUND TO FACILITATE A FULL BODY TURN — AS IN MY CASE WITH THE LONGER CLUBS — THEN LET IT.

IF YOU CAN MAKE A GOOD WIND-UP WITHOUT RAISING THE LEFT HEEL, THEN YOU'VE GOT _TWO_ ADVANTAGES OVER THOSE WHO MUST LET IT LIFT.

ONE IS THAT YOU'LL GET BACK FASTER ONTO YOUR LEFT SIDE COMING DOWN.

THE OTHER IS THAT YOUR LEFT FOOT WILL NOT MOVE OUT OF POSITION AS YOU SHIFT YOUR WEIGHT —— AS SOMETIMES HAPPENS IN MY CASE.

Check Your Knee Flex

HOW MUCH SHOULD YOUR KNEES BEND OR FLEX AT ADDRESS AND THROUGHOUT THE SWING?

THE EXACT DEGREE DEPENDS ON YOUR BUILD AND SWING STYLE, BUT YOU SHOULD WORK WITHIN CERTAIN LIMITS.

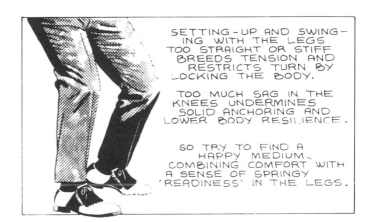

SETTING-UP AND SWINGING WITH THE LEGS TOO STRAIGHT OR STIFF BREEDS TENSION AND RESTRICTS TURN BY LOCKING THE BODY.

TOO MUCH SAG IN THE KNEES UNDERMINES SOLID ANCHORING AND LOWER BODY RESILIENCE.

SO TRY TO FIND A HAPPY MEDIUM, COMBINING COMFORT WITH A SENSE OF SPRINGY 'READINESS' IN THE LEGS.

Work on Your Right-Leg Action

SWAYING AND/OR STIFFENING THE RIGHT LEG GOING BACK CAUSES MUCH HEARTACHE FOR WEEKEND GOLFERS. REASON IS THAT SUCH MOVES PREVENT BOTH PROPER _WEIGHT-SHIFTING_ AND _HIP CLEARANCE_ COMING DOWN.

FLEX YOUR RIGHT KNEE SLIGHTLY AT ADDRESS AND KEEP IT THAT WAY THROUGHOUT THE BACKSWING. DEVELOP THE FEELING OF COILING AROUND A _FIXED BUT FLEXED_ RIGHT KNEE.

PRACTICING WITH A GOLF BALL UNDER THE OUTER EDGE OF THE FOOT WILL QUICKLY TEACH YOU THE PROPER RIGHT LEG ACTION.

BECAUSE IT CAN'T BE DONE WITHOUT THE LEGS MOVING TARGETWARDS, LEARNING TO SHIFT THE WEIGHT FROM THE RIGHT TO THE LEFT FOOT STARTING THE DOWNSWING IS A GREAT WAY TO DEVELOP GOOD LOWER-BODY ACTION.

PRACTICE THE MOTION USING A SHORT-IRON WITH THE BALL TEED AND THE FEET FAIRLY CLOSE TOGETHER. START WITH A LEISURELY HALF-SWING AND BUILD UP, CONCENTRATING ON A DISTINCT TO-AND-FRO WEIGHT SHIFT BY ROLLING THE ANKLES.

TRY TO FINISH EACH SWING WITH 90 PER CENT OF YOUR WEIGHT ON THE OUTSIDE EDGE OF YOUR LEFT FOOT.

14

The Role of the Hands and Wrists

Let Your Hands Follow, Not Lead

WHAT'S THE ROLE OF THE HANDS AND WRISTS IN GOLF?

THAT'S BEEN A SUBJECT OF GREAT DEBATE EVER SINCE THE GAME BEGAN, AND PROBABLY WILL BE AS LONG AS IT'S PLAYED.

BEING ESSENTIALLY A "BODY" RATHER THAN A "HANDS" PLAYER, THE HANDS AND WRISTS IN MY SWING ARE FOLLOWERS RATHER THAN LEADERS. BASICALLY, THEY WORK SIMPLY AS A HINGE TO STORE AND THEN TRANSMIT THE FORCE CREATED BY MY LEG AND BODY ACTION. AS SUCH, THEY COME INTO PLAY REFLEXIVELY RATHER THAN CONSCIOUSLY.

Allow Your Wrists to Cock Reflexively

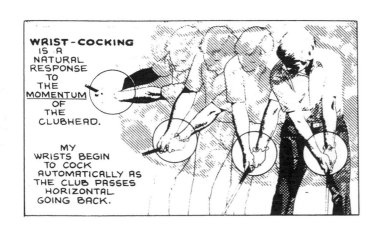

WRIST-COCKING IS A NATURAL RESPONSE TO THE MOMENTUM OF THE CLUBHEAD.

MY WRISTS BEGIN TO COCK AUTOMATICALLY AS THE CLUB PASSES HORIZONTAL GOING BACK.

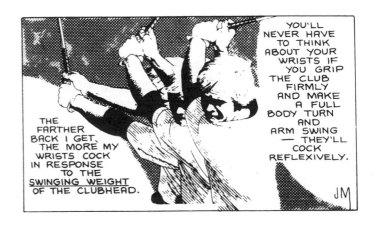

THE FARTHER BACK I GET, THE MORE MY WRISTS COCK IN RESPONSE TO THE SWINGING WEIGHT OF THE CLUBHEAD.

YOU'LL NEVER HAVE TO THINK ABOUT YOUR WRISTS IF YOU GRIP THE CLUB FIRMLY AND MAKE A FULL BODY TURN AND ARM SWING — THEY'LL COCK REFLEXIVELY.

"Reach for the Sky" with Your Hands

THE HIGHER THE HANDS AT THE TOP, THE BETTER THE GOLF SWING AS I SEE IT.

IF YOU HAVE DIFFICULTY CREATING THE FULL BODY TURN AND ARM EXTENSION THAT HIGH HANDS SIGNIFY, HERE'S A TIP THAT MIGHT HELP YOU.

GOING BACK, STRIVE FOR THE FEELING THAT YOUR LEFT ARM AND THE CLUB SHAFT REMAIN IN A STRAIGHT LINE UNTIL THE WEIGHT OF THE SWINGING CLUBHEAD CAUSES YOUR WRISTS TO HINGE INVOLUNTARILY. SWING SMOOTHLY AND DELIBERATELY AND YOU'LL FIND IT MUCH EASIER TO "REACH FOR THE SKY" WITH THIS ONE-PIECE TAKEAWAY FEELING.

Guide with Left, Hit with Right

IS THERE SUCH A THING AS "TOO MUCH RIGHT HAND" IN GOLF?

NOT IN MY VIEW!

IF THE RIGHT HAND OVERPOWERS THE LEFT, IT'S BECAUSE THE LEFT HAS BEEN USED IMPROPERLY.

THE LEFT HAND SHOULD CERTAINLY BE THE DOMINANT FACTOR IN GUIDING AND DIRECTING THE CLUB TO THE BALL. BUT IF IT DOES THAT CORRECTLY, YOU CAN — AND SHOULD — HIT AS HARD AS POSSIBLE WITH THE RIGHT HAND.

IN OTHER WORDS, YOU CAN USE **BOTH** HANDS TO THE UTMOST, SO LONG AS YOU USE THEM UNDERLINE PROPERLY.

Try Bigger Muscles for Better Timing

"HANDS" PLAYERS SEEM TO HAVE MORE TIMING PROBLEMS THAN "BODY" GOLFERS, PERHAPS BECAUSE SMALL MUSCLES OPERATE FASTER AND MORE SPONTANEOUSLY THAN BIG ONES.

THUS LEARNING TO MAKE MORE USE OF THE LEGS AND BACK, AND LESS OF THE HANDS AND WRISTS, IS ONE WAY TO IMPROVE AT GOLF.

IT TAKES TIME AND EFFORT, BUT THE GREATER CONSISTENCY MAY BE WORTH THE PRICE FOR THE AMBITIOUS PLAYER.

15

The All-Important Head

Copy the Masters—Stay Steady

THERE ARE A LOT OF WAYS TO PLAY GOOD GOLF, BUT THEY ALL HAVE ONE THING IN COMMON: A **STEADY HEAD.**

KEEPING YOUR HEAD STEADY ISN'T THE SAME THING AS "KEEPING YOUR EYE ON THE BALL"—I CAN SWAY MY HEAD TWO FEET AND STILL SEE THE BALL.

THE KEY TO HEAD STEADINESS IS NOT ALLOWING THE BACK OF YOUR NECK TO MOVE UP, DOWN OR SIDEWAYS AT ANY POINT FROM TAKEAWAY TO IMPACT.

THAT TAKES DISCIPLINE — AND <u>PRACTICE.</u>

Avoid These 3 Shot-Wreckers

YOUR HEAD IS YOUR SWING FULCRUM. IF IT MOVES SUBSTANTIALLY ONE OR ALL OF THE FOLLOWING WILL HAPPEN:

1. YOUR ARC AND PLANE WILL CHANGE.

2. YOUR EYES WILL RELATE INCORRECTLY TO YOUR TARGET LINE.

3. YOU'LL LOSE BALANCE.

LEARNING TO KEEP THE HEAD STEADY IS ONE OF GOLF'S TOUGHEST CHALLENGES, BUT IT'S AN ABSOLUTE **MUST** IF YOU WISH TO PLAY THE GAME WELL. THE ONLY ANSWERS ARE WILLPOWER AND PRACTICE — SUFFICIENT PRACTICE TO AUTOMATE SWINGING **AROUND** YOUR HEAD, NOT WITH IT.

Swivel Your Chin Going Back . . .

YOU'LL NEVER HIT THE BALL SOLIDLY FORWARD IF YOUR HEAD ISN'T SOLIDLY BEHIND IT AT IMPACT. MY HEAD AT THAT POINT STAYS BEHIND A VERTICAL LINE DRAWN UP FROM THE BALL.

I ENSURE THIS BY POSITIONING MY HEAD BEHIND THE BALL AT ADDRESS.

THEN I ENSURE IT EVEN MORE BY SWIVELING MY CHIN AWAY FROM THE TARGET ON THE TAKEAWAY AND LEAVING IT THERE UNTIL WELL AFTER IMPACT.

. . . and Going Through

A STEADY HEAD IS THE NO. 1 FUNDAMENTAL OF GOLF, BUT IT CAN BE OVERDONE.

IN FACT, TRYING TO LOOK AT THE BALL POSITION TOO LONG AFTER IMPACT ON A FULL SWING CAN ACTUALLY CAUSE YOUR HEAD TO BE FORCED UPWARD BY THE UNWINDING MOTION OF YOUR BODY.

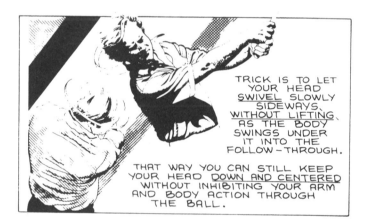

TRICK IS TO LET YOUR HEAD SWIVEL SLOWLY SIDEWAYS, WITHOUT LIFTING, AS THE BODY SWINGS UNDER IT INTO THE FOLLOW-THROUGH.

THAT WAY YOU CAN STILL KEEP YOUR HEAD DOWN AND CENTERED WITHOUT INHIBITING YOUR ARM AND BODY ACTION THROUGH THE BALL.

Beware of Up-and-Down Movement

ALTHOUGH EVEN THE BEST GOLFERS' HEADS DO MOVE A LITTLE DURING THE SWING, I BELIEVE THINKING OF KEEPING THE HEAD IN ONE PLACE, AT LEAST UNTIL IMPACT, DEFINITELY HELPS IN STRIKING THE BALL SOLIDLY.

AVOID UP-AND-DOWN HEAD MOVEMENT AS WELL AS SIDE-TO-SIDE. IF YOUR HEAD GOES DOWN ON THE BACKSWING AND UP ON THE THROUGH-SWING, YOU'LL TOP A LOT OF SHOTS.

IF THE REVERSE HAPPENS — UP IN THE BACKSWING AND DOWN IN THE THROUGH-SWING — YOU'LL HIT A LOT OF SHOTS "FAT" (GROUND BEFORE BALL).

Check Your Head Action the Hard Way

THE BEST WAY TO CHECK HEAD MOVEMENT IS TO HAVE SOMEONE WATCH YOUR HEAD AGAINST A BACKGROUND POINT.

IF YOU HAVE TROUBLE KEEPING THE TOP HALF STEADY, HIT A FEW SHOTS WHILE SOMEONE GRABS YOUR HAIR.

IT MAY BRING TEARS TO YOUR EYES, BUT IT'LL GET THE MESSAGE ACROSS FASTER THAN ANYTHING I KNOW!

SWIVELING THE CHIN TO MAKE ROOM FOR MAXIMUM SHOULDER TURN — AS I DO — IS O.K. SO LONG AS THE BACK OF YOUR NECK REMAINS STEADY.

JM

16

Angled
Lies

Stay Cool in Uneven Situations

Think Hard Before Selecting Club

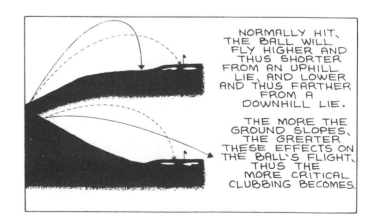

Weight Back When Ground Slopes Down

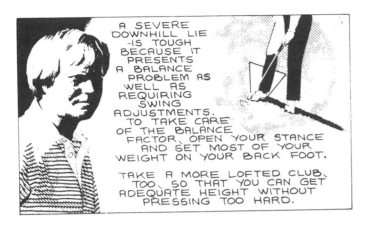

A SEVERE DOWNHILL LIE IS TOUGH BECAUSE IT PRESENTS A BALANCE PROBLEM AS WELL AS REQUIRING SWING ADJUSTMENTS. TO TAKE CARE OF THE BALANCE FACTOR, OPEN YOUR STANCE AND SET MOST OF YOUR WEIGHT ON YOUR BACK FOOT.

TAKE A MORE LOFTED CLUB, TOO, SO THAT YOU CAN GET ADEQUATE HEIGHT WITHOUT PRESSING TOO HARD.

REGARDING SWING ADJUSTMENTS, PLAY THE BALL MORE TOWARD YOUR RIGHT FOOT AND OPEN THE CLUBFACE A LITTLE TO OFFSET A PULLING TENDENCY.

THEN BREAK YOUR WRISTS EARLY ON THE BACKSWING, HIT FIRMLY, AND TRY TO DELAY THE ROLL OF YOUR WRISTS UNTIL WELL AFTER IMPACT.

Allow for Hook When Ball's Higher

A SIDEHILL SHOT WITH THE BALL HIGH ABOVE YOUR FEET IS ONE OF THE TOUGHEST IN GOLF. BEST POLICY IS TO AVOID SUCH LIES BY SHOOTING FOR LEVEL FAIRWAY AREAS.

WHEN THE SHOT DOES PRESENT ITSELF, CHOKE WELL DOWN ON THE CLUB, STAND MORE UPRIGHT THAN NORMAL, AND KEEP YOUR WEIGHT MORE ON YOUR TOES TO OFFSET THE TENDENCY TO FALL BACKWARDS. TRY TO SWING AS SMOOTHLY AND COMPACTLY AS POSSIBLE, WITH A SWEEPING RATHER THAN A PUNCHING ACTION.

ALSO, AIM TO THE RIGHT TO ALLOW FOR THE INEVITABLE HOOK.

Allow for Slice When Ball's Lower

A SIDEHILL SHOT WITH THE BALL WELL BELOW YOUR FEET IS ALWAYS A TESTER.

CAREFUL SHOT-PLANNING FROM THE TEE IS THE BEST WAY TO ENSURE YOU DON'T ENCOUNTER TOO MANY OF THESE POTENTIAL SCORE-WRECKERS.

WHEN YOU DO, GRIP THE CLUB AS CLOSE TO THE END AS POSSIBLE, GET WELL DOWN TO THE SHOT BY FLEXING YOUR KNEES, AND PROTECT YOUR BALANCE BY "SITTING ON YOUR HEELS."

SWING COMPACTLY AND RHYTHMICALLY, **STAY DOWN**, AND AIM LEFT TO ALLOW FOR THE LIKELY FADE.

17

Finessing the Ball

Swing Steeper for Extra "Bite"

MANY CLUB GOLFERS LACK "BITE" ON THEIR APPROACH SHOTS BECAUSE THEY LACK BACKSPIN.

A SURE REDUCER OF BACKSPIN IS GRASS COMING BETWEEN CLUB-FACE AND BALL AT IMPACT, SO CLEAN STRIKING IS YOUR FIRST GOAL.

ANOTHER MIGHT BE TO SWING A LITTLE MORE UPRIGHT, IN THAT THE STEEPER THE ANGLE OF CLUB APPROACH THE MORE POWERFULLY THE BALL WILL BE SPUN UP AND OFF THE CLUBFACE.

HOWEVER, IF YOU GO TO AN UPRIGHT PLANE, BE SURE YOU CONTINUE TO **TURN** AND **EXTEND** FULLY ON THE BACKSWING.

Swing Shorter for "Part" Shots

MANY GOLFERS NEVER TRY ANYTHING LESS THAN A FULL SWING FOR FEAR OF MISSING THE SHOT BY "LETTING UP" ON IT.

BY SO DOING THEY ARE NEEDLESSLY LIMITING THEIR STROKE-MAKING ARSENAL.

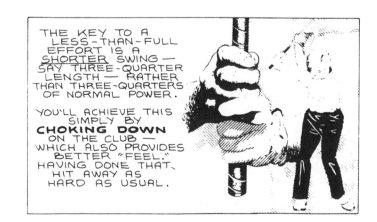

THE KEY TO A LESS-THAN-FULL EFFORT IS A SHORTER SWING — SAY THREE-QUARTER LENGTH — RATHER THAN THREE-QUARTERS OF NORMAL POWER.

YOU'LL ACHIEVE THIS SIMPLY BY **CHOKING DOWN** ON THE CLUB — WHICH ALSO PROVIDES BETTER "FEEL." HAVING DONE THAT, HIT AWAY AS HARD AS USUAL.

"Sweep" Ball with Long Irons

LONG-IRONS AREN'T AS DIFFICULT TO PLAY AS MANY GOLFERS BELIEVE — GIVEN THE RIGHT KIND OF SET-UP AND SWING.

FIRST KEY IS TO POSITION THE BALL FAIRLY WELL FORWARD IN YOUR STANCE, WHERE YOU CAN SWEEP THE CLUBHEAD THROUGH RATHER THAN HITTING DOWN AT THE BALL.

SECOND KEY IS TO SWING ON THE SAME SCALE AND AT THE SAME TEMPO AS YOU SWING A WOODEN CLUB.

THIRD KEY IS TO PRACTICE BOTH TECHNIQUES WITH THE BALL TEED ON A PEG UNTIL YOU BUILD ENOUGH CONFIDENCE IN THE CLUBS TO PLAY THEM FOR REAL OFF THE GROUND.

Waggle as You Want Shot to Fly

YOUR PHYSICAL EXECUTION OF EACH SHOT IS HEAVILY INFLUENCED BY HOW YOU PICTURE IT MENTALLY.

FOR THAT REASON, AND ALSO AS A FORM OF "MINI-REHEARSAL," I WAGGLE AT ADDRESS ACCORDING TO MY INTENDED FLIGHT PATH.

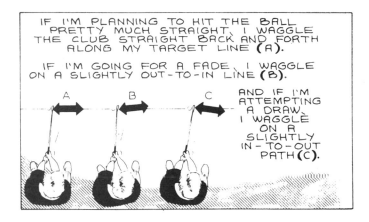

IF I'M PLANNING TO HIT THE BALL PRETTY MUCH STRAIGHT, I WAGGLE THE CLUB STRAIGHT BACK AND FORTH ALONG MY TARGET LINE (A).

IF I'M GOING FOR A FADE, I WAGGLE ON A SLIGHTLY OUT-TO-IN LINE (B).

AND IF I'M ATTEMPTING A DRAW, I WAGGLE ON A SLIGHTLY IN-TO-OUT PATH (C).

To Slice Change Set-up, Not Swing

THERE ARE TWO WAYS TO INTENTIONALLY SLICE A SHOT. ONE IS TO GRIP WITH THE HANDS FARTHER **LEFT** THAN USUAL, THEN SWING **OUT-TO-IN.**

USE THIS IF IT WORKS FOR YOU, BUT IF NOT, TRY MY WAY.

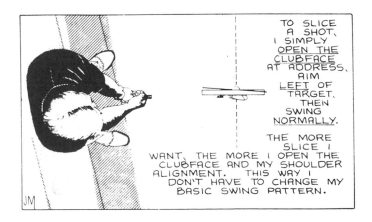

TO SLICE A SHOT, I SIMPLY OPEN THE CLUBFACE AT ADDRESS, AIM LEFT OF TARGET, THEN SWING NORMALLY.

THE MORE SLICE I WANT, THE MORE I OPEN THE CLUBFACE AND MY SHOULDER ALIGNMENT. THIS WAY I DON'T HAVE TO CHANGE MY BASIC SWING PATTERN.

Understand These "Release" Factors

THE LONGER YOU DELAY THE ROLL OF THE RIGHT FOREARM OVER THE LEFT, THE MORE OPEN THE CLUBFACE WILL BE AND THE BETTER YOUR CHANCES OF FADING OR SLICING THE BALL.

CONVERSELY, THE EARLIER THE WRISTS AND FOREARMS ROTATE THROUGH THE IMPACT ZONE, THE BETTER YOUR CHANCES OF DRAWING OR HOOKING THE BALL BECAUSE OF A CLOSING CLUBFACE. EXPERIMENTING WITH THESE ACTIONS IN PRACTICE IS A FINE WAY TO LEARN SHOT FLIGHTING AND BALL CONTROL.

Use Shaft for High and Low Shots

GOLF OFTEN SEEMS A PARADOXICAL GAME, AND THAT'S NOWHERE MORE TRUE THAN WHEN YOU'RE TRYING TO HIT A HARD LOW SHOT OR A SOFT HIGH SHOT. FOLLOWING THEIR INSTINCTS, MANY GOLFERS HOLD THE CLUB EXACTLY OPPOSITE TO THE CORRECT WAY.

HITTING A HARD LOW SHOT BECOMES MUCH EASIER WHEN YOU **CHOKE DOWN** (A) ON THE CLUB. CONVERSELY, USING **ALL THE SHAFT** (B) MAKES PLAYING A SOFT HIGH SHOT MUCH SIMPLER BY ALLOWING A SLOW TEMPO AND A DELIBERATE SWING.

PROVE THIS TO YOURSELF BY PRACTICING BOTH TECHNIQUES.

Move Ball and Hand Back for Less Height

MOVING THE BALL BACK IN YOUR STANCE IS CORRECT PROCEDURE ANY TIME YOU WANT TO HIT IT LOWER, BUT ANOTHER ADJUSTMENT IS NECESSARY TO BE SURE YOU GET THE DESIRED FLIGHT.

IF YOU LEAVE YOUR HANDS WHERE THEY NORMALLY ARE AT ADDRESS WHEN MOVING THE BALL BACK, THE EFFECT WILL BE TO CREATE A STEEPER DOWNSWING ARC WHICH WILL CAUSE MORE BACKSPIN AND THUS GREATER RATHER THAN LESSER HEIGHT. SOLUTION IS TO ALSO MOVE YOUR HANDS BACK PROPORTIONATELY TO THE BALL PLACEMENT, THEN SWING NORMALLY.

7-27

Delay Release to Keep Ball Down

YOU'LL KEEP THE BALL **DOWN** MOST EFFECTIVELY WITH A SLIGHTLY CLOSED CLUBFACE DELIVERY AND A DELAYED RELEASE OF THE CLUBHEAD.

FOR A LOW SHOT, POSITION THE BALL A LITTLE FARTHER BACK IN YOUR STANCE AND HOOD THE CLUBFACE SLIGHTLY.

THEN DELAY THE CLUBHEAD RELEASE BY LEADING THE THROUGH-SWING WITH YOUR LEGS WHILE KEEPING YOUR WRISTS FIRM.

STAY DOWN ON THE SHOT, AND ALLOW FOR A DRAW.

Release Freely to Hit Ball High

HEIGHT IS MOST EASILY ACHIEVED BY A SLIGHTLY <u>OPEN</u> CLUBFACE DELIVERY, COMBINED WITH A <u>VIGOROUS RELEASE</u> OF THE CLUBHEAD THROUGH THE BALL.

WHEN YOU NEED A PARTICULARLY HIGH SHOT, SET THE BALL A LITTLE FARTHER FORWARD IN YOUR STANCE AND OPEN THE CLUBFACE A FEW DEGREES.

THEN BE SURE TO <u>RELEASE</u> THE CLUBHEAD — UNCOCK YOUR WRISTS — FULLY THROUGH IMPACT. STAY <u>BEHIND</u> THE BALL, AND ALLOW FOR A LITTLE FADE.

18

Practice

If You Want to Improve—Practice!

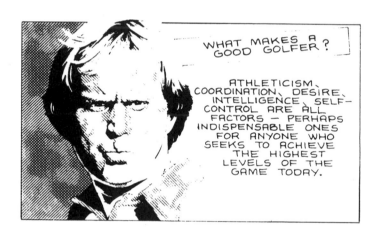

WHAT MAKES A GOOD GOLFER?

ATHLETICISM, COORDINATION, DESIRE, INTELLIGENCE, SELF-CONTROL ARE ALL FACTORS — PERHAPS INDISPENSABLE ONES FOR ANYONE WHO SEEKS TO ACHIEVE THE HIGHEST LEVELS OF THE GAME TODAY.

BUT THERE'S ANOTHER FACTOR, TOO — PRACTICE. THERE'S NEVER BEEN A TOP PLAYER WHO DID NOT HIT TENS OF THOUSANDS OF PRACTICE SHOTS BOTH IN LEARNING AND SUSTAINING HIS OR HER GAME. THE REASON IS THAT THIS IS THE ONLY WAY TO ENSURE THAT FINE SHOTS CAN BE PRODUCED "AUTOMATICALLY" – WHICH IS THE BIG DIFFERENCE BETWEEN THE GOOD CLUB GOLFER AND THOSE WHO PLAY GOLF FOR A LIVING.

Work Most on One Basic "Shape"

WHAT SHOULD A GOLFER BEGINNING A GAME-IMPROVEMENT PROGRAM DO FIRST?
IN MY VIEW, HE SHOULD CONSCIOUSLY DECIDE WHETHER HE IS BASICALLY GOING TO WORK THE BALL FROM RIGHT TO LEFT (**DRAW**) OR FROM LEFT TO RIGHT (**FADE**).

A DEAD STRAIGHT SHOT IS THE TOUGHEST TO HIT ONCE, LET ALONE TO REPEAT CONTINUALLY. FOR THAT AND ALSO FOR STRATEGICAL REASONS, ALMOST ALL TOUR PROS DELIBERATELY EITHER DRAW OR FADE MOST OF THEIR LONG SHOTS. THAT'S HOW YOU SHOULD LEARN TO PLAY GOLF, TOO.

(EVENTUALLY, OF COURSE, IF YOU'RE REALLY SERIOUS ABOUT THE GAME, YOU SHOULD LEARN TO HIT **BOTH** WAYS AT WILL.)

Keep Those Legs Strong

GOOD GOLF IS IMPOSSIBLE IF YOUR LEGS ARE IN LOUSY SHAPE, SO BEING AS ACTIVE AS YOU CAN OFF THE COURSE IS DEFINITELY GOING TO INCREASE YOUR PROWESS AND YOUR PLEASURE ON IT.

GOLF HAS NEVER PROVIDED ME WITH VIGOROUS ENOUGH EXERCISE TO STAY IN THE SHAPE I FEEL NECESSARY TO BE FULLY COMPETITIVE, SO I LIKE TO PLAY MORE STRENUOUS SPORTS AS OFTEN AS POSSIBLE. THE COMPETITION INVOLVED HELPS KEEP ME SHARP FOR GOLF, TOO.

Build Your Game off The Course

ANY TIME YOU CAN'T GET TO THE COURSE FOR A LENGTHY SPELL, DO YOUR DARNDEST TO KEEP AS MANY OF YOUR GOLFING MUSCLES AS POSSIBLE IN THE BEST SHAPE YOU CAN.

IT MIGHT MAKE YOU SWEAT A LITTLE, BUT IT'LL PAY OFF COME PAY-UP TIME!

DO A FEW STRETCHING, BENDING AND TWISTING EXERCISES EACH MORNING FOR THE LOWER BACK AND TORSO. WALK INSTEAD OF RIDING AND TAKE THE STAIRS OVER THE ELEVATOR WHENEVER YOU CAN. ABOVE ALL, TRY TO SWING A CLUB SOMEWHERE PERIODICALLY — AND PREFERABLY A WEIGHTED ONE.

Practice One Thing at a Time

YOU'LL PRACTICE MORE EFFECTIVELY IF YOU CONCENTRATE ON ONE AREA OF THE SWING AT A TIME.

THE FIRST PRIORITIES ARE WHAT MIGHT BE CALLED THE 'STATIC' FUNDAMENTALS — GRIP, AIM AND STANCE, HEAD POSITION, BALL POSITION, AND ADDRESS POSTURE.

ONLY MOVE ON TO THE "ACTION" FUNDAMENTALS WHEN YOU FEEL YOU HAVE THESE 'STATICS' RIGHT. THE ACTION FUNDAMENTALS, TO ME, ARE FULL BACKSWING TURN, HIGH HANDS AT THE TOP, BEGINNING THE DOWNSWING WITH THE LOWER BODY, RELEASING THE CLUBHEAD FULLY, AND SMOOTH OVERALL TEMPO.

Practice on the Course, Too

FIND PRACTICING ON A DRIVING RANGE BORING?

OKAY, THEN DO YOUR PRACTICING ON THE COURSE.

PLAY ALONE WHENEVER THE COURSE ISN'T TOO BUSY, HITTING TWO OR THREE BALLS ON EACH HOLE.

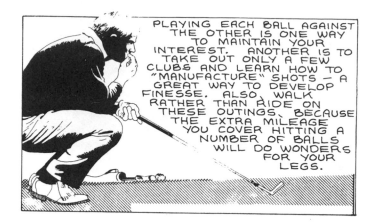

PLAYING EACH BALL AGAINST THE OTHER IS ONE WAY TO MAINTAIN YOUR INTEREST. ANOTHER IS TO TAKE OUT ONLY A FEW CLUBS AND LEARN HOW TO "MANUFACTURE" SHOTS — A GREAT WAY TO DEVELOP FINESSE. ALSO, WALK RATHER THAN RIDE ON THESE OUTINGS, BECAUSE THE EXTRA MILEAGE YOU COVER HITTING A NUMBER OF BALLS WILL DO WONDERS FOR YOUR LEGS.

Warm Up Before You Play

YOU'LL RARELY SEE A HANDICAP GOLFER HIT WARM-UP SHOTS BEFORE HE RUSHES TO THE FIRST TEE. YOU'LL RARELY SEE A PROFESSIONAL NOT DO SO.

MAYBE THAT HAS A LITTLE SOMETHING TO DO WITH THE WAY EACH PLAYS.

START A WARM-UP SESSION WITH A SHORT-IRON AND THEN HIT A FEW SHOTS WITH EVERY SECOND OR THIRD CLUB.

DON'T OVERDO IT!

REMEMBER, YOU'RE WARMING UP, NOT REBUILDING YOUR SWING!

Don't Be Overambitious After Lay-off

TOUGHEST THING TO RECAPTURE AFTER A LONG LAYOFF FROM GOLF IS GOOD SWING TEMPO. GENERALLY, BEING OUT OF PRACTICE AND MAYBE LACKING CONFIDENCE, YOU'LL TEND TO BE JERKY AND FAST.

TO REFIND YOUR TEMPO — AND WITH IT "FEEL" AND CONFIDENCE — DON'T BE TOO AMBITIOUS ON THE PRACTICE RANGE: CONCENTRATE ON BASIC SWING FUNDAMENTALS RATHER THAN WHERE OR HOW FAR THE BALL GOES. AND KEEP EVERYTHING SIMPLE FOR A WHILE, TOO, SAVING THE FANCY SHOTS AND THE FINESSE STROKES UNTIL YOU'VE GOT THE BASICS DOWN PAT AGAIN.

Practice "Finessing" the Ball

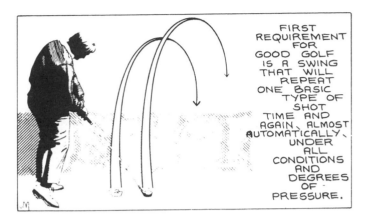

FIRST REQUIREMENT FOR GOOD GOLF IS A SWING THAT WILL REPEAT ONE BASIC TYPE OF SHOT TIME AND AGAIN, ALMOST AUTOMATICALLY, UNDER ALL CONDITIONS AND DEGREES OF PRESSURE.

NEXT REQUIREMENT IS THE ABILITY TO "FINESSE" THE BALL — TO FIT SPECIAL SHOTS TO SPECIAL CIRCUMSTANCES. ADDING THIS CAPABILITY TO ONE'S ARMORY TAKES IMAGINATION AND A CERTAIN AMOUNT OF TRIAL AND ERROR. BUT MOST OF ALL IT TAKES PRACTICE — LOTS AND LOTS OF PRACTICE. SO ALWAYS TRY TO INCLUDE SOME NON-STANDARD OR "TYPE" SHOTS IN YOUR GAME-BUILDING SESSIONS.

Work on Balance This Way

BEST WAY I KNOW TO DEVELOP BALANCE — AND ALSO A GOOD HEAD STEADIER — IS TO PRACTICE SWINGING FROM THE INSIDES OF THE FEET.

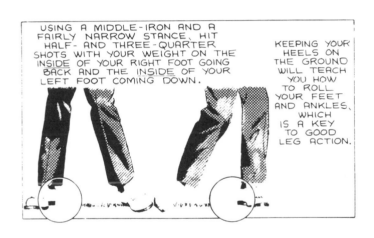

USING A MIDDLE-IRON AND A FAIRLY NARROW STANCE, HIT HALF- AND THREE-QUARTER SHOTS WITH YOUR WEIGHT ON THE INSIDE OF YOUR RIGHT FOOT GOING BACK AND THE INSIDE OF YOUR LEFT FOOT COMING DOWN.

KEEPING YOUR HEELS ON THE GROUND WILL TEACH YOU HOW TO ROLL YOUR FEET AND ANKLES, WHICH IS A KEY TO GOOD LEG ACTION.

Learn to Play Less Than Full Shots

THERE'S NO DOUBT AMPLE SHORT-IRON PRACTICE WILL IMPROVE YOUR SCORING FASTER THAN MOST OTHER TRAINING REGIMENS. BUT THE IMPROVE-MENT WILL BE EVEN GREATER YET IF YOU INCLUDE PLENTY OF 'FINESSE' SHOTS IN THESE SESSIONS.

IN OTHER WORDS, HIT HALF- AND THREE-QUARTER AS WELL AS FULL SHOTS. PRACTICE HITTING YOUR 8-IRON AS FAR AS A FULL WEDGE, THEN YOUR 7-IRON AS FAR AS A FULL 9-IRON, AND SO ON. YOU'LL DEVELOP FEEL AND TOUCH FAST, NOT ONLY FOR REGULAR SHOTS BUT ALSO FOR BAD-WEATHER AND RECOVERY PLAY.

100YDS

Work on _All_ Facets of the Game

WANT TO IMPROVE FAST AT GOLF??
IF YOU CAN'T BREAK 100 BUT ARE CLOSE, A COUPLE OF LESSONS WOULD ALMOST CERTAINLY MOVE YOU INTO THE 90s.

IF YOU'RE A 90s-SHOOTER YEARNING FOR THE 80s, WORKING ON YOUR SHORT GAME WILL GET YOU THERE FASTEST.

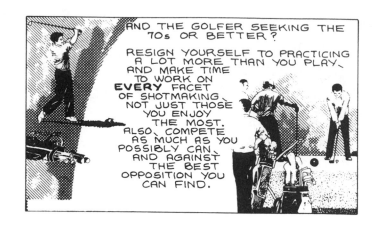

AND THE GOLFER SEEKING THE 70s OR BETTER?

RESIGN YOURSELF TO PRACTICING A LOT MORE THAN YOU PLAY, AND MAKE TIME TO WORK ON **EVERY** FACET OF SHOTMAKING, NOT JUST THOSE YOU ENJOY THE MOST. ALSO, COMPETE AS MUCH AS YOU POSSIBLY CAN, AND AGAINST THE BEST OPPOSITION YOU CAN FIND.

PART TWO

THE SHORT GAME AND SCORING

Introduction

There are two ways to lower your golf score.

The longer and harder way is to improve your full shots: extend your drives, take the bends out of those fairway woods and long irons, sharpen up the medium irons—in effect, build yourself a better swing. This is the longer and harder route because it requires a lot of time, energy, patience and knowledge, not to mention a sound physique and good coordination. However, there's a great satisfaction in becoming a better full-shot golfer, and if that's your aim, now or in the future, I'd refer you to the first section in this book, *The Swing from A-Z.*

The shorter and much easier way to lower your golf score is to improve your short game and your strategizing: to tighten up on your technique around and on the greens, plus the way you think and map yourself around the course. This is the easier and quicker route because, once you know the proper techniques, the shorter shots require much less physical strength and dexterity to play well than the big shots, and because the only things you need to do to improve at course management are look and think a little harder before playing your shots.

This section is for those who would like to take the faster and simpler route to lower scores. In the first half I cover all facets of short-game technique, but with particular emphasis on putting because that's almost fifty percent of the game of golf.

In the second half of this section I've tried to present the specific strategies and tactics that have, I believe, been my greatest personal golfing weapons during my twenty years as a professional.

Jack Nicklaus

CHAPTER **FOUR**

Around
the Green

19

From 100 Yards
on In

Swing Firmly...

ANY TIME YOUR PITCHING GOES SOUR, CHECK THE **FIRMNESS** WITH WHICH YOU PLAY THE LOFTED SHOTS FROM, SAY, 80 YARDS IN TO THE GREEN. OVERSWINGING, RESULTING IN DECELERATION OF THE CLUB-HEAD THROUGH IMPACT, IS A FREQUENT CAUSE OF POOR PITCHING.

JM

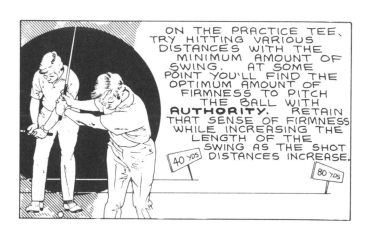

ON THE PRACTICE TEE, TRY HITTING VARIOUS DISTANCES WITH THE MINIMUM AMOUNT OF SWING. AT SOME POINT YOU'LL FIND THE OPTIMUM AMOUNT OF FIRMNESS TO PITCH THE BALL WITH **AUTHORITY**. RETAIN THAT SENSE OF FIRMNESS WHILE INCREASING THE LENGTH OF THE SWING AS THE SHOT DISTANCES INCREASE.

40 YDS

80 YDS

...and Stand Firmly

BE FIRM ON YOUR FEET WHEN PLAYING PITCH SHOTS.

FOR MOST REGULAR SHORT SHOTS WITH THE WEDGES, I SET MOST OF MY WEIGHT ON MY LEFT FOOT AND KEEP IT THERE THROUGHOUT THE SWING.

JM

IF YOU SWING SMOOTHLY THERE WILL NATURALLY BE A LITTLE KNEE ACTION AS YOU GO BACK AND THROUGH, BUT THERE'S NO NEED FOR A LOT OF FOOT ACTION. IN FACT, IF YOU WATCH THE TOUR PLAYERS YOU'LL NOTICE THERE IS VERY LITTLE LIFTING OF THE HEELS ON THESE SHORT, HIGH-FLYING SHOTS.

Set Up Open for Greater Control

WHY DO GOOD GOLFERS USUALLY SET UP A LITTLE OPEN — AIMED LEFT OF TARGET IN THEIR FEET AND HIPS — WHEN PITCHING THE BALL?

THERE ARE TWO REASONS.

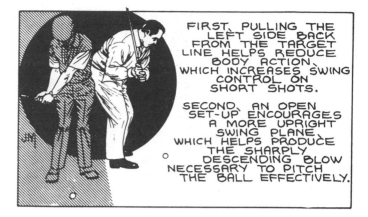

FIRST, PULLING THE LEFT SIDE BACK FROM THE TARGET LINE HELPS REDUCE BODY ACTION, WHICH INCREASES SWING CONTROL ON SHORT SHOTS.

SECOND, AN OPEN SET-UP ENCOURAGES A MORE UPRIGHT SWING PLANE, WHICH HELPS PRODUCE THE SHARPLY DESCENDING BLOW NECESSARY TO PITCH THE BALL EFFECTIVELY.

Meet Ball at Bottom of Arc

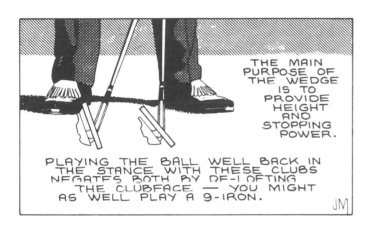

THE MAIN PURPOSE OF THE WEDGE IS TO PROVIDE HEIGHT AND STOPPING POWER.

PLAYING THE BALL WELL BACK IN THE STANCE WITH THESE CLUBS NEGATES BOTH BY DE-LOFTING THE CLUBFACE — YOU MIGHT AS WELL PLAY A 9-IRON.

THAT'S WHY, FOR ALL NORMAL WEDGE PITCH SHOTS, I POSITION THE BALL AS I DO FOR ALL REGULAR SHOTS — OPPOSITE MY LEFT HEEL.

BY MEETING THE BALL JUST BEFORE THE BOTTOM OF THE SWING ARC I AM THEN ASSURED OF BOTH HIGH TRAJECTORY AND GOOD BACKSPIN.

Accelerate the Club Head

AN **ACCELERATING** CLUBHEAD THROUGH IMPACT IS ESSENTIAL ON ALL PITCH AND CHIP SHOTS. IT BECOMES EVEN MORE IMPORTANT WHEN PLAYING **BERMUDA** GRASS COURSES BECAUSE OF THE DECELERATING EFFECT OF THE THICK ROOT SYSTEMS AND TOUGH RUNNERS.

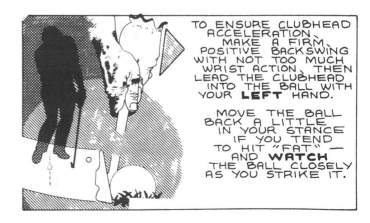

TO ENSURE CLUBHEAD ACCELERATION, MAKE A FIRM, POSITIVE BACKSWING WITH NOT TOO MUCH WRIST ACTION, THEN LEAD THE CLUBHEAD INTO THE BALL WITH YOUR **LEFT** HAND.

MOVE THE BALL BACK A LITTLE IN YOUR STANCE IF YOU TEND TO HIT "FAT" — AND **WATCH** THE BALL CLOSELY AS YOU STRIKE IT.

83

Try These Two Methods.

HOW DO YOU PLAY THOSE PITCHES FROM ABOUT 50 TO 80 YARDS IN TO THE PIN? YOU CAN SWING FULLY BUT SOFTLY (A), OR SHORTER BUT FIRMER THAN NORMAL (B) — EITHER TECHNIQUE WILL WORK.

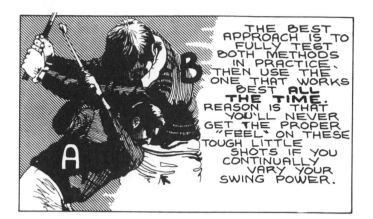

THE BEST APPROACH IS TO FULLY TEST BOTH METHODS IN PRACTICE, THEN USE THE ONE THAT WORKS BEST **ALL THE TIME**. REASON IS THAT YOU'LL NEVER GET THE PROPER "FEEL" ON THESE TOUGH LITTLE SHOTS IF YOU CONTINUALLY VARY YOUR SWING POWER.

Rehearse "Part" Shots Thoroughly

MANY TOUR PLAYERS RARELY TAKE A PRACTICE SWING BEFORE A DRIVE OR OTHER FULL SHOT, BUT YOU'LL NOTICE THAT MOST OF THEM TAKE A NUMBER OF PRACTICE SWINGS BEFORE PLAYING ANY SHOT OF 100 YARDS OR LESS.

WHY?

THE PRACTICE SWINGS ON LESS THAN A FULL SHOT ARE TO 'MEASURE' AND REHEARSE THE LENGTH AND FORCE OF THE STROKE NECESSARY TO HIT THE BALL THE DESIRED DISTANCE.

YOU'LL FIND THE SHORT GAME EASIER IF YOU, TOO, 'FEEL' OUT THE REQUIRED ACTION THOROUGHLY BEFORE STEPPING UP TO THE BALL ON ANYTHING LESS THAN A FULL SHOT.

Don't Neglect the Pitch-and-Run

DON'T OVERLOOK THE PITCH-AND-RUN SHOT WHENEVER HARD GREENS OR HIGH WINDS THREATEN THE HIGH-FLYING PITCH.

PLAY THE SHOT WITH AN EIGHT- OR NINE-IRON, CHOKING WELL DOWN ON THE GRIP AND CONCENTRATING ON MAKING SOLID CONTACT WITH THE BACK OF THE BALL.

ALLOW FOR THE BALL TO RUN ABOUT AS FAR AS IT FLIES IN WINDLESS CONDITIONS, BUT REDUCE OR INCREASE THE ROLL ALLOWANCE FOR HEAD OR TAIL WINDS.

Use Sand-wedge for Extra Height

MANY BEGINNING GOLFERS SEEM TO THINK THE SAND-WEDGE IS LIMITED TO BUNKER PLAY ALONE. NOT SO — I AND MOST OTHER TOUR PLAYERS USE THE SAND-WEDGE FOR ALL KINDS OF SHOTS FROM AROUND THE GREEN.

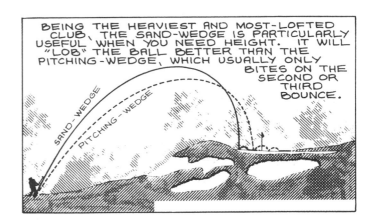

BEING THE HEAVIEST AND MOST-LOFTED CLUB, THE SAND-WEDGE IS PARTICULARLY USEFUL WHEN YOU NEED HEIGHT. IT WILL "LOB" THE BALL BETTER THAN THE PITCHING-WEDGE, WHICH USUALLY ONLY BITES ON THE SECOND OR THIRD BOUNCE.

SAND-WEDGE

PITCHING-WEDGE

Swing Slow and Easy for Short Lob

A SHORT RECOVERY SHOT THAT MUST CLEAR A GREENSIDE OBSTACLE AND STOP QUICKLY REQUIRES A SLOW, EASY SWING WITH VERY FIRM HAND CONTROL. IT NEEDS PRACTICE BECAUSE IT TAKES NERVE, BUT IT'S AN INVALUABLE STROKE-SAVER..ESPECIALLY ON TOUGH COURSES WHERE YOU'RE BOUND TO MISS A NUMBER OF GREENS.

USE A WEDGE, OPEN THE FACE, SWING BACK SLOWLY AND SMOOTHLY WITH THE CLUB FIRMLY GRIPPED IN THE LEFT HAND, THEN MAKE A VERY _POSITIVE_ HIT WITH YOUR **RIGHT** HAND THROUGH IMPACT.

BE SURE NOT TO LET THE LEFT HAND SLACKEN AS THE RIGHT HAND DIRECTS THE BLOW. PROPERLY EXECUTED, THIS SHOT WILL RISE QUICKLY AND SETTLE SOFTLY, EVEN OUT OF FAIRLY HEAVY ROUGH.

Sweep Ball from Uphill Lie

A BALL SITTING CLEANLY ON A GRASSY UPHILL SLOPE NEAR THE GREEN PRESENTS A RELATIVELY EASY SHOT. SIMPLY **SWEEP** THE BALL UP BY LETTING THE CLUB FOLLOW THE SLOPE OF THE GROUND. SWING A LITTLE HARDER TO COMPENSATE FOR A HIGHER TRAJECTORY AND SOFTER LANDING THAN NORMAL.

IF THE BALL IS BURIED IN LONG GRASS, YOU HAVE LITTLE CHOICE BUT TO HIT RIGHT INTO IT AS THOUGH THE LIE WAS LEVEL.

OPEN THE CLUBFACE, KEEP YOUR HEAD VERY STILL, AND TRY TO CATCH THE BALL BEFORE THE CLUB MEETS THE GROUND.

BE **FIRM**.

Stay Ahead of Ball on Downhill Lie

TOP PRIORITY ON ANY DOWNHILL PITCH SHOT IS TO MEET THE BALL BEFORE THE CLUB CONTACTS THE GROUND — WHICH IS NO EASY TASK IF THE SLOPE IS STEEP.

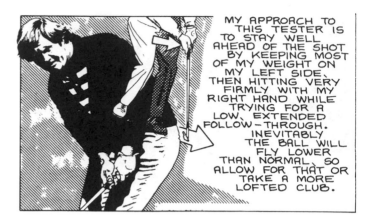

MY APPROACH TO THIS TESTER IS TO STAY WELL AHEAD OF THE SHOT BY KEEPING MOST OF MY WEIGHT ON MY LEFT SIDE, THEN HITTING VERY FIRMLY WITH MY RIGHT HAND WHILE TRYING FOR A LOW, EXTENDED FOLLOW-THROUGH. INEVITABLY THE BALL WILL FLY LOWER THAN NORMAL, SO ALLOW FOR THAT OR TAKE A MORE LOFTED CLUB.

Stand Taller When Ball's Above Feet

FACTOR TO GUARD AGAINST WHEN PITCHING FROM A LIE WHERE THE BALL IS HIGHER THAN YOUR FEET IS CATCHING THE GROUND BEFORE THE CLUB MEETS THE BALL.

COMPENSATE BY STANDING MORE ERECT THAN NORMAL AND POSITIONING THE BALL BACK IN YOUR STANCE WITH YOUR HANDS WELL AHEAD. KEEP YOUR HANDS LEADING THE CLUBFACE THROUGH IMPACT, AND, IF YOU NEED EXTRA HEIGHT, OPEN IT BOTH AT ADDRESS AND AS IT MOVES THROUGH THE BALL.

Keep Clubface Open When Ball's Below Feet

GETTING THE SHOT "UP" AND AVOIDING PUSHING IT RIGHT ARE THE PROBLEMS WHEN CHIPPING OR PITCHING A BALL LYING WELL BELOW YOUR FOOT LEVEL.

ADDRESS THE BALL BACK NEAR YOUR RIGHT FOOT WITH AN OPEN STANCE AND YOUR HANDS WELL AHEAD OF THE CLUBFACE. THEN CUT ACROSS THE BALL BY SWINGING PRONOUNCEDLY FROM OUT TO IN, MAKING SURE YOU DON'T ROLL THE CLUBFACE CLOSED WITH YOUR WRISTS THROUGH IMPACT.

20

From Just Off the Green

Select Club for Maximum Roll

MOST GOLFERS FIND IT EASIER TO JUDGE ROLL THAN FLIGHT, AND IF YOU'RE AMONG THEM THEN SELECTING THE RIGHT CLUB BECOMES THE KEY TO GOOD CHIPPING.

BASIC GOAL IS TO PICK THE CLUB THAT WILL LAND THE BALL A FEW FEET ON THE GREEN AND LET IT ROLL THE REST OF THE WAY TO THE HOLE.

IF YOU WERE SAY 20 YARDS FROM THE PUTTING SURFACE, THIS MIGHT BE AN 8-IRON OR A 9-IRON.

HOWEVER, IF YOU WERE ONLY FOUR OR FIVE YARDS OFF THE GREEN, THEN A LESS LOFTED CLUB WOULD DO THE JOB MORE EASILY — SAY A 5-IRON OR 6-IRON.

"Picture" Shots Mentally

"PICTURING" EACH SHOT IN YOUR MIND'S EYE IS ESSENTIAL ON ALL GOLF STROKES, BUT IT'S PARTICULARLY HELPFUL IN CHIPPING. REASON IS THAT YOU CAN'T PICK THE PRECISE CLUB FOR THE JOB UNTIL YOU MENTALLY "SEE" THE RELATIVE AMOUNTS OF FLIGHT AND ROLL NECESSARY TO GET THE BALL CLOSE.

WHEN PRACTICING CHIPPING I USE VARIOUS CLUBS AND VARIOUS TECHNIQUES, THEN TRY TO COMMIT THE RESULTS TO MEMORY. THIS HELPS GREATLY IN "PICTURING" SHOTS ON THE COURSE ITSELF, NOT LEAST BY REDUCING THE AMOUNT OF GUESSWORK I MUST USE.

Be Deliberate

CHIPPING HAS NEVER COME EASY TO ME, BUT I'VE FOUND OVER THE YEARS THAT THE **SLOWER** MY TEMPO ON THESE LITTLE RECOVERY SHOTS THE BETTER I PLAY THEM.

IT'S ONLY TOO EASY TO JAB OR JERK AT THE BALL WHEN YOU'RE UNDER PRESSURE TO GET IT CLOSE FROM JUST OFF THE GREEN. MY ANTIDOTE TO THAT IS A CONSCIOUS EFFORT TO STROKE DELIBERATELY: TO MAKE AN EASY-YET-FIRM, BUT ABOVE ALL AN **UNHURRIED** SWING.

Find Your Own Best Stroking Style

THERE ARE ALMOST AS MANY WAYS TO CHIP AS THERE ARE TO PUTT, BUT MOST GOOD PLAYERS SEEM TO PREFER EITHER AN ALL-WRIST ACTION OR A FAIRLY STIFF-WRISTED ARM STROKE.

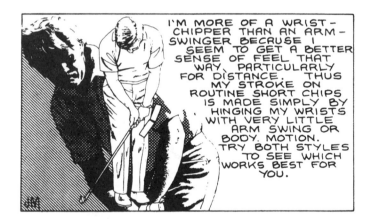

I'M MORE OF A WRIST-CHIPPER THAN AN ARM-SWINGER BECAUSE I SEEM TO GET A BETTER SENSE OF FEEL THAT WAY, PARTICULARLY FOR DISTANCE. THUS MY STROKE ON ROUTINE SHORT CHIPS IS MADE SIMPLY BY HINGING MY WRISTS WITH VERY LITTLE ARM SWING OR BODY MOTION. TRY BOTH STYLES TO SEE WHICH WORKS BEST FOR YOU.

Keep Grip Pressure Consistent

SOME GOLFERS SEEM TO THINK THEY SHOULD GRIP TIGHTER ON A CHIP SHOT, WHILE OTHERS FEEL A LOOSER-THAN-NORMAL GRIP WILL WORK BETTER. BOTH ARE WRONG.

CRISPNESS OF STRIKE IS ESSENTIAL ON CHIP SHOTS, AND YOU WON'T ACHIEVE IT EITHER WITH THE CHOPPY SWING THAT COMES FROM AN OVER-TIGHT GRIP OR THE FLOPPY MOTION THAT COMES FROM A SLOPPY HOLD ON THE CLUB. WHAT WILL ACHIEVE IT IS THE SAME DEGREE OF FIRMNESS IN THE HANDS THAT YOU USE FOR FULL SHOTS.

Choke Down for Better "Touch"

DON'T MAKE THE COMMON MISTAKE OF ROUTINELY HOLDING AS HIGH ON THE CLUB AS YOU DO FOR FULL SHOTS WHEN CHIPPING AND PITCHING.

THE CLOSER YOUR HANDS ARE TO THE CLUBHEAD, THE GREATER YOUR CONTROL AND THE MORE DELICATE YOUR TOUCH. SO LEARN TO CHOKE DOWN ON THE LITTLE SHOTS — USING LESS SHAFT THE MORE GENTLY YOU MUST STROKE AND/OR THE LESS DISTANCE THE BALL MUST TRAVEL.

Stand Close for Maximum Control

IF YOUR CHIPPING IS LESS THAN YOU'D LIKE IT TO BE, CONSIDER YOUR DISTANCE FROM THE BALL.

THE FARTHER AWAY YOU STAND, THE MORE THE CLUBHEAD MUST SWING OFF THE TARGET LINE ON BOTH SIDES OF THE BALL, AND THUS THE MORE ITS FACE MUST OPEN AND CLOSE.

STANDING AS CLOSE AS IS COMFORTABLY POSSIBLE FACILITATES A MORE DIRECTLY BACK- AND THROUGH-SWING PATH, AND THUS A BETTER CHANCE OF MEETING THE BALL WITH THE CLUBFACE SQUARE TO THE TARGET LINE.

Swing Through, Not At, Ball

A QUICK AND JERKY CHIPPING STROKE CAN CAUSE YOU A LOT OF PAIN AT GOLF. SO, TOO, CAN AN OVER-DELIBERATE STROKING MOTION BY CAUSING YOU TO DECELERATE THE CLUBHEAD THROUGH THE BALL.

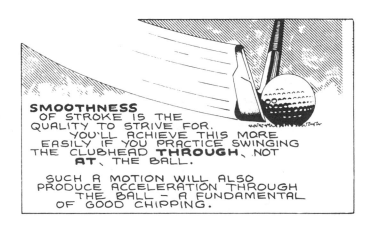

SMOOTHNESS OF STROKE IS THE QUALITY TO STRIVE FOR. YOU'LL ACHIEVE THIS MORE EASILY IF YOU PRACTICE SWINGING THE CLUBHEAD **THROUGH**, NOT **AT**, THE BALL.

SUCH A MOTION WILL ALSO PRODUCE ACCELERATION THROUGH THE BALL — A FUNDAMENTAL OF GOOD CHIPPING.

Don't Roll Right Over Left

A LOT OF CHIP SHOTS ARE PULLED LEFT OF TARGET BECAUSE THE RIGHT HAND ROLLS OVER THE LEFT THROUGH IMPACT, CLOSING THE CLUBFACE.

THE FAULT ALSO CAUSES THE BALL TO FLY TOO LOW AND ROLL TOO FAR.

IF YOU'RE PULLING ANY OF THE LITTLE SHOTS, CHECK YOUR HAND ACTION THROUGH IMPACT.

THE FEELING TO STRIVE FOR IS OF THE RIGHT HAND MOVING **UNDER**, NOT OVER, AS IT HITS AGAINST A FIRM, GUIDING LEFT HAND.

Hold Extra Firmly from Rough

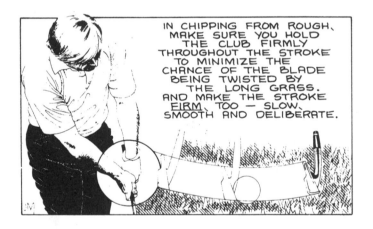

IN CHIPPING FROM ROUGH, MAKE SURE YOU HOLD THE CLUB FIRMLY THROUGHOUT THE STROKE TO MINIMIZE THE CHANCE OF THE BLADE BEING TWISTED BY THE LONG GRASS. AND MAKE THE STROKE FIRM, TOO — SLOW, SMOOTH AND DELIBERATE.

I FIND FIRMING UP EVEN MORE WITH MY RIGHT HAND JUST BEFORE IMPACT HELPS ME KEEP THE CLUBFACE SQUARE AND ACCELERATING ON THESE TRICKY LITTLE SHOTS.

BUT PRACTICE THIS TECHNIQUE A WHILE BEFORE YOU TAKE IT ONTO THE COURSE.

Putt from Off Green When Possible

I'LL "TEXAS WEDGE" A SHOT FROM JUST OFF THE GREEN — PUTT THE BALL INSTEAD OF CHIPPING OR PITCHING IT — ANY TIME CONDITIONS ALLOW. THESE ARE GENERALLY IDEAL WHEN THE TURF IS FIRM AND DRY AND FAIRLY EVEN.

TO PLAY THIS SHOT, USE YOUR NORMAL PUTTING TECHNIQUE BUT HIT A LITTLE HARDER THAN YOU NORMALLY WOULD. AND **KEEP YOUR HEAD AND BODY STILL** — THERE'S A GREAT TEMPTATION ON THIS KIND OF STROKE TO "PEEK" TOO EARLY. YOU'LL FIND THIS SHOT PARTICULARLY VALUABLE FROM A THIN LIE.

21

From the Sand

Get Out at First Attempt

THE FIRST RULE OF BUNKER PLAY IS, 'GET OUT AT THE FIRST ATTEMPT.'

SO DON'T TRY SHOTS THAT ARE BEYOND YOUR CAPABILITY OR EXPERIENCE UNTIL YOU'VE LEARNED HOW TO PLAY THEM AND PUT IN SOME PRACTICE TIME.

THE SAFEST WAY BACK TO MOWN GRASS FROM A FAIRWAY BUNKER IS USUALLY THE SHORTEST. TAKE IT IF YOU'RE NOT A GOOD SAND PLAYER.

LIKEWISE, BE CONTENT SIMPLY TO GET THE BALL SOMEWHERE ON THE PUTTING SURFACE FROM A GREENSIDE BUNKER, RATHER THAN CLOSE TO THE PIN, IF THE LIE OR THE LAND CONTOURS OVER-EXTEND YOUR CAPABILITIES.

Use the Proper Sand Club

THE WIDER AND DEEPER THE FLANGE OF A SAND-WEDGE, THE MORE IT WILL BOUNCE ON CONTACT WITH THE SAND, AND THUS THE LESS IT WILL 'KNIFE' UNDER THE BALL. CONVERSELY, THE NARROWER AND SHALLOWER THE FLANGE, THE LESS THE CLUB WILL BOUNCE AND THE MORE IT WILL DIG AND STOP AS IT STRIKES THE SAND.

IN SELECTING A SAND-WEDGE, IT PAYS TO RELATE THESE FACTORS TO THE TYPE OF BUNKERS YOU GENERALLY ENCOUNTER.

HAVING TO COPE WITH ALL KINDS OF SAND TYPES AND CONDITIONS, I AND MOST OTHER TOUR PLAYERS FAVOR A MEDIUM WIDTH AND DEPTH OF FLANGE.

Learn to Hit Sand, Not Ball

A LOT OF THE MISSED BUNKER SHOTS I SEE IN PRO-AMS ARE THE RESULT OF TRYING TO "PICK" THE BALL, WHICH IN TURN RESULTS FROM A FEAR OF HITTING SAND INSTEAD OF BALL.

THIS FEAR WILL VANISH IF YOU UNDERSTAND THAT HITTING FIRMLY INTO THE SAND A COUPLE OF INCHES OR SO BEHIND THE BALL CREATES SUFFICIENT PRESSURE TO "EXPLODE" THE BALL UPWARD AND FORWARD. BETTER THAN SIMPLY UNDERSTANDING THE CONCEPT MENTALLY, PROVE IT TO YOURSELF PHYSICALLY BY PRACTICING IT AWHILE.

Think and Swing in Slow Motion

BECAUSE THEY FEAR SAND SHOTS SO DEEPLY, MOST GOLFERS RUSH BOTH THEIR PREPARATION AND THE SWING ITSELF IN AN EFFORT TO GET THE EXPERIENCE OVER AND DONE WITH.

IT'S FREQUENTLY A VERY COSTLY MISTAKE.

APPROACH A BUNKER SHOT BOTH MENTALLY AND PHYSICALLY AS THOUGH YOU WERE THINKING AND PLAYING IN **SLOW MOTION**. REMEMBER, YOU RARELY NEED FORCE TO REMOVE THE BALL A SHORT DISTANCE FROM SAND — JUST REASONABLY ACCURATE CLUB-HEAD DELIVERY.

SO STAY CALM AND KEEP THE TEMPO SLOW, LOOSE AND EASY.

Read Green Slopes Carefully

PLAYED CORRECTLY, ALL NORMAL GREENSIDE BUNKER SHOTS ARE STRUCK WITH A CUTTING OR SLICING ACTION, CAUSING THE BALL TO BREAK TO YOUR RIGHT UPON LANDING.

CAREFUL READING OF GREEN SLOPES IS THUS A KEY ELEMENT IN SUCH SHOTS.

ALLOW FOR CONSIDERABLY MORE LEFT-TO-RIGHT BREAK THAN NORMAL WHEN THE GROUND SLOPES IN THAT DIRECTION. CONVERSELY, ALLOW FOR LITTLE IF ANY BREAK WHEN HITTING INTO A PRONOUNCED RIGHT-TO-LEFT SLOPE.

Keep Clubface Open

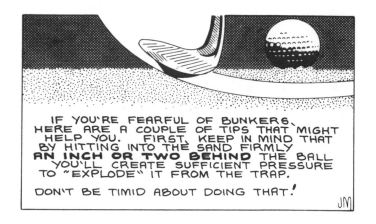

IF YOU'RE FEARFUL OF BUNKERS, HERE ARE A COUPLE OF TIPS THAT MIGHT HELP YOU. FIRST, KEEP IN MIND THAT BY HITTING INTO THE SAND FIRMLY **AN INCH OR TWO BEHIND** THE BALL YOU'LL CREATE SUFFICIENT PRESSURE TO "EXPLODE" IT FROM THE TRAP.

DON'T BE TIMID ABOUT DOING THAT!

SECOND, IN MAKING THE SHOT, UNTIL YOU GAIN CONFIDENCE FOCUS MOST OF YOUR EFFORT ON **NOT CLOSING THE CLUBFACE** AS IT SLICES THROUGH THE SAND.

IN OTHER WORDS, DON'T LET YOUR WRISTS ROLL OVER OR YOUR HANDS FLIP THE CLUBFACE SHUT AS YOU FOLLOWTHROUGH.

Dig Yourself a Firm Footing

A BASIC OF BUNKER PLAY, APPLICABLE TO EVERY TYPE OF SHOT, IS TO ESTABLISH A FIRM STANCE BY DIGGING AND SHUFFLING YOUR FEET WELL INTO THE SAND.

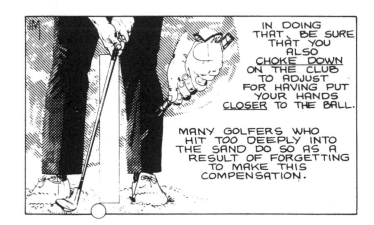

IN DOING THAT, BE SURE THAT YOU ALSO CHOKE DOWN ON THE CLUB TO ADJUST FOR HAVING PUT YOUR HANDS CLOSER TO THE BALL.

MANY GOLFERS WHO HIT TOO DEEPLY INTO THE SAND DO SO AS A RESULT OF FORGETTING TO MAKE THIS COMPENSATION.

Test Sand Texture with Feet

TESTING THE TEXTURE OF BUNKER SAND WITH YOUR HANDS OR THE CLUB IS ILLEGAL, BUT THE RULES DO ALLOW WIGGLING THE FEET AROUND AS MUCH AS YOU LIKE.

SO, WHILE THEY'RE BUILDING YOU A NICE FIRM STANCE, USE THEM ALSO TO TRANSMIT INFORMATION ABOUT THE SAND TEXTURE.

A GOOD 'RULE OF FOOT' IS THAT THE SOFTER THE SUBSURFACE OF THE SAND, THE LESS THE CLUB WILL BOUNCE OR KNIFE THROUGH IT, THUS THE HARDER YOU MUST SWING.

AND, OF COURSE, VICE VERSA IN FIRM SAND.

Decide Your Preferred Method

TO VARY DISTANCE ON "EXPLOSION"-TYPE SHOTS FROM SAND, YOU CAN VARY EITHER THE FORCE OF THE SWING OR THE DEPTH OF THE CUT YOU TAKE — OR A COMBINATION OF BOTH.

TOUR PLAYERS USE ALL THREE TECHNIQUES.

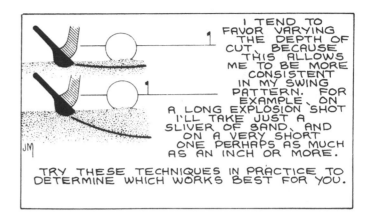

I TEND TO FAVOR VARYING THE DEPTH OF CUT, BECAUSE THIS ALLOWS ME TO BE MORE CONSISTENT IN MY SWING PATTERN. FOR EXAMPLE, ON A LONG EXPLOSION SHOT I'LL TAKE JUST A SLIVER OF SAND, AND ON A VERY SHORT ONE PERHAPS AS MUCH AS AN INCH OR MORE.

TRY THESE TECHNIQUES IN PRACTICE TO DETERMINE WHICH WORKS BEST FOR YOU.

Picture Removing Area of Sand

HERE'S A SAND-SHOT TIP THAT HELPED ME TREMENDOUSLY SOME YEARS AGO, AND THAT COULD DO THE SAME FOR YOU. INSTEAD OF THINKING OF HITTING AT A CERTAIN POINT BEHIND THE BALL, CONCENTRATE INSTEAD ON AN **AREA** OF SAND.

ENVISION A RECTANGLE ABOUT SIX INCHES LONG AND THREE INCHES WIDE OF WHICH THE BALL IS PART. REMOVE THIS AREA FROM THE BUNKER AND YOU'LL ALSO REMOVE THE BALL.

CUT OUT A SHALLOWER SLAB THE FARTHER YOU WANT THE BALL TO GO, OR TAKE THE SAME CUT AND HIT HARDER.

Vary Depth of Cut for Special Effects

VARYING THE DEPTH YOU HIT UNDER THE BALL PRODUCES VARYING EFFECTS FROM SAND. FOR EXAMPLE, HIT SHALLOW AND WELL BEHIND THE BALL AND YOU'LL PRODUCE A SOFT SHOT WITH LITTLE BACKSPIN.

HIT DEEP AND FAR BEHIND THE BALL (AS FOR A BURIED LIE) AND THE BALL WILL RUN ON LANDING. HIT SHALLOW AND CLOSE AND THE HEAVY BACKSPIN IMPARTED WILL STOP THE BALL QUICKLY.

OCCASIONALLY PRACTICING THESE DIFFERENT TECHNIQUES WILL VASTLY IMPROVE YOUR "RECOVERY" GAME.

12-14

Relate Swing Force to Chipping

IF YOUR BUNKER-SHOT TECHNIQUE IS TO VARY DISTANCES BY THE FORCE OF THE SWING, HERE'S A MEANS OF GUAGING HOW MUCH POWER IS REQUIRED THAT HAS HELPED ME OVER THE YEARS.

SIMPLY PROGRAM YOURSELF TO SWING AS HARD FROM SAND AS YOU WOULD FOR A CHIP SHOT FROM DOUBLE THE DISTANCE.

FOR INSTANCE, IF YOU HAVE A 30-FOOT SAND SHOT, THINK OF THE FORCE NEEDED FOR A 60-FOOT CHIP SHOT, AND SO ON.

Hit Steeply under Buried Lie

GETTING THE BALL CLOSE TO THE PIN FROM A BURIED LIE WHEN YOU HAVE VERY LITTLE GREEN TO WORK WITH IS ONE OF THE TOUGHEST SHOTS IN GOLF — SOMETIMES TO THE POINT OF BEING IMPOSSIBLE.

MY TECHNIQUE ON THIS SHOT STARTS WITH A WIDE-OPEN CLUBFACE AT ADDRESS, PLUS A QUICK WRIST-BREAK GOING BACK TO CREATE A VERY STEEP ANGLE OF ATTACK COMING DOWN. THEN I CONCENTRATE ON GETTING <u>WELL UNDER</u> THE BALL BY DRIVING THE CLUBHEAD DEEP INTO THE SAND ABOUT AN INCH BEHIND IT, HITTING VERY FORCEFULLY WITH MY RIGHT HAND.

Swing "Low" to Beat Wet Sand

WET COMPACTED SAND IS OFTEN EASIER TO PLAY FROM THAN DRY, POWDERY SAND, SO LONG AS YOU KNOW HOW. START BY POSITIONING THE BALL OPPOSITE YOUR LEFT HEEL AND SET THE SAND-WEDGE FACE WIDE OPEN.

THEN MAKE A SHORT, **OUTSIDE** AND **LOW** BACKSWING, HITTING ABOUT AN INCH BEHIND THE BALL.

THE CUSHIONING EFFECT OF THE SAND, PLUS THE LOW BACKSWING AND OPEN FACE, WILL KEEP THE CLUB FROM DIGGING TOO DEEPLY.

Adjust Posture When Ball's Below . . .

KEY TO **THIS** SHOT IS ADJUSTING YOUR BODY SO YOU CAN SWING PRETTY MUCH AS YOU WOULD FROM A LEVEL LIE.

GRIP THE CLUB CLOSE TO ITS END, THEN BEND YOUR KNEES AS FAR AS NECESSARY TO GET FULLY **DOWN** TO THE BALL.

AIM MORE TO THE LEFT THAN USUAL TO ALLOW FOR THE BALL'S TENDENCY TO FLY RIGHT, THEN SWING AS FOR A NORMAL SAND SHOT.

ABOVE ALL, KEEP YOUR HEAD STILL UNTIL WELL AFTER IMPACT.

. . . or Above Feet

AS WHEN THE BALL IS BELOW YOUR FEET, THE WAY YOU SET UP IS THE KEY TO THIS FREQUENTLY-ENCOUNTERED SAND SHOT.

'DISTANCE' YOURSELF CORRECTLY FROM THE BALL BY CHOKING DOWN ON THE CLUB AND STANDING MORE ERECT THAN NORMAL. AIM RIGHT TO ALLOW FOR THE BALL'S TENDENCY TO FLY LEFT, THEN SWING AS YOU USUALLY DO ON A BUNKER SHOT. BE SURE NOT TO LET THE CLUBFACE CLOSE AS YOU HIT THROUGH THE SAND.

Don't Give Up on This One

DON'T GIVE UP ON THE SHOT PICTURED HERE, BECAUSE GETTING IT WITHIN AT LEAST TWO-PUTT DISTANCE IS (A) NOT IMPOSSIBLE, AND (B) WILL GIVE YOU A NICE PSYCHOLOGICAL BOOST.

TAKE A SOLID STANCE, CHOKE DOWN ON THE CLUB, OPEN THE FACE WIDE, COCK YOUR WRISTS SHARPLY WHILE SWINGING BACK TO THE OUTSIDE, THEN HIT INTO THE SAND VERY FIRMLY WITH YOUR RIGHT HAND AS CLOSE TO THE BALL AS POSSIBLE.

Consider a Chip Shot

IN CERTAIN CONDITIONS, A CHIP SHOT CAN OFFER BETTER PERCENTAGES FROM A BUNKER THAN THE MORE NORMAL BLAST OR EXPLOSION SHOT.
THESE ARE WHEN THE SAND IS FIRM AND THE LIE GOOD, THERE IS LITTLE OR NO LIP AHEAD, AND THE PIN IS WELL BACK ON THE GREEN.

TO PLAY THIS SHOT, ADDRESS THE BALL OPPOSITE YOUR RIGHT HEEL, CHOKE DOWN ON THE CLUB, AND HOOD THE FACE SLIGHTLY.

THEN, WITH **A VERY STEADY HEAD**, HIT DOWN ONTO THE BACK OF THE BALL WITH A FIRM PUNCHING-TYPE STROKE.

ALLOW FOR LOTS OF RUN.

Putt Ball When Conditions Allow

DON'T DISCOUNT PUTTING OUT OF SAND IF YOUR LIE IS GOOD AND THE BUNKER IS RELATIVELY FLAT WITH LITTLE OR NO LIP.

IT CAN BE A REAL PERCENTAGE SHOT.

I USE MY NORMAL STROKE, BUT TRY TO HIT THE BALL OFF THE **TOE** RATHER THAN THE CENTER OF THE BLADE. I DON'T KNOW WHY, BUT I'VE FOUND THIS GIVES THE BALL A BETTER ROLLING ACTION.

HOWEVER, BECAUSE OF THE OFF-CENTER STRIKE, IT'S IMPORTANT TO HIT A LITTLE MORE FIRMLY THAN NORMAL.

Swallow Pride—and Play Safe

MIRACLES RARELY HAPPEN AT GOLF, AND ALMOST NEVER FROM BUNKERS. SO DON'T BE FOOLHARDY IN A SITUATION LIKE THIS. TAKE YOUR PUNISHMENT AND TAKE THE **SAFE** WAY ONTO THE GREEN.

PLAYING AWAY FROM THE HOLE WILL CERTAINLY GIVE YOU A LONGER PUTT THAN YOU'D LIKE.

BUT, NO MATTER HOW LONG IT IS, IT'S BETTER THAN FACING THE SAME SHOT OVER AGAIN... AND AGAIN... AND AGAIN...

Never Forget These Four Basics

FOUR BASICS ARE COMMON TO ALMOST EVERY SHORT BUNKER SHOT. FIRST, YOU HIT INTO AND THROUGH THE SAND BENEATH THE BALL, NOT THE BALL ITSELF.

SECOND, YOU WORK YOUR FEET WELL INTO THE SAND IN ORDER TO ESTABLISH A FIRM SWING BASE.

THIRD, YOU CREATE A MORE ABRUPT ARC THAN NORMAL BY PLAYING FROM AN OPEN STANCE AND MAKING AN EARLY WRIST COCK GOING BACK.

FOURTH, YOU CUT ACROSS THE BALL BY SWINGING ON AN OUTSIDE-IN ARC (ANOTHER REASON FOR TAKING AN OPEN STANCE).

CHAPTER FIVE
On the Green

22

Six Principles for Good Putting

Find Style That Works Best for You

WHAT'S THE BEST PUTTING STYLE: A STIFF-WRISTED ARM-AND-SHOULDER STROKE, A COMBINED WRIST-FOREARM ACTION, OR A WRISTS-ONLY METHOD? THE ONLY WAY TO FIND OUT IS TO EXPERIMENT INTELLIGENTLY TO DISCOVER WHAT WORKS BEST FOR YOU PERSONALLY.

SOME OF THE GREATEST PUTTERS HAVE BEEN ARM-AND-SHOULDER STROKERS, BUT MOST TOUR PLAYERS TODAY (INCLUDING ME) SEEM TO FAVOR A COMBINED WRIST-FOREARM ACTION...AND VERY FEW THE WRISTS-ONLY TECHNIQUE. REASON PROBABLY IS THAT SWINGING WITH THE WRISTS AND THE ARMS IS THE MOST NATURAL WAY TO STROKE A PUTT, AND THEREFORE THE EASIEST TO REPEAT CONSISTENTLY.

Know How You Control Distance

STROKER

RAPPER

THERE ARE BASICALLY TWO WAYS TO CONTROL THE DISTANCE THE BALL ROLLS IN PUTTING. ONE IS BY FORCE OF HIT, WHICH IS COMMON TO THE "RAPPING" TECHNIQUE. THE OTHER IS BY LENGTH OF BACKSWING, WHICH USUALLY GOES WITH MORE OF A "STROKING" ACTION.

I'M PRINCIPALLY A STROKER. AS PUTTS LENGTHEN, SO OBVIOUSLY THE FORCE YOU APPLY IS BOUND TO INCREASE. HOWEVER, I GOVERN DISTANCE CHIEFLY BY VARYING THE LENGTH OF MY BACKSWING, TRYING TO SUSTAIN A CONSTANT PACE AND STRENGTH OF STROKE ON ALL PUTTS.

SHORT PUTT

LONGER PUTT

Be Consistent in Your Method

YOU'LL APPROACH PUTT MORE CONSISTENTLY IF YOU MAKE YOUR MIND UP WHETHER YOU'RE BASICALLY A "CHARGE" OR "DIE" PUTTER.

"CHARGE" PUTTERS — **ARNOLD PALMER** WAS THE GREATEST — AIM TO HIT THE BACK OF THE HOLE HARD AND TRUE ENOUGH TO "TRAP" THE BALL INTO THE CUP.

I'M A DIE PUTTER BECAUSE I THINK IT OFFERS BETTER PERCENTAGES.

I AIM TO DROP THE BALL JUST OVER THE FRONT EDGE OF THE CUP WHEN I STROKE IT PERFECTLY, OR TOPPLE IT IN THE SIDES WHEN I DON'T.

Find and Stick to Ideal Putter

I'VE CHANGED PUTTERS ON ONLY TWO OR THREE OCCASIONS DURING MY CAREER, BECAUSE I BELIEVE IT'S THE "PUTTEE," NOT THE PUTTER, THAT DETERMINES WHAT WILL HAPPEN TO THE BALL.

SO MY ADVICE IS TO FIND A PUTTER YOU LIKE — THAT GIVES YOU THE BEST **FEEL** DAY IN, DAY OUT — AND STICK TO IT. ONE FACTOR TO WATCH FOR IN SELECTING A PUTTER IS WEIGHT: IF YOUR GREENS ARE NORMALLY FAST, THEN YOU'LL PROBABLY DO BEST WITH A LIGHT PUTTER, AND THE REVERSE IF THEY ARE GENERALLY SLOW.

Look for Good Balance, Proper Lie

FINDING A WEIGHT AND BALANCE OF CLUB THAT FEELS GOOD IS A BIG FACTOR IN SELECTING A PUTTER.

AN EQUALLY IMPORTANT POINT IS HOW THE HEAD SITS WHEN YOU ASSUME YOUR MOST EFFECTIVE PUTTING STANCE.

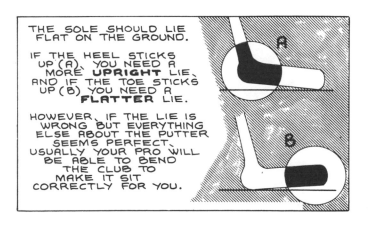

THE SOLE SHOULD LIE FLAT ON THE GROUND.

IF THE HEEL STICKS UP (A), YOU NEED A MORE **UPRIGHT** LIE, AND IF THE TOE STICKS UP (B) YOU NEED A **FLATTER** LIE.

HOWEVER, IF THE LIE IS WRONG BUT EVERYTHING ELSE ABOUT THE PUTTER SEEMS PERFECT, USUALLY YOUR PRO WILL BE ABLE TO BEND THE CLUB TO MAKE IT SIT CORRECTLY FOR YOU.

Build Confidence in Your Stroke

DON'T GET INTO THE HABIT OF DISCOUNTING OR DISLIKING PUTTING AS A PART OF THE GAME OF GOLF.

REMEMBER, YOU MAY BE ABLE TO RECOVER FROM A MISSED DRIVE OR APPROACH, BUT A MISSED PUTT IS A STROKE GONE FOREVER.

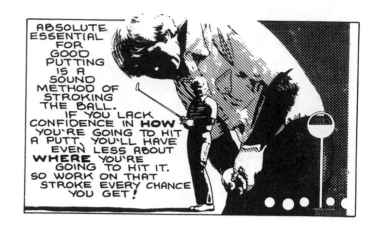

ABSOLUTE ESSENTIAL FOR GOOD PUTTING IS A SOUND METHOD OF STROKING THE BALL. IF YOU LACK CONFIDENCE IN **HOW** YOU'RE GOING TO HIT A PUTT, YOU'LL HAVE EVEN LESS ABOUT **WHERE** YOU'RE GOING TO HIT IT. SO WORK ON THAT STROKE EVERY CHANCE YOU GET!

23

The Basics of Putting Technique

Six Factors for Good Putting

WHAT MAKES A GOOD PUTTER?

HERE ARE SOME OF THE PHYSICAL FACTORS THAT I HAVE NOTED OVER THE YEARS.
1. VERY STILL HEAD AND BODY.
2. SMOOTHNESS OF STROKE, EVENNESS OF TEMPO.
3. PUTTERHEAD ACCELERATES THROUGH BALL.

AND ON THE MENTAL SIDE:
1. A GENERALLY POSITIVE ATTITUDE TO THIS CRITICAL PART OF THE GAME.
2. CARE, PRECISION AND SKILL IN READING ALL TYPES OF GREENS.
3. CONFIDENCE.

Grip to Stroke Ball Squarely

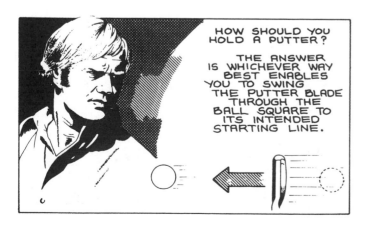

HOW SHOULD YOU HOLD A PUTTER?

THE ANSWER IS WHICHEVER WAY BEST ENABLES YOU TO SWING THE PUTTER BLADE THROUGH THE BALL SQUARE TO ITS INTENDED STARTING LINE.

MOST PEOPLE FIND THIS HAPPENS WHEN THEIR PALMS ARE SQUARELY ALIGNED WITH THE PUTTER BLADE. IN MY CASE, IT'S PARTICULARLY IMPORTANT TO HAVE THE **RIGHT** HAND FACING THUS, SO I CAN IN EFFECT USE IT TO "PUSH" THE PUTTER HEAD THROUGH THE BALL DIRECTLY ALONG ITS STARTING LINE.

105

Work for a Fluid Motion

HOW TIGHTLY SHOULD YOU HOLD YOUR PUTTER?

TO ME, THE MOST IMPORTANT CONSIDERATION IN PUTTING IS **FLUIDITY** OF STROKE, AND GRIP FIRMNESS HAS A BIG INFLUENCE ON THAT.

I TRY TO HOLD THE PUTTER SUFFICIENTLY FIRMLY TO BE ABLE TO CONTROL ITS PATH AND FACE ALIGNMENT. BUT NOT SO FIRMLY THAT IT CAN'T SWING NATURALLY OF ITS OWN WEIGHT. YOU MIGHT FIND IT WORTH SOME EXPERIMENTATION TO DISCOVER EXACTLY WHAT "WEIGHT" OF GRIP ALLOWS YOU TO MEET THOSE STROKING IDEALS.

Guide with Left, Hit with Right

WHICH IS THE MASTER HAND IN PUTTING?

AS WITH SO MANY GOLFING QUESTIONS, THE ANSWER HAS TO BE "THAT DEPENDS..."

SOME GREAT PUTTERS HAVE FELT THE LEFT HAND TO BE IN COMMAND. OTHERS HAVE SWORN THAT THE RIGHT WAS THE KEY.

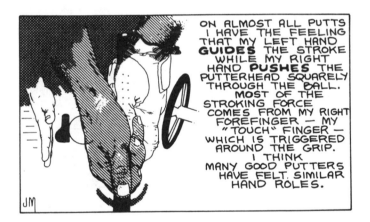

ON ALMOST ALL PUTTS I HAVE THE FEELING THAT MY LEFT HAND **GUIDES** THE STROKE WHILE MY RIGHT HAND **PUSHES** THE PUTTERHEAD SQUARELY THROUGH THE BALL. MOST OF THE STROKING FORCE COMES FROM MY RIGHT FOREFINGER — MY "TOUCH" FINGER — WHICH IS TRIGGERED AROUND THE GRIP. I THINK MANY GOOD PUTTERS HAVE FELT SIMILAR HAND ROLES.

Align Putter for True Roll

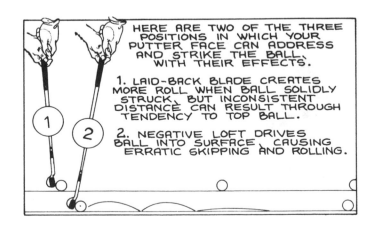

HERE ARE TWO OF THE THREE POSITIONS IN WHICH YOUR PUTTER FACE CAN ADDRESS AND STRIKE THE BALL, WITH THEIR EFFECTS.

1. LAID-BACK BLADE CREATES MORE ROLL WHEN BALL SOLIDLY STRUCK, BUT INCONSISTENT DISTANCE CAN RESULT THROUGH TENDENCY TO TOP BALL.

2. NEGATIVE LOFT DRIVES BALL INTO SURFACE, CAUSING ERRATIC SKIPPING AND ROLLING.

I FIND I'M MOST CONSISTENT IN BOTH STRIKING THE BALL SOLIDLY AND ROLLING IT TRULY WHEN THE BLADE IS VERTICAL AT ADDRESS AND IMPACT.

BUT EXPERIMENT WITH ALL THREE TECHNIQUES TO SEE WHICH WORKS BEST FOR YOU.

Meet These Two Set-Up Goals

WHAT'S THE PROPER STANCE AND POSTURE FOR PUTTING?

FRANKLY, I DON'T THINK SUCH THINGS EXIST. WATCH THE **PGA TOUR** AND YOU'LL SEE JUST ABOUT AS MANY VARIATIONS AS THERE ARE PLAYERS.

ALL, HOWEVER, TRY TO MEET AT LEAST TWO GOALS.

NUMBER ONE IS GOOD BALANCE — A FEELING OF COMFORT AND STABILITY. NUMBER TWO IS A SET-UP THAT POSITIONS THE EYES DIRECTLY OVER THE BALL AND ALLOWS THE HEAD TO REMAIN VERY STILL THROUGHOUT THE STROKE — "MUSTS" FOR GOOD STROKING.

Set Weight to Stabilize Body

HOW SHOULD YOUR WEIGHT BE DISTRIBUTED WHEN PUTTING?

WHICHEVER WAY BEST ALLOWS YOU TO KEEP YOUR HEAD AND BODY **PERFECTLY STILL** THROUGHOUT THE STROKE.

USUALLY, I CAN BEST ACHIEVE THAT ABSOLUTE PUTTING FUNDAMENTAL BY FEELING A PREDOMINANCE OF WEIGHT ON MY LEFT FOOT — AND PARTICULARLY ON THE **HEEL**.

EXPERIMENT TO DISCOVER THE SET-UP THAT GIVES YOU THE GREATEST **STABILITY** OVER THE BALL.

Look to Target from Behind Ball

I'LL VARY MY PUTTING STANCE A LITTLE FROM DAY TO DAY IN THE SEARCH FOR COMFORT, BUT BASICALLY I GET THE BEST RESULTS FROM REASONABLY SQUARE ALIGNMENT OF MY BODY TO THE TARGET LINE.

GENERALLY, I POSITION THE BALL OPPOSITE THE INSTEP OF MY LEFT FOOT, AND I **ALWAYS** SET MY HEAD BEHIND IT SO THAT I'M LOOKING DOWN THE LINE FROM **BEHIND** RATHER THAN ON TOP OF THE BALL.

107

Find Your Own Best Posture

HOW TALL OR CROUCHED YOU SET UP TO PUTT IS A MATTER OF PERSONAL PREFERENCE.

WATCH THE TOUR PROS AND YOU'LL SEE ALL SORTS OF STYLES, FROM VERY UPRIGHT TO ALMOST DOUBLED OVER.

I'M ESSENTIALLY A CROUCHER BECAUSE, BY GETTING WELL DOWN TO AND BEHIND THE BALL, I FEEL I CAN GET A BETTER SIGHTING OF THE LINE. WHICHEVER WAY YOU STAND, HOWEVER, BE SURE THAT YOUR EYES ARE **DEAD OVER** THE BALL AT ADDRESS, BECAUSE THAT'S FUNDAMENTAL TO ALMOST ALL FINE PUTTERS.

Check Your Right Elbow Position

I USE MY RIGHT ELBOW AS A SORT OF FULCRUM, OR GUIDE, TO STABILIZE MY PUTTING STROKE. HOLDING IT CLOSE TO MY RIGHT SIDE THROUGHOUT THE STROKE HELPS ME TO KEEP THE PUTTER BLADE SQUARE AND MOVING DIRECTLY ALONG THE TARGET LINE.

LETTING THE RIGHT ELBOW STRAY FROM THE SIDE TENDS TO CLOSE THE PUTTER FACE AND THROW THE CLUBHEAD OUTSIDE THE LINE.

SO, IF YOU PULL A LOT OF PUTTS LEFT OF THE HOLE, TRY KEEPING YOUR RIGHT ARM TUCKED WELL IN THROUGHOUT THE STROKE.

Forward-Press for Fluid Takeaway

IF YOU HAVE TROUBLE TAKING THE PUTTER AWAY SMOOTHLY, A FORWARD PRESS MIGHT HELP YOU DEVELOP A MORE FLUID START-BACK MOTION.

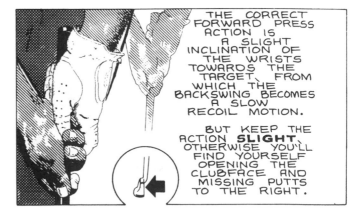

THE CORRECT FORWARD PRESS ACTION IS A SLIGHT INCLINATION OF THE WRISTS TOWARDS THE TARGET, FROM WHICH THE BACKSWING BECOMES A SLOW RECOIL MOTION.

BUT KEEP THE ACTION **SLIGHT**, OTHERWISE YOU'LL FIND YOURSELF OPENING THE CLUBFACE AND MISSING PUTTS TO THE RIGHT.

Swing Blade Low to Ground

TRUE END — OVER — END BALL ROLL IS THE FIRST GOAL IN PUTTING. THE **HEIGHT** OF YOUR STROKE HAS A BEARING ON THIS.

LIFTING THE CLUB ON THE BACKSWING CAUSES A CHOPPING — DOWN TYPE IMPACT THAT CREATES BACKSPIN (AND SOMETIMES ALSO SIDESPIN). LIFTING THE CLUB ON THE THROUGH-STROKE CREATES A SCOOPING TYPE ACTION THAT BREEDS "THIN" OR SEMI-TOPPED CONTACT. SO TRY TO KEEP THE BLADE AS LOW AS POSSIBLE BOTH SIDES OF THE BALL FOR A SQUARE, SOLID HIT.

Set-Up and Stroke to a *Specific Plan*

CONFIDENCE IS THE PRIMARY REQUIREMENT IN PUTTING.

IF YOU THINK YOU'LL MAKE A PUTT, YOU PROBABLY WILL.

IF YOU DON'T THINK YOU'LL MAKE IT, YOU ALMOST CERTAINLY WON'T.

PROPER PLANNING BREEDS CONFIDENCE.

STUDY LINE, BREAK AND SPEED, AND FORM A POSITIVE PICTURE IN YOUR MIND OF HOW THE BALL MUST BEHAVE TO DROP INTO THE HOLE.

THEN **STICK TO YOUR PLAN** AS YOU SET UP TO AND STROKE THE BALL.

24

Strategy and Tactics

Habitualize a "Reading" Routine

ALL GOOD GOLFERS DEVELOP A SET OF ROUTINES THAT BEST ENABLE THEM TO PREPARE PROPERLY FOR SHOTS. HERE'S MINE ON THE PUTTING GREEN. FIRST, AS I WALK ONTO THE GREEN, I CHECK OVERALL SLOPE OF THE LAND, THE GRAIN DIRECTION, AND ANY WIND FACTOR.

NEXT, I ASSESS THE SPECIFIC ANGLES AND BREAKS BETWEEN BALL AND CUP, AT THE SAME TIME EXAMINING THE LENGTH AND TEXTURE OF THE GRASS TO DETERMINE THE PROPER SPEED OF THE PUTT.

FINALLY, I COMPUTE THESE FACTORS INTO A COMPLETE MENTAL PICTURE OF THE PUTT AS I STEP UP TO THE BALL.

"See" Ball Dropping as You Plan

I PUTT BEST WHEN I CAN ALMOST LITERALLY "SEE" THE BALL RUNNING TO AND DROPPING INTO THE CUP IN MY MIND'S EYE AS I PLAN THE SHOT.

CONFIDENCE IN ONE'S STROKE IS A PREREQUISITE TO PAINTING SUCH PRETTY PICTURES, BUT SO EQUALLY IS PROPER SURVEYING OF EACH AND EVERY PUTT. DON'T HOLD UP PLAY, BUT **DO** TAKE ENOUGH TIME TO PROPERLY IDENTIFY THE BALL'S LINE AND COMPUTE ITS SPEED. IDEALLY, DO THAT SURVEYING WHILE YOUR PLAYING PARTNERS ARE SUMMING UP THEIR PUTTS.

Make Your Own Decisions

FRIENDLY AND WELL-MEANING ADVICE IS USUALLY IN PLENTIFUL SUPPLY ON GOLF COURSES, ESPECIALLY ON THE GREENS FROM PLAYING PARTNERS AND CADDIES.

THIS, HOWEVER, IS A TIME TO "SHUT OUT THE WORLD" IN MY BOOK.

AS ALL PUTTS IN THE FINAL ANALYSIS ARE "SPEED" PUTTS, AND AS NO ONE ELSE KNOWS HOW HARD YOU ARE GOING TO HIT THE BALL, I DON'T SEE HOW THEY CAN EFFECTIVELY ADVISE ON BREAK OR ANY OTHER FACTORS.

SO BE A LONER ON THE GREENS — DO YOUR OWN READING, AS YOU MUST DO YOUR OWN STROKING.

Squat for Best Angle on Slopes

STAND ERECT IN ASSESSING THE LINE OF THE PUTT AND THE MORE SUBTLE UNDULATIONS IN THE GREEN WILL TEND TO FLATTEN OUT.

LIE ON YOUR BELLY AND ALL YOU'LL SEE CLEARLY IS THE UPS AND DOWNS IN THE IMMEDIATE FOREGROUND.

THAT'S WHY I PREFER TO SQUAT OR BEND OVER FROM THE WAIST IN READING GREENS.

WITH MY HEAD AT ABOUT THREE FEET OFF THE GROUND, I SEEM TO GET THE BEST PERSPECTIVE ON BOTH SLOPE AND LINE, ESPECIALLY ON MIDDLE-DISTANCE PUTTS.

Focus Chiefly on Distance

WHAT'S MORE IMPORTANT IN PUTTING, **DIRECTION** OR **DISTANCE**? MOST PEOPLE CAN INTUITIVELY JUDGE THE LINE TO THE HOLE ON APPROACH PUTTS SUFFICIENTLY WELL TO STROKE THE BALL WITHIN REASONABLE PROXIMITY OF THE CUP. MANY, HOWEVER, SEEM TO HAVE MUCH GREATER PROBLEMS JUDGING DISTANCE.

IF YOU'RE ONE OF THOSE, AFTER HAVING DECIDED THE LINE, FIX YOUR MIND AS YOU PREPARE TO PUTT CHIEFLY ON **DISTANCE**, NOT DIRECTION. THINK LAST BEFORE YOU SWING ABOUT THE FORCE OR "WEIGHT" OF THE STROKE, TRYING TO SENSE IT IN YOUR HANDS AS YOU MAKE YOUR PRACTICE MOTIONS.

I THINK SO DOING WILL DEFINITELY CUT DOWN ON THOSE THREE-PUTT HORRORS.

Don't Be Over-Ambitious

SOME GREAT PUTTERS WILL TELL YOU THEY TRY TO HOLE EVERYTHING ON THE GREENS, BUT IT'S MY BELIEF THAT MOST TOUR PLAYERS, PUTTING FROM MORE THAN 30 OR SO FEET, ARE GENERALLY THINKING TWO PUTTS, NOT ONE.

TWO-FOOT RADIUS

DANGER IN BEING TOO AMBITIOUS IS OVER-HITTING THE PUTT AND THEN FACING A LONG ONE COMING BACK. IT'S BETTER IN MY BOOK — UNLESS YOU ACTUALLY HAVE TO HOLE A "SNAKE" TO WIN — TO THINK OF GETTING THE BALL WITHIN A TWO-FOOT RADIUS OF THE CUP, RATHER THAN ACTUALLY IN THE HOLE.

AT LEAST, YOU'LL DEFINITELY THREE-PUTT LESS WITH SUCH AN APPROACH.

Never Overlook Grain Factors

ALMOST ALL TYPES OFF GRASS HAVE SOME DEGREE OF GRAIN, AND AN AWFUL LOT OF MAKEABLE PUTTS ARE MISSED BY GOLFERS WHO DON'T NOTICE IT OR KNOW HOW TO READ IT.

WITH

AGAINST

MOST GRASSES GROW EITHER TOWARD THE NEAREST WATER OR IN THE DIRECTION OF DRAINAGE. IN CERTAIN PARTS OF THE WORLD THEY GROW PREDOMINANTLY TOWARD THE SETTING SUN. ONE VISUAL TEST IS THE SHEEN OF THE GRASS. IF IT'S LIGHT AND SILVERY, THEN YOU'RE GENERALLY WITH THE GRAIN, AND IF IT'S DARK OR MATT-LOOKING THEN YOU'RE USUALLY AGAINST IT.

Know How Grain Influences Ball

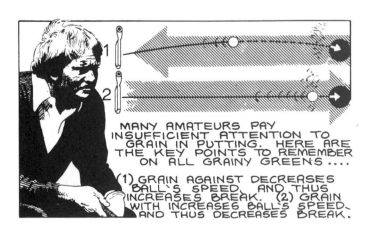

1

2

MANY AMATEURS PAY INSUFFICIENT ATTENTION TO GRAIN IN PUTTING. HERE ARE THE KEY POINTS TO REMEMBER ON ALL GRAINY GREENS ....

(1) GRAIN AGAINST DECREASES BALL'S SPEED AND THUS INCREASES BREAK. (2) GRAIN WITH INCREASES BALL'S SPEED, AND THUS DECREASES BREAK.

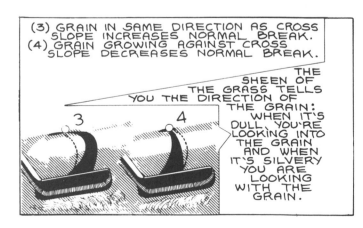

(3) GRAIN IN SAME DIRECTION AS CROSS SLOPE INCREASES NORMAL BREAK.
(4) GRAIN GROWING AGAINST CROSS SLOPE DECREASES NORMAL BREAK.

3   4

THE SHEEN OF THE GRASS TELLS YOU THE DIRECTION OF THE GRAIN: WHEN IT'S DULL, YOU'RE LOOKING INTO THE GRAIN AND WHEN IT'S SILVERY YOU ARE LOOKING WITH THE GRAIN.

Observe Closely Around Hole

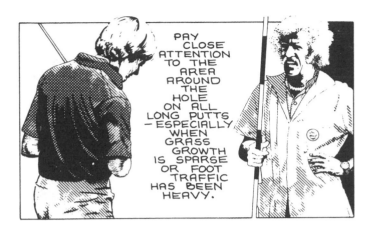

PAY CLOSE ATTENTION TO THE AREA AROUND THE HOLE ON ALL LONG PUTTS — ESPECIALLY WHEN GRASS GROWTH IS SPARSE OR FOOT TRAFFIC HAS BEEN HEAVY.

THE BARER THE GROUND OR THE WORSE THE IRREGULARITIES, THE MORE THE BALL WILL WANDER OFF LINE AS IT LOSES MOMENTUM.

PLAN FOR THAT IN ASSESSING SPEED AND LINE, NOT JUST FOR THE AREA OF TRAVEL YOU CAN EASILY SEE WHILE STANDING OVER THE PUTT.

Try This Method on Double-Breakers

DOUBLE-BREAKING PUTTS NEED EXTRA CARE.

HERE'S A SYSTEM THAT MIGHT HELP YOU TAKE SOME OF THE COMPLEXITY OUT OF THEM.

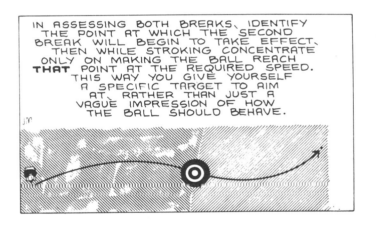

IN ASSESSING BOTH BREAKS, IDENTIFY THE POINT AT WHICH THE SECOND BREAK WILL BEGIN TO TAKE EFFECT, THEN WHILE STROKING CONCENTRATE ONLY ON MAKING THE BALL REACH **THAT** POINT AT THE REQUIRED SPEED. THIS WAY YOU GIVE YOURSELF A SPECIFIC TARGET TO AIM AT, RATHER THAN JUST A VAGUE IMPRESSION OF HOW THE BALL SHOULD BEHAVE.

Get Aid from Overall Terrain

OCCASIONALLY YOU WILL ENCOUNTER A PUTT WHERE THE BREAK APPEARS TO DIFFER GREATLY WHEN VIEWED FROM OPPOSITE SIDES OF THE HOLE.

THE BEST ANSWER TO THIS CONFUSING SITUATION LIES IN THE SURROUNDING TERRAIN. GENERALLY, YOU'LL FIND THE BALL MORE LIKELY TO TURN **WITH** THE GENERAL SLOPE THAN AGAINST IT. SO LOOK AROUND AT THE OVERALL LIE OF THE LAND BEFORE YOU MAKE A DECISION.

Take Relief from Standing Water

DEMANDING AS THEY MAY SOMETIMES SEEM TO BE, ONE THING THE **R**ULES OF **G**OLF DON'T REQUIRE YOU TO DO IS PLAY FROM OR THROUGH STANDING WATER — UNLESS YOU'VE LANDED IN AN ACTUAL WATER HAZARD, THAT IS. BE AWARE OF THIS ON THE GREENS AS WELL AS 'THROUGH THE GREEN.'

IF WATER HAS VISIBLY ACCUMULATED BETWEEN YOU AND THE HOLE, THEN TAKE THE RELIEF AVAILABLE UNDER **R**ULE 32.

BASICALLY, THIS INVOLVES MOVING THE BALL TO THE NEAREST SPOT THAT AVOIDS THE WATER WITHOUT MOVING IT NEARER THE HOLE.

Don't Let Moisture Fool You

DON'T LET MOISTURE FOOL YOU ON THE GREENS. THERE ARE TWO TYPES — RECOGNIZE THE DIFFERENCE.

WHEN THE GROUND ITSELF IS THOROUGHLY SOAKED, THE BALL WILL NEITHER ROLL NOR BREAK AS MUCH AS NORMAL, THUS REQUIRING A **FIRMER** STROKE.

WHEN THE GROUND IS BASICALLY FIRM, BUT THE SURFACE HAS BEEN DAMPENED BY DEW OR A SHOWER, THE BALL GENERALLY WILL BOTH ROLL AND BREAK ALMOST AS MUCH AS IN DRY CONDITIONS.

SO HIT PRETTY MUCH WHAT YOU SEE IN TERMS OF BREAK, AND GO EASY ON THE POWER.

Play to Putt Out Uphill on Fast Greens

HERE'S A TIP THAT WILL HELP YOU ANY TIME YOU PUTT VERY FAST GREENS.

IN THINKING DISTANCE, PLAN TO LEAVE YOURSELF AN **UPHILL** PUTT SHOULD YOU MISS THE HOLE ON THE PRESENT ATTEMPT.

ON VERY SLICK GREENS I'D RATHER HAVE EVEN A SIDEHILL PUTT THAN ONE GOING STRAIGHT DOWN A PRONOUNCED SLOPE, BECAUSE THOSE "SLIDERS" ARE THE TRICKIEST TO JUDGE AND STROKE IN THE GAME.

SO PLAN CAREFULLY SLOPE-WISE, ESPECIALLY ON LONG APPROACH PUTTS — AND ON CHIP SHOTS, TOO.

Try This Tactic on Short Downhillers

MOST GOLFERS FEAR DOWNHILL PUTTS, AND MISS THEM BECAUSE THE FEAR BREEDS HESITANT STROKING. HERE'S THE WAY I'VE ALWAYS TAKEN THE ANXIETY OUT OF THESE SHOTS.

INSTEAD OF WORRYING ABOUT THE SLOPE, COMPUTE AND PLAY THE PUTT AS IF IT WERE ON LEVEL GROUND.

FOR EXAMPLE, IF THE PUTT IS ACTUALLY 10 FEET BUT WILL REACH THE HOLE WITH THE FORCE NEEDED FOR A 3-FOOTER ON LEVEL GROUND, THEN AIM AT A POINT 3 FEET AWAY AND STROKE FOR THAT DISTANCE.

THE MORE PRECISE FEEL FOR THE SHOT THIS APPROACH GIVES YOU WILL MAKE YOUR ACTION A LOT MORE POSITIVE.

Be Firm on Short Uphillers

GOLF IS A GAME OF PERCENTAGES. BEING **FIRM** ON SHORT UP-HILLERS PUTS THEM IN YOUR FAVOR, BOTH BECAUSE THERE IS LITTLE DANGER OF RUNNING A LONG WAY PAST, AND BECAUSE THE HIGHER REAR EDGE OF THE HOLE MAKES FOR A BETTER BACKSTOP.

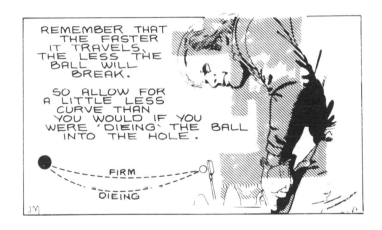

REMEMBER THAT THE FASTER IT TRAVELS, THE LESS THE BALL WILL BREAK.

SO ALLOW FOR A LITTLE LESS CURVE THAN YOU WOULD IF YOU WERE 'DIEING' THE BALL INTO THE HOLE.

FIRM

DIEING

Make Hole Look Like a Bucket

IF YOU'RE SUFFERING FROM PUTTING BLUES, TRY PRACTICING TO A **TEE** STUCK IN THE GROUND INSTEAD OF TO A HOLE.

BY MAKING YOU LESS "CUP CONSCIOUS," THIS WILL HELP YOU CONCENTRATE BETTER ON STROKE MECHANICS AND TEMPO. ALSO, ONCE YOU GET BACK ON THE COURSE, THE HOLE WILL LOOK LIKE A BUCKET!

SMOOTHNESS...

Practice the Putts You Plan to Hole

WATCHING AMATEURS PRACTICE BEFORE PRO-AMS, I OFTEN SEE THEM PUTTING CONTINUOUSLY FROM 40 FEET OR MORE.

I SOMETIMES WONDER HOW MANY SUCH MONSTERS THEY ACTUALLY EXPECT TO HOLE.

HITTING A FEW ROLLER-COASTERS IS GOOD FOR GETTING THE OVERALL PACE OF THE GREENS AND FOR DEVELOPING A FLUID STROKING MOTION.

BUT FROM ABOUT **12** FEET IN IS WHERE YOU MOST NEED ACCURACY AND CONFIDENCE. AND DON'T NEGLECT THOSE THREE- AND FOUR- FOOTERS, EITHER, IF YOU'D LIKE LESS PRESSURE ON YOUR CHIPS AND LONG PUTTS.

4 FEET

12 FEET

Don't Try to Be a Hero...

N MATCH-PLAY, DON'T TRY TO BE A HERO ON THE GREENS WHEN THERE IS NO NEED FOR HEROICS.

IF YOUR OPPONENT IS 20 FEET AWAY AND YOU ARE 40 FEET, WORK AT LAGGING YOUR PUTT "DEAD" RATHER THAN RISKING THREE- PUTTING BY TRYING TO HOLE IT.

JUST GET IT CLOSE!

THE PERCENTAGES ARE THAT YOUR OPPONENT WILL MISS. IF THAT HAPPENS AND YOU THREE- PUTT, YOU'LL FEEL YOU'VE GIVEN HIM THE HOLE AND RISK GETTING DOWN ON YOURSELF AS A RESULT.

SHOULD HE HOLE OUT, THEN HE'S SIMPLY BEATEN THE ODDS AND YOU HAVE NOTHING TO HURT ABOUT INSIDE.

WOW! NICE PUTT!

25

Faults and Cures

Accelerate the Putterhead

Change Grip to Stop Pulling

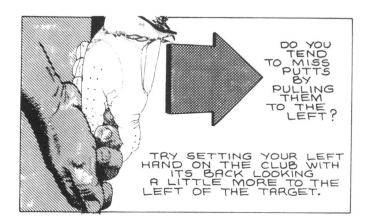

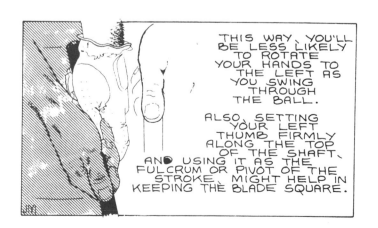

Watch Blade to Correct Mishits

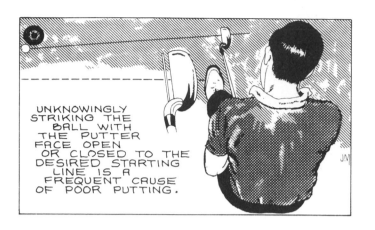

UNKNOWINGLY STRIKING THE BALL WITH THE PUTTER FACE OPEN OR CLOSED TO THE DESIRED STARTING LINE IS A FREQUENT CAUSE OF POOR PUTTING.

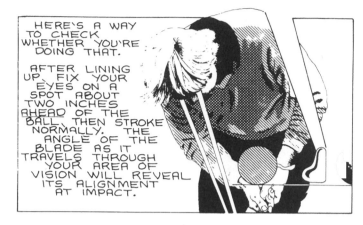

HERE'S A WAY TO CHECK WHETHER YOU'RE DOING THAT.

AFTER LINING UP, FIX YOUR EYES ON A SPOT ABOUT TWO INCHES AHEAD OF THE BALL, THEN STROKE NORMALLY. THE ANGLE OF THE BLADE AS IT TRAVELS THROUGH YOUR AREA OF VISION WILL REVEAL ITS ALIGNMENT AT IMPACT.

Try More Backswing, Not More Force

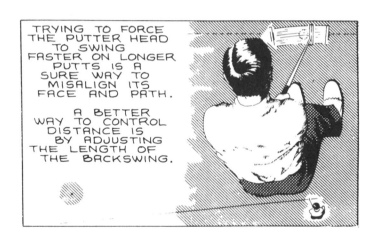

TRYING TO FORCE THE PUTTER HEAD TO SWING FASTER ON LONGER PUTTS IS A SURE WAY TO MISALIGN ITS FACE AND PATH.

A BETTER WAY TO CONTROL DISTANCE IS BY ADJUSTING THE LENGTH OF THE BACKSWING.

I TRY TO SWING THE PUTTER HEAD AT MORE OR LESS THE SAME PACE ON ALL PUTTS — THE IDEAL PACE IN MY CASE BEING A SENSE OF THE CLUB VIRTUALLY 'SWINGING ITSELF.' DISTANCE IS THEN VARIED SIMPLY BY INCREASING OR DECREASING THE LENGTH OF THE BACKSWING.

Check Your Follow-Through

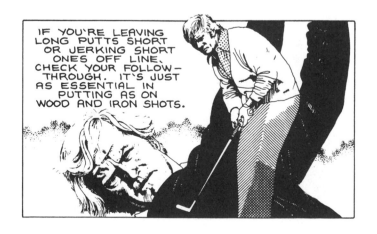

IF YOU'RE LEAVING LONG PUTTS SHORT OR JERKING SHORT ONES OFF LINE, CHECK YOUR FOLLOW-THROUGH. IT'S JUST AS ESSENTIAL IN PUTTING AS ON WOOD AND IRON SHOTS.

DRAW AN IMAGINERY LINE ALONG THE STARTING PATH OF THE PUTT AND TRY TO CARRY THE PUTTER BLADE STRAIGHT ALONG IT AFTER IMPACT FOR AT LEAST FIVE OR SIX INCHES. YOU'LL STRIKE THE BALL MORE FIRMLY AND SQUARELY BY **ACCELERATING** THROUGH IT BETTER.

Keep Shoulders Still to Steady Head

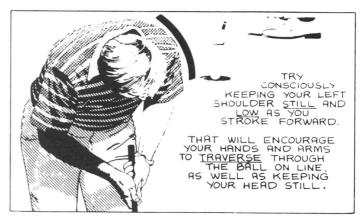

Let Putterhead Do the Work

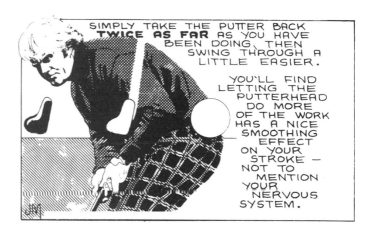

Stay on Path to Drop Those Shorties

CHAPTER SIX

Managing Your Game from Tee to Green

26

Fundamentals of Good Strategy

Observe and Plan Before You Hit

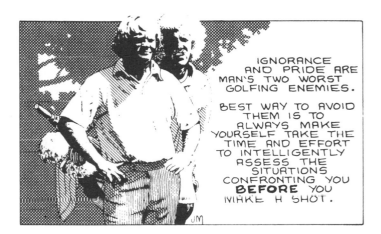

IGNORANCE AND PRIDE ARE MAN'S TWO WORST GOLFING ENEMIES.

BEST WAY TO AVOID THEM IS TO ALWAYS MAKE YOURSELF TAKE THE TIME AND EFFORT TO INTELLIGENTLY ASSESS THE SITUATIONS CONFRONTING YOU **BEFORE** YOU MAKE A SHOT.

STUDY WHAT LIES AHEAD PRUDENTLY AND UNEMOTIONALLY. WEIGH THE CONSEQUENCES OF THE SHOT YOU'D IDEALLY LIKE TO HIT, AND THEN THE ONE YOU ACTUALLY HAVE A REASONABLE CHANCE OF EXECUTING. IN SHORT, LOOK AND THINK, AND THEN BE TOTALLY REALISTIC IN BASING YOUR DECISIONS ON YOUR TRUE CAPABILITIES. MAKE A HABIT OF SO DOING AND YOUR HANDICAP WILL TUMBLE WITHOUT ANY IMPROVEMENT IN YOUR SHOT-MAKING SKILLS.

"Blank Out" the Bad Shots

TOO OFTEN ONE BAD GOLF SHOT IMMEDIATELY LEADS TO ANOTHER AT LEAST AS BAD OR EVEN WORSE. THE REASON IS ALMOST ALWAYS ANGER AND FRUSTRATION, NOT SUDDEN LOSS OF SWING SKILLS.

I'VE GENERALLY MANAGED TO AVOID THIS TRAP BY "BLANKING OUT" THE BAD SHOT BY CONSCIOUSLY FORCING MY MIND TO FOCUS IMMEDIATELY ON THE RECOVERY I NOW HAVE TO PLAY. IN OTHER WORDS, I SWITCH OFF THE FAULT AND SWITCH ON TO THE REMEDY AS FAST AS I POSSIBLY CAN. IT TAKES DISCIPLINE, BUT IT ALSO PAYS BIG DIVIDENDS.

Try to Stay Relaxed

A COUPLE OF FRIENDS MENTIONED RECENTLY THAT THEY PLAYED MUCH BETTER UPON FIRST COMING BACK FROM A LAY-OFF THAN WHEN THEY WERE TEEING IT UP REGULARLY. I DON'T THINK THE REASON IS HARD TO GUESS.

PLAYING FREQUENTLY, YOU PUT YOURSELF UNDER PRESSURE TO PLAY WELL, WHICH BREEDS BOTH MENTAL AND PHYSICAL TENSION.

NOT EXPECTING TO DO MUCH AFTER A LAY-OFF, YOU'RE **RELAXED** — AND YOU PLAY WELL AS A RESULT.

IF THAT'S AS TRUE AS I THINK IT IS, THEN OBVIOUSLY ANYTHING YOU CAN DO TO **STAY** RELAXED ONCE YOU'RE BACK IS GOING TO MAKE YOU A BETTER PLAYER.

Work on Your "Vizualization"

IF YOU GENERALLY STRIKE THE BALL PRETTY WELL BUT FALL SHORT, LONG OR WIDE OF A LOT OF TARGETS, DO SOME WORK ON YOUR VISUALIZATION PROCESSES <u>BEFORE</u> YOU HIT — AND, PREFERABLY, EVEN BEFORE YOU SELECT A CLUB.

START BY FULLY ANALYZING ALL THE FACTORS THAT WILL DECIDE THE TYPE OF SHOT YOU'LL PLAY. NEXT, VISUALIZE THAT SPECIFIC SHOT FLYING TO YOUR TARGET — ACTUALLY "SEE" IT IN YOUR MIND'S EYE. FINALLY, IMAGINE AND MENTALLY "FEEL" THE SWING YOU NEED TO MAKE THE SHOT. ONLY THEN DRAW OUT A CLUB AND GO INTO ACTION.

Think "Target," Not "Trouble"

THINK **TARGET**, NOT "TROUBLE" IN SETTING UP TO EVERY SHOT.

BLOT OUT THE POTENTIAL HAZARDS BY CONCENTRATING HARD ON THE AREA YOU WANT TO HIT, NOT THOSE YOU WANT TO MISS.

OVER-CONSCIOUSNESS OF HAZARDS IS A PRIME CAUSE OF BOTH MUSCULAR TENSION AND TRYING TO "GUIDE" THE BALL AMONG WEEKEND GOLFERS. THINK ONLY OF THE RESULTS YOU SEEK AND YOU WILL BOTH AIM AND ALIGN MORE ACCURATELY AND SWING MORE FREELY.

Go with Your Natural "Shape"

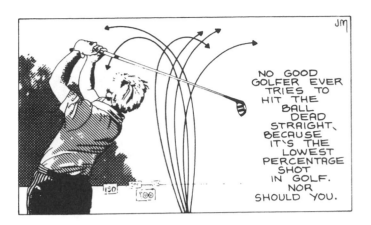

NO GOOD GOLFER EVER TRIES TO HIT THE BALL DEAD STRAIGHT, BECAUSE IT'S THE LOWEST PERCENTAGE SHOT IN GOLF. NOR SHOULD YOU.

IF YOU'VE BEEN PLAYING GOLF AWHILE, YOU'LL HAVE DEVELOPED A NATURAL TENDENCY EITHER TO FADE OR DRAW MOST SHOTS. UNLESS YOU ARE SKILLED ENOUGH TO BE ABLE TO MOVE THE BALL EITHER WAY AT WILL, YOUR NATURAL 'SHAPE' IS THE ONE TO GO WITH IN PLANNING ALL YOUR LONG-SHOT STRATEGY.

USE IT PARTICULARLY TO CURVE THE BALL **AWAY FROM** SEVERE TROUBLE.

Don't Fight the Inevitable

MANY AMATEURS SLICE THE BALL TO THE RIGHT REPEATEDLY, BUT CONTINUALLY AIM STRAIGHT IN THE HOPE THAT **THIS TIME** IT WILL FLY STRAIGHT.

UNFORTUNATELY, THEIR OPTIMISM FAR EXCEEDS THE LAWS OF CHANCE.

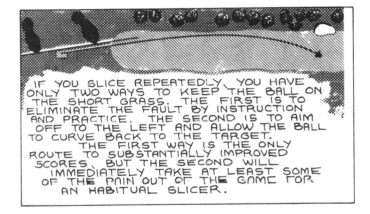

IF YOU SLICE REPEATEDLY, YOU HAVE ONLY TWO WAYS TO KEEP THE BALL ON THE SHORT GRASS. THE FIRST IS TO ELIMINATE THE FAULT BY INSTRUCTION AND PRACTICE. THE SECOND IS TO AIM OFF TO THE LEFT AND ALLOW THE BALL TO CURVE BACK TO THE TARGET.

THE FIRST WAY IS THE ONLY ROUTE TO SUBSTANTIALLY IMPROVED SCORES, BUT THE SECOND WILL IMMEDIATELY TAKE AT LEAST SOME OF THE PAIN OUT OF THE GAME FOR AN HABITUAL SLICER.

Play the Percentages

MY APPROACH TO TROUBLE IS TO GAMBLE AS MUCH AS POSSIBLE WITHOUT BEING FLAT-OUT FOOLISH. FOR EXAMPLE, IF I'M IN A DENSE FOREST AND THERE IS OUT-OF-BOUNDS OR WATER CLOSE BY, I'LL PLAY THE SAFEST POSSIBLE "GET OUT" SHOT.

HOWEVER, IF I'M BEHIND JUST A FEW TREES WITH NOT MUCH OTHER TROUBLE AROUND, I'LL USUALLY TRY TO WORK THE BALL THROUGH AN OPENING, THE PERCENTAGES BEING THAT I'LL HAVE AS GOOD A NEXT SHOT AS I'D HAVE HAD BY CHIPPING OUT, EVEN IF I DO CATCH SOME PART OF THE WOODWORK.

Beware Those Easy-Looking Holes

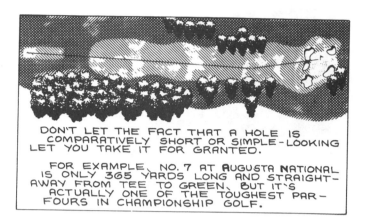

DON'T LET THE FACT THAT A HOLE IS COMPARATIVELY SHORT OR SIMPLE-LOOKING LET YOU TAKE IT FOR GRANTED.

FOR EXAMPLE, NO. 7 AT AUGUSTA NATIONAL IS ONLY 365 YARDS LONG AND STRAIGHT-AWAY FROM TEE TO GREEN, BUT IT'S ACTUALLY ONE OF THE TOUGHEST PAR-FOURS IN CHAMPIONSHIP GOLF.

THE NARROW, TREE-LINED FAIRWAY DEMANDS GREAT ACCURACY FROM THE TEE, BUT YOU ALSO NEED GOOD DISTANCE SO AS TO BE ABLE TO THROW A HIGH, SOFT SHOT INTO THE VERY SHALLOW, SAND-SURROUNDED, STEEPLY-ANGLED GREEN.

IN OTHER WORDS, LIKE A LOT OF SHORT PAR FOURS, THIS EASY-LOOKING HOLE ACTUALLY DEMANDS MAXIMUM THINKING AND STRIKING EFFORT ON EVERY SHOT.

Take It Easy After a Lay-Off

STARTING GOLF AGAIN AFTER A LONG LAYOFF?

DON'T GO OUT THE FIRST TIME AND BEAT A THOUSAND RANGE BALLS: YOUR MUSCLES AREN'T READY FOR IT AND THEY WILL DEFINITELY PUNISH YOU!

INSTEAD, DO WHAT YOU'VE BEEN DYING TO DO, WHICH IS **PLAY**, NOT PRACTICE. USE AN OUTING OR TWO ON THE COURSE TO REKINDLE YOUR ENTHUSIASM, AND ALSO TO TELL YOU WHAT AREAS OF YOUR SWING OR GAME PARTICULARLY NEED WORK. BY USING THIS EXPERIENCE TO CREATE A PRACTICE PLAN, YOU CAN THEN GO SERIOUSLY TO WORK WITH SOME **CLEAR** OBJECTIVES IN MIND.

27

From the Tee

Never Rush the Opening Drive

ONE OF GOLF'S MOST IMPORTANT SHOTS IS THE OPENING DRIVE.

HIT IT WELL AND ALL SEEMS RIGHT WITH THE WORLD. HIT IT POORLY AND, AS LIKE AS NOT, YOU'VE SET THE TONE FOR A FRUSTRATING DAY.

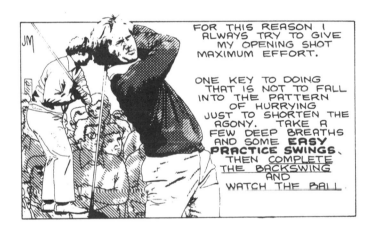

FOR THIS REASON I ALWAYS TRY TO GIVE MY OPENING SHOT MAXIMUM EFFORT.

ONE KEY TO DOING THAT IS NOT TO FALL INTO THE PATTERN OF HURRYING JUST TO SHORTEN THE AGONY. TAKE A FEW DEEP BREATHS AND SOME **EASY PRACTICE SWINGS**, THEN <u>COMPLETE THE BACKSWING</u> AND <u>WATCH THE BALL</u>.

Think Positively

IN PLANNING TEE SHOTS, DON'T THINK OF THINGS TO AVOID LIKE WOODS OR BUNKERS. INSTEAD, IDENTIFY AND THEN MENTALLY FOCUS ON THE AREA OF THE FAIRWAY **YOU WANT TO HIT.**

HAVING DONE THAT, PICTURE THE SHOT THAT WILL GET YOU THERE IN YOUR MIND'S EYE, THEN MENTALLY REHEARSE THE SWING THAT WILL EXECUTE THE IMAGINED SHOT.

IN OTHER WORDS THINK **POSITIVELY**, NEVER NEGATIVELY, IN YOUR SHOT-PLANNING.

Be Observant

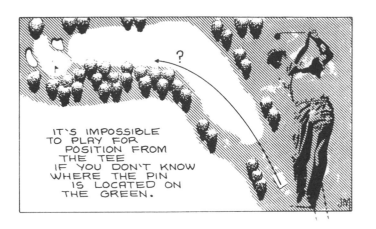

IT'S IMPOSSIBLE TO PLAY FOR POSITION FROM THE TEE IF YOU DON'T KNOW WHERE THE PIN IS LOCATED ON THE GREEN.

CADDIES SUPPLY THIS INFORMATION TO TOUR PLAYERS. IF THAT'S BEYOND YOUR RESOURCES, THEN AT LEAST BE SURE TO CHECK PIN LOCATIONS ON UPCOMING HOLES AS YOU PASS ADJACENT TO THEM OR WHENEVER THEY BECOME VISIBLE.

IN OTHER WORDS, BE OBSERVANT.

NO. 3
375 YDS
PAR 4

Don't Fret About Being Out-Hit

DOES BEING OUTHIT FROM THE TEE UPSET YOU?

DON'T LET IT -- ESPECIALLY IF YOUR OPPONENT IS WILD AS WELL AS. LONG (AS IS OFTEN THE CASE). REASON #1 IS THAT YOU GAIN A PSYCHOLOGICAL EDGE BY GETTING YOUR BALL ON THE GREEN FIRST.

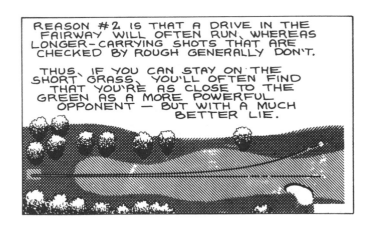

REASON #2 IS THAT A DRIVE IN THE FAIRWAY WILL OFTEN RUN, WHEREAS LONGER-CARRYING SHOTS THAT ARE CHECKED BY ROUGH GENERALLY DON'T.

THUS, IF YOU CAN STAY ON THE SHORT GRASS, YOU'LL OFTEN FIND THAT YOU'RE AS CLOSE TO THE GREEN AS A MORE POWERFUL OPPONENT — BUT WITH A MUCH BETTER LIE.

Put Position Ahead of Distance

DISTANCE IS VALUABLE IN GOLF, BUT ONLY IN TERMS OF MAKING THE NEXT SHOT EASIER — NEVER FOR ITS OWN SAKE.

EVEN MORE IMPORTANT IS POSITION — FOR EXAMPLE, A 7-IRON FROM A DOWNHILL/SIDEHILL LIE IS A TOUGHER SHOT THAN A 5-IRON FROM A LEVEL LIE.

SO DON'T JUST WHACK AWAY FROM THE TEE — REMEMBER THAT NEARNESS TO THE HOLE DOESN'T ALWAYS SET UP THE BEST APPROACH SITUATION.

Always Target Specifically

EVEN IF YOU'RE NOT A GOOD ENOUGH STRIKER TO FREQUENTLY HIT A SPECIFIC AREA OF THE FAIRWAY, I STILL THINK YOU SHOULD **TRY** TO DO SO ON EVERY TEE SHOT.

WHY? BECAUSE THE MORE SPECIFICALLY YOU "TARGET" MENTALLY, THE MORE ACCURATELY YOU WILL PHYSICALLY AIM THE CLUBFACE AND ALIGN YOURSELF AT ADDRESS. AND THE MORE PRECISELY YOU DO BOTH THOSE THINGS, THE BETTER YOUR CHANCES OF HITTING THE BALL WHERE YOU'D LIKE IT TO GO.

Hit Away from Trouble Areas

NOTHING CREATES TENSION IN A CLUB GOLFER FASTER THAN AN OUT-OF-BOUNDS AREA CLOSE UP TO ONE OR OTHER SIDE OF THE FAIRWAY.

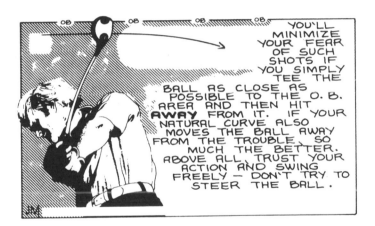

YOU'LL MINIMIZE YOUR FEAR OF SUCH SHOTS IF YOU SIMPLY TEE THE BALL AS CLOSE AS POSSIBLE TO THE O.B. AREA AND THEN HIT **AWAY** FROM IT. IF YOUR NATURAL CURVE ALSO MOVES THE BALL AWAY FROM THE TROUBLE, SO MUCH THE BETTER. ABOVE ALL, TRUST YOUR ACTION AND SWING FREELY — DON'T TRY TO STEER THE BALL.

Beware the "Driver Syndrome"

COULD YOU GET MY DRIVER, PLEASE..

BEWARE THE SYNDROME OF **ALWAYS** HITTING A DRIVER SIMPLY BECAUSE A HOLE IS A PAR-4 OR A PAR-5. GET INTO THE HABIT OF LOOKING AT AND THINKING ABOUT WHAT LIES IMMEDIATELY AHEAD BEFORE SELECTING A TEE-SHOT CLUB.

IF THE HAZARDS ARE PARTICULARLY SEVERE, OR YOU GET THAT "CLOSED IN" FEELING, CONSIDER PLAYING A SHORTER AND THEREFORE MORE CONTROLLABLE WOODEN CLUB — OR EVEN AN IRON.

REMEMBER, YOUR CHANCES ARE ALWAYS A LOT BETTER FROM SHORT GRASS, EVEN IF THE APPROACH SHOT IS LONGER, THAN THEY ARE FROM WATER, SAND OR TALL TIMBER.

Play Short of Severe Hazards

CONSIDER GOING WITH LESS THAN YOUR MAXIMUM-DISTANCE TEE-SHOT WHENEVER THERE IS POTENTIAL TREE TROUBLE UP AHEAD.

FOR EXAMPLE, IF THERE ARE A COUPLE OF TREES TO ONE SIDE OF THE FAIRWAY, A WELL-HIT BUT SLIGHTLY OFF-LINE DRIVE MIGHT PUT YOU SO CLOSE THAT YOU CAN NEITHER GO OVER OR AROUND THEM. A THREE- OR FOUR-WOOD FROM THE TEE, ON THE OTHER HAND, COULD LEAVE YOU FAR ENOUGH BACK TO TAKE ONE OF THOSE OPTIONS AND STILL GET HOME.

3-WOOD DRIVER

Make Fairway Slopes Work for You

DON'T HAUL OFF AND FIRE CASUALLY TO A SLOPING FAIRWAY, ESPECIALLY IN DRY OR RUNNING GROUND CONDITIONS. MAKE THE SLOPE WORK **FOR**, NOT AGAINST YOU.

FOR EXAMPLE, IF THE LANDING AREA SLOPES UP FROM RIGHT TO LEFT, TRY EITHER TO DRAW THE BALL INTO IT OR AIM TO THE LEFT SIDE. CONVERSELY, PLAY A FADE OR AIM TO THE RIGHT SIDE OF THE FAIRWAY IN A LEFT-TO-RIGHT UP-SLOPING SITUATION. IN OTHER WORDS, BE OBSERVANT AND PLAN THE BEST PERCENTAGE SHOT BEFORE YOU SWING.

Tackle Dog-Legs This Way

A BASIC RULE OF DOG-LEG STRATEGY IS TO TRY TO "BEND" THE TEE-SHOT **WITH** RATHER THAN AGAINST THE FAIRWAY ANGLE: IN OTHER WORDS, FADE AROUND A LEFT-TO-RIGHT DOG-LEG, AND DRAW ON A RIGHT-TO-LEFT CURVE.

HOWEVER, IF YOU'RE TRYING TO CUT THE CORNER BY PLAYING OVER TREES OR OTHER "ELBOW" TROUBLE THEN **REVERSING** THIS STRATEGY CAN GIVE YOU A LITTLE INSURANCE BY MOVING THE BALL AWAY FROM THE TROUBLE.

Tee Ball in Most Level Area

MY FIRST CONCERN IN LOOKING FOR A SPOT TO TEE THE BALL IS FINDING A TRULY LEVEL AREA.

GOLF'S DIFFICULT ENOUGH, WITHOUT PLAYING TEE SHOTS FROM ANGLED LIES. PAYING ATTENTION TO SEEMINGLY SMALL DETAILS LIKE THIS COULD IMPROVE YOUR SCORE WITHOUT HITTING ONE MORE PRACTICE SHOT.

Position Ball for Solid Strike

HOW HIGH SHOULD YOU TEE THE BALL INTO A HEADWIND?

MY ADVICE IS HIGH ENOUGH TO BE SURE OF GETTING ALL OF THE **CLUBFACE** ON IT.

REMEMBER, THE PRIME REQUIREMENT HERE IS A TRULY **SOLID** HIT, MUCH MORE THAN A LOW FLIGHT.

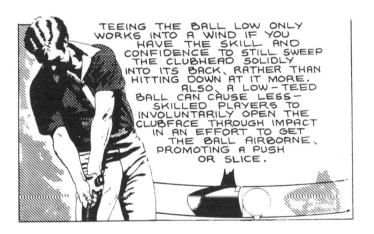

TEEING THE BALL LOW ONLY WORKS INTO A WIND IF YOU HAVE THE SKILL AND CONFIDENCE TO STILL SWEEP THE CLUBHEAD SOLIDLY INTO ITS BACK, RATHER THAN HITTING DOWN AT IT MORE. ALSO, A LOW-TEED BALL CAN CAUSE LESS-SKILLED PLAYERS TO INVOLUNTARILY OPEN THE CLUBFACE THROUGH IMPACT IN AN EFFORT TO GET THE BALL AIRBORNE, PROMOTING A PUSH OR SLICE.

Peg Ball on All Tee Shots

TEE THE BALL ON A PEG EVEN WHEN YOU'RE PLAYING IRON SHOTS TO PAR-THREE HOLES.

I USUALLY SET THE BALL ABOUT ¼ INCH ABOVE THE GROUND FOR A SHORT IRON SHOT, AND ABOUT ½ INCH UP FOR A LONG IRON.

NO. 4
56 YDS.
AR 3

TEEING THE BALL NOT ONLY INCREASES YOUR CHANCE OF STRIKING IT SOLIDLY, BUT ALSO MINIMIZES THE RISK OF HITTING A "FLIER" AS THE RESULT OF GRASS INTERVENING BETWEEN THE BALL AND CLUB-FACE. ALWAYS TAKE ADVANTAGE OF SUCH "PERCENTAGES."

Don't "Reload" Too Hastily

VERY OFTEN, WHEN A GOLFER DRIVES OUT-OF-BOUNDS, HE WILL RE-LOAD AND HIT AGAIN BEFORE THE REST OF THE GROUP HAS TEED OFF.

THAT'S VERY POOR STRATEGY AS WELL AS LOUSY ETIQUETTE.

HASTE AND IRRITATION IN THIS SITUATION CAN EASILY CAUSE YOU TO TURN A MISCUE INTO A DISASTER.

BY REPLAYING IN THE PROPER ORDER — LAST, IN THIS CASE — YOU GIVE YOURSELF TIME TO CALM DOWN A LITTLE, PLUS BREATHING SPACE TO CONSEQUENTLY PLAN THE SECOND DRIVE WITH GREATER CARE.

Always Play the Easier Shot

HOW OFTEN HAVE YOU (OR A FELLOW GOLFER) HIT INTO A WATER HAZARD FROM A 3-PAR TEE AREA, AND PROCEEDED TO HIT YOUR NEXT SHOT FROM THE SAME PLACE?

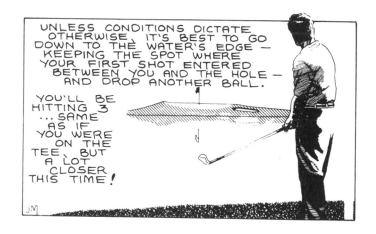

UNLESS CONDITIONS DICTATE OTHERWISE, IT'S BEST TO GO DOWN TO THE WATER'S EDGE — KEEPING THE SPOT WHERE YOUR FIRST SHOT ENTERED BETWEEN YOU AND THE HOLE — AND DROP ANOTHER BALL.

YOU'LL BE HITTING 3 ...SAME AS IF YOU WERE ON THE TEE, BUT A LOT CLOSER THIS TIME!

Never Drive without a Plan

NEVER BEGIN A HOLE WITHOUT FIRST HAVING AT LEAST A GENERAL IDEA OF YOUR PLAYING STRATEGY. TRY ON THE TEE TO DETERMINE THE BEST AND SAFEST ROUTE TO THE CUP RELATIVE TO THE DESIGN OF THE HOLE, ITS HAZARDS, THE PIN POSITION, AND GROUND AND WEATHER CONDITIONS.

ABOVE ALL, BE REALISTIC ABOUT YOUR OWN CAPABILITIES. DON'T BITE OFF MORE THAN YOU CAN GENUINELY HOPE TO CHEW. AND IF YOU DO ENCOUNTER TROUBLE, USE YOUR INTELLIGENCE AHEAD OF YOUR MUSCLES IN RECOVERING FROM IT.

REMEMBER, MIRACLES DON'T HAPPEN IN GOLF ANY MORE OFTEN THAN THEY DO IN LIFE.

28

Into the Green

Know How Far You Hit Each Club

Figure Distances Carefully

Stop Under-Clubbing Yourself!

STATISTICS PROVE THAT TOUR PROS GENERALLY DRIVE THE BALL SHORTER THAN MANY FANS IMAGINE THEY DO — ONLY ABOUT 250 YARDS ON AVERAGE.

WATCHING PRO-AM PARTNERS PROVES TO ME THAT MOST HANDICAP GOLFERS ALSO DRIVE THE BALL SHORTER THAN THEY THINK THEY DO — WHICH IS ONE REASON THEY'RE SO CONSISTENTLY SHORT ON SECOND SHOTS. SO BE REALISTIC — USE ENOUGH CLUB.

5-IRON

NOPE... THIS 6 WILL DO IT...

Consider Putts When Planning Approaches

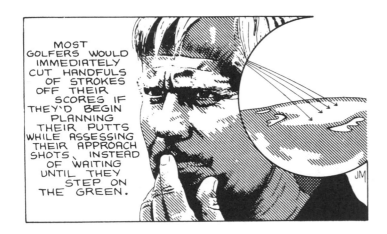

MOST GOLFERS WOULD IMMEDIATELY CUT HANDFULS OF STROKES OFF THEIR SCORES IF THEY'D BEGIN PLANNING THEIR PUTTS WHILE ASSESSING THEIR APPROACH SHOTS, INSTEAD OF WAITING UNTIL THEY STEP ON THE GREEN.

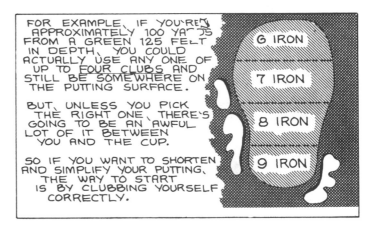

FOR EXAMPLE, IF YOU'RE APPROXIMATELY 100 YARDS FROM A GREEN 125 FEET IN DEPTH, YOU COULD ACTUALLY USE ANY ONE OF UP TO FOUR CLUBS AND STILL BE SOMEWHERE ON THE PUTTING SURFACE.

BUT, UNLESS YOU PICK THE RIGHT ONE, THERE'S GOING TO BE AN AWFUL LOT OF IT BETWEEN YOU AND THE CUP.

SO IF YOU WANT TO SHORTEN AND SIMPLIFY YOUR PUTTING, THE WAY TO START IS BY CLUBBING YOURSELF CORRECTLY.

6 IRON

7 IRON

8 IRON

9 IRON

Give Yourself Margin for Error

AT BEST, I HIT ONLY FOUR OR FIVE SHOTS A ROUND EXACTLY AS I'VE PLANNED THEM MENTALLY. FOR THAT REASON, I TRY TO LEAVE MYSELF SOME MARGIN FOR ERROR ON ALL APPROACHES.

WITH THE PIN ON THE RIGHT, FOR EXAMPLE, I'LL AIM FOR THE GREEN CENTER AND ATTEMPT TO FADE THE BALL TO THE HOLE. WITH THE PIN ON THE LEFT, I REVERSE THE PROCEDURE BY TRYING TO DRAW THE BALL IN. THIS WAY, I'LL GENERALLY BE PUTTING EVEN IF I DON'T FADE OR DRAW AS MUCH AS PLANNED.

Know When Not to Attack

KNOWING WHERE **NOT** TO ATTACK IN GOLF IS AS CRITICAL AS KNOWING WHEN TO PLAY BOLDLY.

NO. 11 AT AUGUSTA NATIONAL IS A GOOD EXAMPLE.

THERE IS A STRONG RISK HERE OF A LONG SECOND EITHER FALLING SHORT OR KICKING AND ROLLING INTO THE WATER IMMEDIATELY FRONTING THE GREEN.

THUS I ALMOST ALWAYS PLAY THE HOLE AS A "PAR 4½," APPROACHING TO THE **RIGHT SIDE** OF THE GREEN AND RELYING ON A CHIP OR LONG PUTT TO GET MY PAR.

Keep an Eye on Upcoming Holes

YOU CAN SAVE A LOT OF SHOTS ON DOG-LEG HOLES BY KNOWING THE PIN POSITION IN ADVANCE.

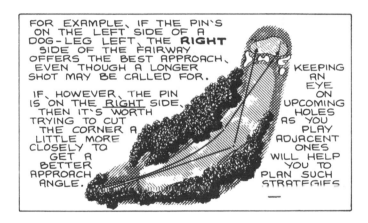

FOR EXAMPLE, IF THE PIN'S ON THE LEFT SIDE OF A DOG-LEG LEFT, THE **RIGHT** SIDE OF THE FAIRWAY OFFERS THE BEST APPROACH, EVEN THOUGH A LONGER SHOT MAY BE CALLED FOR.

IF, HOWEVER, THE PIN IS ON THE RIGHT SIDE, THEN IT'S WORTH TRYING TO CUT THE CORNER A LITTLE MORE CLOSELY TO GET A BETTER APPROACH ANGLE.

KEEPING AN EYE ON UPCOMING HOLES AS YOU PLAY ADJACENT ONES WILL HELP YOU TO PLAN SUCH STRATEGIES.

Don't Give Yourself "Flier" Lies

PLAYERS WHO SET THE BALL UP ON GRASSY TUFTS AT EVERY OPPORTUNITY SHOW LACK OF GOLFING SOPHISTICATION AS WELL AS LACK OF CONFIDENCE.

WHAT THEY'RE DOING IS CREATING EXACTLY THE SITUATION THAT ALL FINE PLAYERS HATE AND AVOID — THE "FLIER LIE."

SO LONG AS THE BALL IS SITTING CLEANLY, THE SHORTER AND DRIER THE GRASS UNDER AND AROUND IT, THE MORE ACCURATELY IT CAN BE STRUCK AND THUS THE BETTER IT CAN BE SPUN.

SO, IF YOU WANT TO IMPROVE AS A SHOT-MAKER, RELISH THOSE TIGHT LIES AND USE THEM AS A CHALLENGE TO LEARN TO "WORK" THE BALL.

Bear This Clubbing Factor in Mind

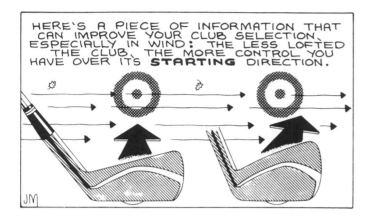

HERE'S A PIECE OF INFORMATION THAT CAN IMPROVE YOUR CLUB SELECTION, ESPECIALLY IN WIND: THE LESS LOFTED THE CLUB, THE MORE CONTROL YOU HAVE OVER ITS **STARTING** DIRECTION.

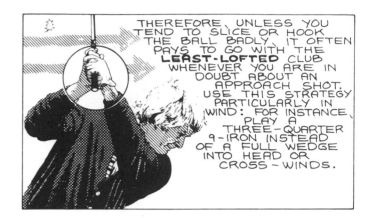

THEREFORE, UNLESS YOU TEND TO SLICE OR HOOK THE BALL BADLY, IT OFTEN PAYS TO GO WITH THE **LEAST-LOFTED** CLUB WHENEVER YOU ARE IN DOUBT ABOUT AN APPROACH SHOT. USE THIS STRATEGY PARTICULARLY IN WIND: FOR INSTANCE, PLAY A THREE-QUARTER 9-IRON INSTEAD OF A FULL WEDGE INTO HEAD OR CROSS-WINDS.

Restrict Long-Irons to Good Lies

IF YOU HAVE DIFFICULTY WITH THE LONG IRONS — AND MOST HIGH HANDICAPPERS DO — THEN MAKE IT A RULE NEVER TO PLAY THEM FROM A POOR OR "TIGHT" LIE. USE A FAIRWAY WOOD INSTEAD.

3-IRON, PLEASE.... NO, LET'S GO WITH THE 5-WOOD!

GIVEN A GOOD LIE, THINK "**SWEEP**" NOT "PUNCH" IN PLAYING A LONG-IRON. TRY TO SWING AS YOU DO WITH THE DRIVER, BRUSHING THE BALL CLEANLY FROM THE SURFACE OF THE GRASS RATHER THAN HITTING SHARPLY DOWN INTO IT. PRACTICE WITH BALLS TEED TO GAIN CONFIDENCE.

Keep Asking Yourself This Question

WHEN INDECISIVE ABOUT SACRIFICING DISTANCE FOR ACCURACY, ASK YOURSELF THIS: "IS THE POSSIBLE REWARD FOR ADDED DISTANCE WORTH THE RISK I MUST TAKE TO GET IT?"

REMEMBER, PLAYING A WEDGE TO THE GREEN WOULD BE WONDER-FUL, BUT A 7-IRON APPROACH FROM SHORT GRASS IS BETTER THAN CHIPPING OUT OF THE FOREST OR BLASTING A FEW YARDS OUT OF A FAIRWAY BUNKER.

PUT COMMON SENSE AHEAD OF PRIDE AND PLAY FOR <u>POSITION</u>.

29

In the Wind and Wet

Be Patient, Keep Control

EVER NOTICED THAT THE BEST PLAYERS ALMOST ALWAYS COME TO THE TOP WHEN THE WIND BLOWS HARD?

ONE REASON IS THEIR TECHNICAL SHOT-MAKING ABILITY, BUT THERE'S MORE TO IT THAN THAT.

THE INTELLIGENT GOLFER RECOGNIZES WIND AS ONE OF THE GAME'S TOUGHEST CHALLENGES, WHICH CAUSES HIM TO BE **MORE PATIENT** AND EXERCISE EVEN **GREATER SELF-CONTROL** THAN NORMAL.

THE LESS SAVVY PLAYER LETS WIND MAKE HIM ANGRY AND FEARFUL, WHICH EMOTIONS ARE RAPIDLY REFLECTED IN HIS SOARING SCORES.

Check the Tree-Tops

DO YOU LIKE TO TEST WIND STRENGTH AND DIRECTION BY TOSSING GRASS IN THE AIR?

THAT DEFINITELY CAN HELP IN PROVIDING INFORMATION, BUT SOMETIMES IT DOESN'T PROVIDE ENOUGH FOR MY LIKING.

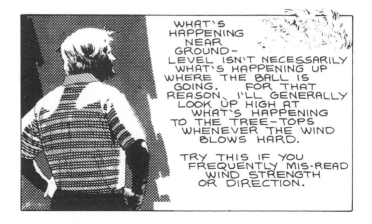

WHAT'S HAPPENING NEAR GROUND-LEVEL ISN'T NECESSARILY WHAT'S HAPPENING UP WHERE THE BALL IS GOING. FOR THAT REASON, I'LL GENERALLY LOOK UP HIGH AT WHAT'S HAPPENING TO THE TREE-TOPS WHENEVER THE WIND BLOWS HARD.

TRY THIS IF YOU FREQUENTLY MIS-READ WIND STRENGTH OR DIRECTION.

Resist Urge to Hurry Shots

ONE OF THE GREATEST DANGERS YOU FACE WHEN PLAYING IN BAD WEATHER IS HURRYING — A STRONG WIND OR WATER RUNNING DOWN YOUR NECK CREATES AN INVOLUNTARY URGE TO "GET IT OVER WITH."

I TRY TO COUNTERACT THIS BY MAKING A CONSCIOUS EFFORT TO BE VERY DELIBERATE ABOUT MY SET-UP, THEN TO SWING AS **SMOOTHLY** AND **FULLY** AS POSSIBLE.

"COMPLETE THE BACKSWING" IS ONE OF MY KEY THOUGHTS WHENEVER THE CONDITIONS ARE AGAINST ME.

Don't Tee Lower into the Wind

DON'T MAKE THE MISTAKE OF TEEING THE BALL LOWER WHEN HITTING INTO A HEADWIND OR SIDEWIND.

THE LOWER YOU TEE THE BALL, THE MORE LIKELY YOU ARE TO HIT DOWN INTO IT, AND THE MORE YOU HIT DOWN INTO IT THE HIGHER IT WILL FLY AND THE MORE IT WILL BE BLOWN OFF LINE.

INSTEAD, TEE THE BALL YOUR NORMAL HEIGHT, THEN MAKE YOUR BEST EFFORT TO **SWEEP** THE DRIVER THROUGH TRAVELING AT GROUND LEVEL.

MOVING THE BALL A LITTLE FARTHER FORWARD IN YOUR STANCE MAY PROMOTE A MORE SWEEPING HIT, BUT DON'T OVERDO IT.

Swing Easier with More Club

BIG PROBLEM WHEN PLAYING INTO A STRONG HEADWIND IS THE RISK OF "BALLOONING" SHOTS. FREQUENTLY THE BALL'S TENDENCY TO SOAR IS INCREASED BY THE EXTRA BACKSPIN IMPARTED BY YOUR NATURAL TENDENCY TO HIT IT HARDER.

I GENERALLY ATTEMPT TO COUNTER BOTH TENDENCIES BY HITTING EASIER RATHER THAN HARDER. IF THE SHOT NORMALLY WOULD CALL FOR SAY A 6-IRON I'LL TAKE A 4-IRON AND SWING SOFTLY. THIS IMPARTS LESS BACKSPIN, WHICH KEEPS THE BALL LOWER AND THUS MAKES IT BORE BETTER THROUGH THE WIND.

Consider Wind's Stopping Effect

REMEMBER THAT, INTO A HEADWIND, LESS LOFT GENERALLY MEANS GREATER CONTROL. SO, IF THE SHOT NORMALLY WOULD CALL FOR A WEDGE, CONSIDER USING THE NINE-IRON INSTEAD.

IF UNDER STILL CONDITIONS YOU'D HIT A THREE-QUARTER WEDGE, MAKE A HALF-SWING WITH THE NINE-IRON. IF THE WIND IS EXTREMELY STRONG, CONSIDER EVEN GOING TO THE EIGHT-IRON. REMEMBER THAT, THE STRONGER THE WIND, THE GREATER ITS STOPPING EFFECT ON THE BALL, EVEN THOUGH YOU HIT IT LOW.

Swing More Compact for Better Balance

BALANCE IS A CRITICAL FACTOR ON ALL GOLF SHOTS. BUT SOMETIMES — SUCH AS IN WINDY OR WET WEATHER — IT'S VERY DIFFICULT TO ACHIEVE USING YOUR NORMAL SWING. IN THOSE INSTANCES, CONSIDER COMPACTING YOUR SWING.

MY WAY IS GENERALLY TO USE LESS BODY MOTION AND MORE HAND ACTION. THE CHIEF ADJUSTMENT IS TO RELAX MY WRISTS MORE GOING BACK, WHICH ALLOWS THEM TO COCK EARLIER AND MORE FULLY. THIS IN TURN CREATES A MATCHING LIVELINESS OF WRIST ACTION THROUGH IMPACT, CREATING GOOD CLUBHEAD SPEED WITHOUT A GREAT DEAL OF BODY MOVEMENT.

Adjust Like This for Wider Stance

A WIDER STANCE WILL GIVE YOU BETTER ANCHORAGE AND BALANCE WHEN PLAYING IN A STRONG WIND, BUT IT ALSO CREATES A RESTRICTION THAT NEEDS TO BE COMPENSATED FOR.

WIDENING THE STANCE SHORTENS THE BACKSWING BY REDUCING BODY TURN, WHICH GENERALLY REDUCES DISTANCE. THE ANSWER IS TO TAKE AT LEAST ONE MORE CLUB THAN NORMAL — WHICH ALSO HAS THE ADDITIONAL BENEFIT OF FLYING THE BALL LOWER.

Try These Approaches Downwind

THERE ARE TWO WAYS TO PLAY A DOWNWIND APPROACH. THE SAFEST AND EASIEST WAY, WHEN THERE ARE NO FRONTAL HAZARDS, IS TO LAND THE BALL SHORT AND LET IT ROLL ONTO THE GREEN.

WITH TROUBLE IN FRONT OF THE GREEN, A HIGH, SOFT-LANDING SHOT IS NECESSARY. YOU CAN INCREASE STOPPING POWER BY FADING THE BALL IN WHEN THE GREEN SLOPES TO THE LEFT, AND DRAWING IT WHEN THE GREEN SLOPES TO THE RIGHT.

Accept the Extra Challenge

THERE ARE THREE WAYS TO APPROACH WET WEATHER GOLF.

ONE IS TO STAY HOME UNTIL CONDITIONS DRY UP, AND THE SECOND IS TO PLAY BUT WITH A NEGATIVE ATTITUDE AND A LOT OF GRIPING — AND, INVARIABLY, POOR SCORES.

THE THIRD WAY, WHICH I FAVOR, IS TO ACCEPT THE RAIN AS JUST ANOTHER OF THE GAME'S MANY CHALLENGES AND ENJOY MEETING IT AS BEST YOU CAN. HOWEVER RECOGNIZING THAT YOU AREN'T LIKELY TO SHOOT YOUR RECORD SCORE IS CRITICAL TO PLAYING INTELLIGENT SHOTS UNDER SUCH CONDITIONS.

Ensure a Solid Footing

WATCH THE P G A TOUR AND YOU'LL NOTICE HOW METICULOUS ALL THE PLAYERS ARE ABOUT CLEANING OFF THEIR GOLF SHOE SPIKES, ESPECIALLY IN WET OR SLOPPY CONDITIONS.

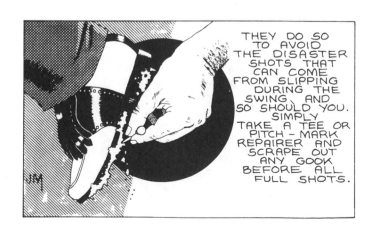

THEY DO SO TO AVOID THE DISASTER SHOTS THAT CAN COME FROM SLIPPING DURING THE SWING, AND SO SHOULD YOU. SIMPLY TAKE A TEE OR PITCH - MARK REPAIRER AND SCRAPE OUT ANY GOOK BEFORE ALL FULL SHOTS.

Drive for Maximum Carry

HOW DO YOU GET MAXIMUM DISTANCE WHEN HITTING TO A SOFT FAIRWAY?

SOME GOLFERS TRY TO GAIN EXTRA RUN BY PLAYING A LOW HOOKING SHOT, AND IF THAT'S AN EASY SHOT FOR YOU TO MAKE THEN THAT'S THE ONE TO PLAY.

MY PREFERENCE IS TO SEEK MAXIMUM **CARRY** IN THAT FLIGHT IS MORE PREDICTABLE AND CONTROLLABLE THAN RUN.

TO ACHIEVE THAT, I CONCENTRATE ON MEETING THE BALL SQUARELY AT THE BOTTOM OF THE SWING ARC AND STAYING WELL BEHIND IT FOR AS LONG AS POSSIBLE INTO THE FOLLOW-THROUGH.

Don't Be Too Fancy

NEVER TRY TO BE TOO FANCY WITH THE LONGER CLUBS OFF WET TURF OR WHEN PLAYING IN RAIN.

WHEN WATER COMES BETWEEN THE CLUBFACE AND THE BALL IT DIMINISHES SIDESPIN, AS WELL AS HEIGHT.

THUS AN ATTEMPTED FADE WILL OFTEN FLY PRETTY MUCH STRAIGHT LEFT IN WET CONDITIONS, AND AN ATTEMPTED DRAW STRAIGHT RIGHT. BEST POLICY IS A STRAIGHT SHOT, WITH AS AMPLY LOFTED A CLUB AS POSSIBLE RELATIVE TO THE DISTANCE TO BE COVERED.

30

Getting Out of
Trouble

Focus on Recovery, Not Mistake

TASK NO. 1, WHENEVER YOU STRAY FROM THE SHORT GRASS, IS: **STAY COOL**.

THE MORE YOU LET ANGER OR FEAR INFLUENCE YOUR ACTIONS, THE GREATER YOUR CHANCE OF COMPOUNDING THE ERROR INTO A DISASTER.

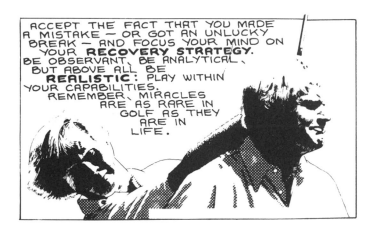

ACCEPT THE FACT THAT YOU MADE A MISTAKE — OR GOT AN UNLUCKY BREAK — AND FOCUS YOUR MIND ON YOUR **RECOVERY STRATEGY**. BE OBSERVANT, BE ANALYTICAL, BUT ABOVE ALL BE **REALISTIC**: PLAY WITHIN YOUR CAPABILITIES. REMEMBER, MIRACLES ARE AS RARE IN GOLF AS THEY ARE IN LIFE.

Take Less Club for "Flier" Lie

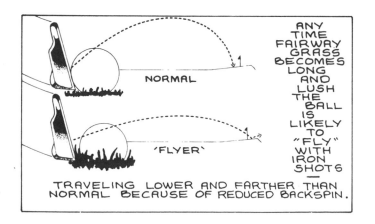

NORMAL

'FLYER'

TRAVELING LOWER AND FARTHER THAN NORMAL BECAUSE OF REDUCED BACKSPIN.

ANY TIME FAIRWAY GRASS BECOMES LONG AND LUSH THE BALL IS LIKELY TO "FLY" WITH IRON SHOTS —

I COUNTERACT THAT BY GOING DOWN A CLUB — SAY FROM A SIX- TO A SEVEN-IRON — WHICH AUTOMATICALLY PRODUCES LESS DISTANCE.

THEN, TO GAIN MAXIMUM HEIGHT, I MOVE THE BALL A LITTLE FORWARD AT ADDRESS AND MAKE SURE I **RELEASE** FULLY WITH THE WRISTS GOING THROUGH.

Know This Key Rule in Rough

BY WRAPPING AROUND THE HOSEL OF THE CLUB, LONG GRASS OR OTHER ROUGH GENERALLY HAS THE EFFECT OF TWISTING THE CLUBFACE CLOSED THROUGH IMPACT.

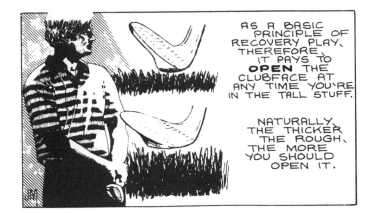

AS A BASIC PRINCIPLE OF RECOVERY PLAY, THEREFORE, IT PAYS TO **OPEN** THE CLUBFACE AT ANY TIME YOU'RE IN THE TALL STUFF.

NATURALLY, THE THICKER THE ROUGH, THE MORE YOU SHOULD OPEN IT.

Fit Shot to Grass Direction

IN ROUGH, THE DIRECTION OF GRASS GROWTH WILL OFTEN AFFECT THE BEHAVIOR OF THE BALL. FOR INSTANCE, WHEN THE GRASS LIES **AGAINST** THE SHOT IT WILL TEND TO CHECK AND CLOSE THE CLUBFACE MORE THAN USUAL, SO CLUB YOURSELF AND AIM ACCORDINGLY.

THERE'S LESS RESISTANCE WHEN THE GRASS LIES **TOWARDS** THE TARGET, BUT THE BALL WILL OFTEN TEND TO "FLY" BECAUSE OF REDUCED BACKSPIN. THEREFORE, FROM THIS TYPE OF LIE IT GENERALLY PAYS TO TAKE LESS CLUB THAN NORMAL, AND TO ALLOW FOR EXTRA RUN.

Master the High-Flier . . .

I PLAY BASICALLY TWO TYPES OF SHOT FROM ROUGH.

HERE'S MY TECHNIQUE WHEN NEEDING A HIGH-FLYING, SOFT-LANDING SHOT WITH AS MUCH SPIN AS I CAN GENERATE DESPITE GRASS GETTING BETWEEN THE CLUBFACE AND BALL AT IMPACT.

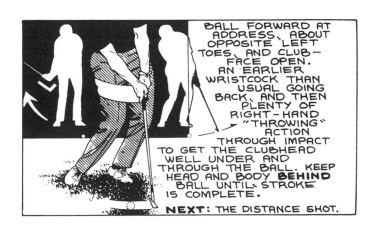

BALL FORWARD AT ADDRESS, ABOUT OPPOSITE LEFT TOES, AND CLUBFACE OPEN. AN EARLIER WRISTCOCK THAN USUAL GOING BACK, AND THEN PLENTY OF RIGHT-HAND "THROWING" ACTION THROUGH IMPACT TO GET THE CLUBHEAD WELL UNDER AND THROUGH THE BALL. KEEP HEAD AND BODY **BEHIND** BALL UNTIL STROKE IS COMPLETE.

NEXT: THE DISTANCE SHOT.

. . . and the Low Runner

SO LONG AS YOU DON'T HAVE TO FLY THE BALL HIGH OR LAND IT SOFTLY, THERE'S A WAY TO GET DISTANCE FROM HEAVY, GRASSY LIES.

TAKE A CLUB OR TWO LESS THAN YOU'D NORMALLY PLAY, MOVE THE BALL WELL BACK IN YOUR STANCE, THEN HIT STEEPLY DOWN ONTO IT WITH A HARD, PUNCHING DELIVERY. IT'S A FAIRLY UNCONTROLLED AND CERTAINLY AN INELEGANT SHOT, BUT PLAYED CORRECTLY IT WILL SQUIRT THE BALL OUT LOW AND WITH LOTS OF RUN.

Aim Off for Angled Lies

WHEN THE BALL IS BELOW YOUR FEET YOU'LL TEND TO SWING MORE UPRIGHT, WHICH MAY PRODUCE A FADE OR SLICE. WHEN THE BALL IS ABOVE YOUR FEET YOU'LL NORMALLY SWING FLATTER, WHICH USUALLY CREATES A DRAW OR HOOK.

EASIEST WAY TO COUNTERACT THIS IS SIMPLY TO AIM OFF AT ADDRESS TO ALLOW FOR THE CURVE — TO THE LEFT WHEN THE BALL IS BELOW YOUR FEET, AND TO THE RIGHT WHEN IT'S ABOVE. REMEMBER, HOWEVER, THAT THE MORE ANGLED THE LIE THE MORE SUCH SHOTS WILL CURVE, SO ALLOW ACCORDINGLY.

Bear Down When "Divotted"

DON'T GIVE UP WHEN YOUR BALL LANDS IN A DIVOT HOLE.

THERE ARE TWO WAYS TO BEAT THIS UNLUCKY BREAK. FIRST, IF YOU CAN RUN THE BALL ONTO THE GREEN, PLAY A PUNCH SHOT — BALL BACK, HANDS AHEAD AT ADDRESS AND IMPACT, THREE-QUARTER SWING, FIRM HIT.

IF YOU MUST FLY THE BALL TO THE TARGET, MOVE THE BALL FORWARD, OPEN THE CLUBFACE, SWING FULLY, AND HIT HARD WITH THE RIGHT HAND WITHOUT ALLOWING IT TO ROLL OVER THE LEFT UNTIL WELL AFTER IMPACT. ALLOW FOR A FADE — AND, IN BOTH CASES, KEEP YOUR HEAD STILL.

Use Woods to "Dig" for Distance

GETTING DISTANCE FROM A DIVOT MARK, OR OTHER SHALLOW DEPRESSION, IS MUCH EASIER WITH THE FAIRWAY WOODS THAN THE LONG IRONS FOR MOST PLAYERS.

TAKE THE WOOD WITH THE MOST ROUNDED SOLE, OPEN THE CLUBFACE A LITTLE AT ADDRESS, PLAY THE BALL A LITTLE FARTHER BACK THAN NORMAL, THEN SWING THE CLUBHEAD FIRMLY DOWN INTO IT.

AND ALLOW FOR A FADE.

Try This from Deep Depressions

GETTING THE BALL OUT OF A DITCH, OR ANY OTHER PLACE WHERE IT'S WELL BELOW YOUR FEET, IS A VERY TOUGH SHOT.

OFTEN IT'S BEST TO TAKE A DROP AND THE UNPLAYABLE - LIE PENALTY.

IF YOU WANT TO GAMBLE, GET AS LOW TO THE SHOT AS YOU CAN BY BENDING YOUR KNEES, PICK THE CLUB UP SHARPLY WITH A QUICK WRIST BREAK, AND PUNCH STRAIGHT DOWN ON THE BALL.

KEEP YOUR HEAD STILL AND DON'T WORRY ABOUT FOLLOWING - THROUGH.

Let Club Loft Lift ball from Hard-Pan

THERE'S ONE ABSOLUTE RULE WHENEVER YOU ARE OBLIGED TO HIT FROM ANY FORM OF HARDPAN.

THAT IS TO ALLOW THE **LOFT OF THE CLUB** TO LIFT THE BALL, RATHER THAN TRYING TO DO IT WITH YOUR SWING.

THE MORE CLEANLY YOU CAN "PINCH" THE BALL OFF THE HARD STUFF, THE MORE EFFECTIVE THE SHOT WILL BE. I MAKE ONLY ONE SWING MODIFICATION TO ACHIEVE THIS, WHICH IS TO CONSCIOUSLY KEEP MY HANDS WELL AHEAD OF THE CLUBFACE THROUGH IMPACT BY SWINGING MORE FIRM-WRISTEDLY THAN NORMAL. PRACTICE THE TECHNIQUE AWHILE, PARTICULARLY IF YOU'VE BEEN A "SCOOPER."

Use Sand-Shot Technique from Water

WHAT SHOULD YOU DO WHEN THE BALL IS IN WATER BUT STILL VISIBLE AND REACHABLE?

IF IT'S TOTALLY SUBMERGED, MY ADVICE IS DROP CLEAR AND TAKE YOUR PENALTY, BECAUSE THE CHANCES OF A DECENT RECOVERY ARE DEFINITELY AGAINST YOU.

HOWEVER, IF PART OF THE BALL PROTRUDES ABOVE WATER — AND YOU DON'T MIND GETTING WET — THEN YOU MIGHT WANT TO HAVE A GO AT IT. PLAY THE SHOT LIKE A BURIED SAND LIE, SLICING THE BLADE THROUGH THE WATER AND UNDER THE BALL AT AN OBLIQUE ANGLE. USE A 9-IRON, WHICH WON'T BOUNCE OFF THE WATER AS MUCH AS A WEDGE.

AND GOOD LUCK!

Release *Fully* to Clear Tree-Tops

HITTING OVER TREES IS LESS OF A PROBLEM THAN MOST AMATEURS BELIEVE IT TO BE, GIVEN THE MINOR SWING MODIFICATIONS THAT PRODUCE HIGHER-FLYING SHOTS.

OPEN THE CLUBFACE SLIGHTLY AND ALLOW FOR A FADE. COMING DOWN, KEEP YOUR HEAD WELL BEHIND THE BALL AND BE SURE TO GET WELL UNDER IT BY RELEASING YOUR WRISTS A LITTLE EARLIER THAN USUAL.

FOR EVEN GREATER HEIGHT, MOVE THE BALL FARTHER FORWARD IN YOUR STANCE.

Concentrate on Swing, Not Lie

THE TRICK TO MAKING GOOD CONTACT WHEN THE ACTION IS RESTRICTED, AS HERE, IS TO CONCENTRATE ON THE **EXECUTION OF THE SWING**, RATHER THAN ON THE LIE OF THE BALL.

TAKE YOUR TIME AND MAKE ENOUGH PRACTICE SWINGS TO FULLY "MEASURE" HOW FAR BACK YOU CAN ALLOW THE CLUB TO MOVE. THEN, WHEN YOU SET UP FOR REAL, FOCUS ON MAKING THE SWING YOU'VE REHEARSED, RATHER THAN ON HITTING AT THE BALL, AND DON'T RUSH THE ACTION — TRY TO BE SMOOTH BOTH BACK AND THROUGH.

Don't Risk a Penalty Here

IT'S EASY TO INCUR A PENALTY BY CAUSING THE BALL TO MOVE WHEN IT'S SITTING ON LOOSE MATERIALS, LIKE LEAVES OR PINE NEEDLES.

TO MINIMIZE THAT RISK I AVOID GROUNDING THE CLUB AT ADDRESS.

BECAUSE THE BALL CAN'T BE "GRIPPED" AS CLEANLY ON THE CLUBFACE, IT WILL USUALLY FLY LOWER AND RUN FARTHER FROM SUCH A LIE.

ALLOW FOR THAT IN ASSESSING THE SHOT.

"Explode" Ball from "Straw" Lie

LOTS OF PINE NEEDLES WHERE YOU PLAY?

HERE'S A WAY TO PITCH THE BALL OUT OF A "STRAW" LIE THAT IS PARTICULARLY USEFUL WHEN YOU MUST GET IT UP FAST.

PLAY A BUNKER-TYPE **EXPLOSION** SHOT. USING A SAND- OR PITCHING-WEDGE, PICK THE CLUB UP QUICKLY WITH AN OPEN FACE, AND HIT DOWN AND THROUGH ABOUT AN INCH BEHIND THE BALL.

SWING A LITTLE HARDER THAN YOU WOULD FOR THE SAME DISTANCE FROM GRASS.

Meet Ball before Sand

A FUNDAMENTAL OF ACHIEVING DISTANCE FROM BUNKERS IS MEETING THE BALL BEFORE THE CLUBHEAD CATCHES THE SAND.

MOVING THE HANDS FORWARD AND/OR THE BALL BACK AT ADDRESS FACILITATES THIS CLEAN "PICKING" ACTION.

HOWEVER, BOTH THESE SET-UP ADJUSTMENTS ALSO HAVE THE EFFECT OF REDUCING EFFECTIVE CLUBFACE LOFT. SO CONSIDER TAKING A MORE LOFTED CLUB THAN YOU NORMALLY WOULD ANY TIME YOU HAVE A HIGH LIP AHEAD OF YOU.

Select Club with Sufficient Loft

YOU WON'T ALWAYS REACH THE GREEN FROM A FAIRWAY BUNKER, BUT YOU CAN OFTEN GET CLOSE ENOUGH TO IT TO SALVAGE PAR IF YOU HAVE DEVELOPED A BASIC "ESCAPE" SHOT.

ABSOLUTE **MUST** IS TO CHOOSE A CLUB THAT WILL ENABLE YOU TO EASILY CLEAR THE FRONT LIP. AFTER THAT, CHOKE DOWN ON THE CLUB A LITTLE (TO MAKE UP FOR YOUR FEET HAVING WRIGGLED DOWN INTO THE SAND), LOOK AND AIM AT THE TOP OF THE BALL, AND SWING **FREELY**.

ATTEMPT THIS SHOT ONLY FROM A GOOD LIE.

Consider the "Long Explosion"...

DON'T GIVE UP ON REACHING THE GREEN IF YOU'RE FACED WITH A POOR LIE IN A FAIRWAY BUNKER WITHIN NORMAL SHORT-IRON RANGE OF THE GREEN. TRY A LONG EXPLOSION SHOT.

TAKE TWO CLUBS MORE THAN THE DISTANCE WOULD NORMALLY REQUIRE. PLANT YOURSELF FIRMLY, OPEN THE CLUBFACE WIDE, AIM LEFT TO ALLOW FOR THE INEVITABLE FADE, MAKE A FULL SWING, AND HIT HARD INTO THE SAND AS CLOSE TO THE BALL AS YOU CAN.

THIS IS A VALUABLE RECOVERY SHOT TECHNIQUE, BUT IT NEEDS PRACTICE TO BE PLAYED CONFIDENTLY.

...and the "Cut Blast"

IF CIRCUMSTANCES DEMAND THAT YOU MUST GO FOR DISTANCE FROM A "FLUFFY" BUNKER LIE, TRY HITTING A **CUT BLAST SHOT** WITH A ROUND-SOLED FOUR- OR FIVE-WOOD.

THE HEAVY, ROUNDED SOLE OF THE WOOD GIVES YOU A BETTER CHANCE OF BLASTING THROUGH INTERVENING SAND THAN A LIGHT-HEADED, STRAIGHT-SOLED MEDIUM- OR LONG-IRON. CUTTING ACROSS THE SHOT A LITTLE FROM OUT TO IN REDUCES THE AMOUNT OF SAND YOU TAKE BY STEEPENING YOUR SWING ARC.

Play Normal Bunker Shot from Sand-spill

A BALL LAYING ON SAND SPILL NEAR THE EDGE OF A BUNKER IS EASIER TO PLAY THAN IT LOOKS.

NORMALLY FROM SAND THE DEPTH OF CUT IS CRITICAL TO PROVIDING THE CLUBHEAD BOUNCE NECESSARY TO GET BENEATH THE BALL. BUT IN THIS SITUATION THE GROUND BELOW THE LIGHT SAND LAYER IS A NICE INSURANCE AGAINST DIGGING TOO DEEPLY.

SO GO AHEAD AND USE YOUR SAND-WEDGE AND JUST PLAY THE SHOT AS YOU WOULD FROM A NORMAL GREENSIDE BUNKER LIE, HITTING A COUPLE OF INCHES BEHIND THE BALL AND MAKING SURE TO FOLLOW-THROUGH.

Try the "Bounce-and-Run"

THERE ARE MANY SITUATIONS IN GOLF THAT PROHIBIT A HIGH PITCH:
1) A VERY TIGHT LIE,
2) A MOUND GUARDING A TIGHT PIN PLACEMENT,
3) OVERHANGING LIMBS, ETC.

SUCH CHALLENGES CALL FOR A LOW BOUNCE-AND-RUN SHOT WITH A LONG-IRON. POSITION THE BALL BACK NEAR YOUR RIGHT FOOT WITH YOUR HANDS WELL FORWARD OF IT, THEN HIT CRISPLY DOWN INTO ITS BACK WITH A SHORT, FIRM SWING.

PRACTICE THE SHOT TO GET A FEEL FOR HOW FAR THE BALL WILL RUN.

Be Firm on This Tough Pitch

IMPARTING HEAVY BACKSPIN TO A PITCH SHOT FROM ROUGH ISN'T EASY, BUT IT CAN BE DONE IF THE LIE IS NOT TOO TERRIBLE.

TRICK IS TO OPEN THE CLUBFACE AT ADDRESS, THEN PICK THE CLUB UP WITH THE WRISTS VERY ABRUPTLY AND HIT SHARPLY DOWN INTO THE BALL.

THE STEEPER THE ANGLE OF ATTACK, THE BETTER YOUR CHANCE OF GETTING BALL BEFORE GRASS.

BUT THIS IS A SHOT WHERE YOU REALLY DO HAVE TO STRIKE FIRMLY — AND LOOK AT THE BALL WHILE DOING SO.

Use Your Imagination

DEPENDING ON YOUR SKILL AND NERVE, IT'S POSSIBLE TO 'MANUFACTURE' SHOTS TO GET THE BALL OUT OF SEEMINGLY IMPOSSIBLE PLACES.

FOR EXAMPLE, A BALL THAT YOU CAN'T HIT RIGHT-HANDED CAN OFTEN BE MOVED FORWARD BY SWINGING LEFT-HANDED WITH A WELL-LOFTED CLUB TURNED UPSIDE DOWN.

THE PUTTER CAN COME IN HANDY IN THESE SITUATIONS IF NOTHING ELSE CAN WORK. AND I'VE SAVED A FEW SHOTS IN MY TIME SIMPLY BY REBOUNDING THE BALL OFF SOME AWKWARD OBSTACLE.

31

Tournament Play

Try the Walter Hagen Philosophy

MOST CLUB GOLFERS PLAY LESS WELL IN TOURNAMENTS THAN THEY DO IN REGULAR GAMES WITH PALS.

EXTRA MENTAL AND PHYSICAL TENSION CREATED BY WANTING TO EXCEL IS GENERALLY THE CHIEF CAUSE.

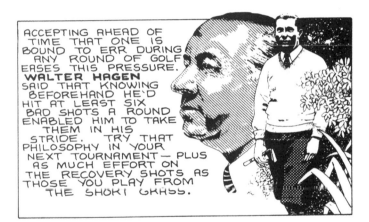

ACCEPTING AHEAD OF TIME THAT ONE IS BOUND TO ERR DURING ANY ROUND OF GOLF EASES THIS PRESSURE. **WALTER HAGEN** SAID THAT KNOWING BEFOREHAND HE'D HIT AT LEAST SIX BAD SHOTS A ROUND ENABLED HIM TO TAKE THEM IN HIS STRIDE. TRY THAT PHILOSOPHY IN YOUR NEXT TOURNAMENT — PLUS AS MUCH EFFORT ON THE RECOVERY SHOTS AS THOSE YOU PLAY FROM THE SHORT GRASS.

Put Safety First in Stroke-Play

BE REALISTIC, ESPECIALLY IN STROKE-PLAY WHERE THE RESULT DOESN'T DEPEND ON ANY ONE SHOT OR SINGLE HOLE.

BE SAFE RATHER THAN SORRY ANY TIME YOU'RE FACED WITH A TRULY RISKY SITUATION.

FOR EXAMPLE, IF YOUR BALL IS IN A TIGHT LIE JUST SHORT OF A DEEP, WIDE TRAP WITH THE PIN TUCKED JUST BEYOND IT, THE PERCENTAGES IN TRYING TO GET CLOSE ARE DEFINITELY WAY AGAINST YOU.

DON'T COMPOUND THE ERROR: PLAY TO BE **ON THE GREEN SOMEWHERE**, EVEN IF THAT MEANS BEING LONG OR SHOOTING AWAY FROM THE HOLE.

Don't Forget to Hit the Ball

BEWARE BECOMING "TENTATIVE" AS THE COMPETITIVE SCREWS TIGHTEN. MANY MORE MATCHES ARE LOST THROUGH TRYING TO STEER THE BALL THAN BY OPENING THE SHOULDERS AND SWINGING FREELY.

MAKING MYSELF CONSCIOUSLY AWARE OF THE NEED TO ACTUALLY HIT THE BALL HAS HELPED ME A LOT AT SUCH TIMES.

I'LL CERTAINLY TRY FOR THE SMOOTHEST AND FULLEST SWING, OF COURSE, BUT THE THING I'LL TRY FOR MOST IS TO MAKE THAT SWING PRODUCE A HARD AND SOLID **HIT THROUGH**, RATHER THAN A FEARFUL JAB AT, THE BALL.

"Complete the Backswing"

BECAUSE FEAR MAKES FOR HASTE, IT'S EASY TO "START DOWN BEFORE YOU'VE GONE BACK" ANY TIME YOU'RE UNDER PRESSURE OR FACING AN UNUSUALLY DIFFICULT SHOT.

"COMPLETE THE BACKSWING" IS MY FAVORITE THOUGHT AT SUCH TIMES.

CONSCIOUSLY CONCENTRATING ON SWINGING MY LEFT SHOULDER WELL UNDER MY CHIN, AND MY HANDS WELL ABOVE MY HEAD, ENSURES THAT I GO BACK BEFORE I TRY TO COME DOWN.

Win With Your Clubs Only

I HAVE NEVER KNOWINGLY USED "GAMESMAN-SHIP" AGAINST AN OPPONENT, BECAUSE I DON'T BELIEVE IT SHOULD PLAY A PART IN GOLF. SELF-RESPECT TO ME DEPENDS ON ACCOUNTING FOR MYSELF WITH MY CLUBS, NOT THROUGH SOME KIND OF PSYCHOLOGICAL WARFARE.

HOWEVER, RESPECTING YOUR OPPONENT ISN'T THE SAME THING AS FEARING HIM. SO LONG AS IT IS APPLIED ONLY INTERNALLY, I'VE ALWAYS LIKED THE OLD SENTIMENT, "A SECRET DISBELIEF IN THE ENEMY'S ABILITY IS VERY USEFUL." SO BE COURTEOUS, BUT ALSO BE CONFIDENT INSIDE THAT YOU POSSESS THE GREATER SKILLS.

Play the Course Rather Than the Man

BASICALLY YOU'LL FARE BEST BY PLAYING THE COURSE RATHER THAN THE MAN IN MATCH-PLAY, SO CONCENTRATE CHIEFLY ON YOUR OWN GAME, NOT YOUR OPPONENT'S.

TIME TO PLAY THE MAN IS WHEN, HITTING FIRST, HE ENCOUNTERS SERIOUS TROUBLE LIKE OUT-OF-BOUNDS OR AN OBVIOUSLY UNPLAYABLE LIE.

WHEN THAT HAPPENS, DON'T TAKE ANY CHANCES.

SWALLOW YOUR PRIDE AND PLAY FOR A SURE WINNING SCORE, EVEN IF IT'S A BOGEY.

Don't Fear a "Better" Golfer

IN MATCH-PLAY, TRY NOT TO LET YOURSELF GET PSYCHED OUT BEFORE YOU BEGIN BY THE PROSPECT OF PLAYING A BETTER GOLFER. FORM ON THE DAY IS ALL THAT MATTERS, AND YOU WON'T KNOW HIS UNTIL PLAY BEGINS.

HE COULD BE "OFF" JUST AS YOU COULD BE "ON."

BE SOCIABLE, BUT STRIVE TO PLAY YOUR OWN GAME AGAINST THE COURSE RATHER THAN AGAINST THE MAN. DON'T GAMBLE UNLESS AND UNTIL YOU ARE FORCED TO. MATCH-PLAY RECORDS SHOW THAT PAR GOLF GENERALLY WINS OVER THE LONG HAUL, SO PLAY FOR THAT FIRST — USING YOUR STROKES TO THAT END IF THE CONTEST INVOLVES HANDICAPS.

Never Coast in Match-Play

IN MATCH-PLAY, YOU GAIN A USEFUL PSYCHOLOGICAL ADVANTAGE BY DRAWING FIRST BLOOD, SO THE EARLIER YOU CAN GET AHEAD THE BETTER.

IN OTHER WORDS, TRY YOUR HARDEST FROM THE OPENING TEE SHOT.

ALSO, ONCE AHEAD, DON'T BE CONTENT TO SIMPLY STAY THERE — TRY TO GET EVEN FARTHER AHEAD. THE MORE HOLES YOU CAN WIN, THE FASTER TIME RUNS OUT FOR YOUR OPPONENT. SO, EVEN THOUGH YOU MAY BE FOUR UP, DON'T COAST. MAKE IT YOUR GOAL TO GO FIVE UP, THEN SIX, THEN SEVEN... IF YOU SUCCEED YOU CAN ALWAYS SYMPATHIZE WITH YOUR OPPONENT **AFTER** THE MATCH.

Gamble Only When You Must

IN MATCH-PLAY, YOU MUST SOMETIMES GAMBLE HEAVILY IN RESPONSE TO YOUR OPPONENT'S PLAY.

FOR EXAMPLE, IF YOU'RE ONE DOWN WITH ONE TO PLAY AND HE'S ON THE GREEN, THEN YOU'VE GOT TO GO FOR IT, TOO, WHATEVER THE RISK.

WHEN THE GAME IS STROKE-PLAY, HOWEVER, KEEP IN MIND THE FACT THAT THE DECISION IS MADE OVER 18 HOLES, NEVER ON ANY ONE SHOT.

SO DON'T WRECK YOUR CHANCES BY TAKING NEEDLESS GAMBLES — PLAY THE PERCENTAGE SHOT OVER THE RISKY ONE AND STAY AWAY FROM DISASTERS.

BOGEY

Keep Cool—and Keep Trying

NICKLAUS +5 +4
TH 0 -2

GOLF IS A GREAT GAME FOR PEOPLE WHO DON'T KNOW WHEN TO 'QUIT.' I'VE WON A LOT OF TOURNAMENTS SIMPLY BY 'HANGING IN THERE' WHILE OTHERS FALTERED, INCLUDING A FEW MAJOR CHAMPIONSHIPS.

THE KEY IS FIGHTING DEMORALIZATION BY PLAYING THE GAME ONE SHOT AT A TIME AND GIVING EACH YOUR MAXIMUM EFFORT. REMEMBER THAT GOLF IS NEVER OVER UNTIL THE LAST PUTTS HAVE ACTUALLY BEEN HOLED — ESPECIALLY ON TOUGH COURSES OR IN ROUGH CONDITIONS. SO KEEP YOUR COOL AND KEEP ON TRYING.

THREE

SHORT CUTS TO LOWER SCORES

Introduction

One of the most frustrating—and fascinating—things about golf is its impermanence. One day you "have it" and the next you don't. This is true of every element of the game from driving the ball to holing it out. I've gradually improved in just about every area of technique over the years, but never in all the 30 and more years I've played golf have I been able to hold top form for more than comparatively short periods. Everything always goes in cycles—peaks and valleys. That's one reason I gear my playing schedule around the major championships. Knowing it's impossible to maintain top form for an entire season, I try to build and tune my game for the events that are the most important to me.

The number one reason why no golfer can stay at his or her peak indefinitely is that human beings aren't machines. Our ability to exactly repeat a certain set of actions is limited, and thus our abilities as shot-makers are bound to fluctuate. This is compounded by the tendency, present in all of us, to eventually overdo or exaggerate whatever we have found to be successful. In terms of the golf swing this tendency often creeps up on us subconsciously, but it is none the less destructive for that. And, when it has done its dirty work, reality has to be faced: if we want once more to play up to our maximum potential, the rebuilding or retuning process must begin all over again.

This final section of PLAY BETTER GOLF is designed to help take a lot of the pain out of this most basic of golfing challenges by providing answers to the shot-making problems all of us encounter at some time or another. As before, I've tried to be as clear and precise as possible, and also in this case to organize the material for quick and easy problem-solving reference. However, as almost every element of shot-making is covered, I feel this section could also be very helpful as an overall guide for anyone seeking all-around improvement at the game.

Jack Nicklaus

CHAPTER SEVEN

Preparing
to Play

32

Getting Properly Equipped

Correct Clubs Make Golf Easier

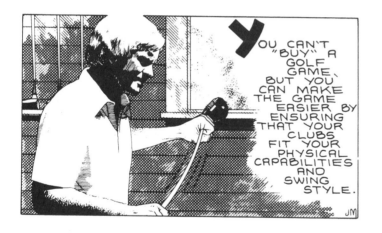

YOU CAN'T "BUY" A GOLF GAME, BUT YOU CAN MAKE THE GAME EASIER BY ENSURING THAT YOUR CLUBS FIT YOUR PHYSICAL CAPABILITIES AND SWING STYLE.

FOR EXAMPLE, IF DIRECTION IS YOUR CHIEF PROBLEM, THEN STIFFER SHAFTS MIGHT TAKE SOME OF THE BEND OUT OF YOUR LONG SHOTS. CONVERSELY, LIGHTER OR MORE FLEXIBLE SHAFTS CAN HELP THE WEAKER GOLFER ADD VALUABLE YARDAGE — AND ALSO FLY THE BALL HIGHER.

ASK YOUR PRO FOR ADVICE AND FOR HELP IN EXPERIMENTING.

Fit Driver to Swing Style

HAVING TEE-SHOT TROUBLES ??

LOOKING FOR A NEW DRIVER ??

DON'T BE HASTY... TALK TO YOUR PRO AND EXPERIMENT UNTIL YOU FIND ONE THAT MATCHES YOUR SWING CHARACTERISTICS -- ESPECIALLY YOUR <u>TEMPO</u>.

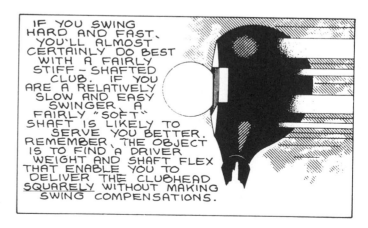

IF YOU SWING HARD AND FAST, YOU'LL ALMOST CERTAINLY DO BEST WITH A FAIRLY STIFF - SHAFTED CLUB. IF YOU ARE A RELATIVELY SLOW AND EASY SWINGER, A FAIRLY "SOFT" SHAFT IS LIKELY TO SERVE YOU BETTER. REMEMBER, THE OBJECT IS TO FIND A DRIVER WEIGHT AND SHAFT FLEX THAT ENABLE YOU TO DELIVER THE CLUBHEAD <u>SQUARELY</u> WITHOUT MAKING SWING COMPENSATIONS.

Experiment with Grip Thickness

IF YOU'RE SERIOUS ABOUT GOLF, FIND A WAY TO EXPERIMENT WITH VARYING GRIP THICKNESSES.

YOU MIGHT BE SURPRISED AT THE DIFFERENCE A SLIGHTLY THINNER OR FATTER GRIP CAN MAKE TO YOUR GAME.

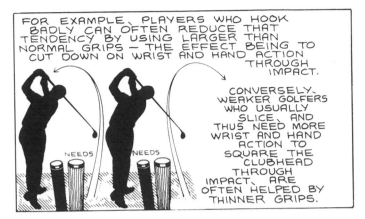

FOR EXAMPLE, PLAYERS WHO HOOK BADLY CAN OFTEN REDUCE THAT TENDENCY BY USING LARGER THAN NORMAL GRIPS — THE EFFECT BEING TO CUT DOWN ON WRIST AND HAND ACTION THROUGH IMPACT.

CONVERSELY, WEAKER GOLFERS WHO USUALLY SLICE, AND THUS NEED MORE WRIST AND HAND ACTION TO SQUARE THE CLUBHEAD THROUGH IMPACT, ARE OFTEN HELPED BY THINNER GRIPS.

NEEDS   NEEDS

Keep Your Grips in Good Condition

THE CONDITION OF YOUR CLUB GRIPS CAN BEAR HEAVILY ON HOW YOU SCORE.

CLUB SLIPPAGE IS FATAL AT ANY POINT IN THE SWING, AND IT'S BOUND TO HAPPEN SOMETIME IF YOUR GRIPS ARE SLICK OR DRIED OUT.

ALSO, WORN AND SLIPPERY GRIPS WILL FORCE YOU TO HOLD THE CLUB TOO TIGHTLY, INHIBITING PROPER SWING ACTION.

TO KEEP RUBBER OR COMPOSITION GRIPS IN GOOD SHAPE, SIMPLY SCRUB THEM PERIODICALLY WITH SOAP AND WATER. IF YOUR PREFERENCE IS LEATHER (MY CHOICE), THEN KEEP THE GRIPS SUPPLE AND TACKY WITH PERIODIC APPLICATIONS OF CONDITIONING OIL.

Check Flange to Solve Sand Problems

HAVING BUNKER PROBLEMS?

CHECK YOUR SAND-WEDGE.

IF YOU'RE DIGGING TOO DEEPLY, IT COULD BE THAT THE CLUB HAS INSUFFICIENT FLANGE TO LET IT "BOUNCE" THROUGH THE SAND EASILY.

CONVERSELY, IF YOU'RE "BLADING" OR CATCHING THE BALL THIN, IT'S POSSIBLE THAT A CLUB WITH A SHALLOWER FLANGE WOULD TAKE SOME OF THE PAIN OUT OF THOSE SAND SHOTS.

SHOW YOUR CLUB AND YOUR BUNKER ACTION TO THE PRO, AND TAKE HIS ADVICE.

33

Getting More from Practice

When in Trouble, Go Back to Basics

GOING THROUGH A SLUMP ??

TRIED EVERYTHING AND NOTHING WORKS ??

WHEN THIS HAPPENS — AS IT DOES TO ALL GOLFERS AT TIMES — THE FASTEST REMEDY IS USUALLY A LESSON FROM A TEACHER WHO KNOWS YOUR GAME.

F THAT'S NOT POSSIBLE, THEN GO BACK TO BASICS. FORGET ALL THE GIMMICKS OR **BAND-AID** REMEDIES YOU MAY HAVE BEEN TRYING, AND WORK THROUGH THE FUNDAMENTALS, STARTING WITH YOUR GRIP, SET-UP AND POSTURE.

FREQUENTLY YOU'LL FIND THE PROBLEM IN ONE OF THESE "STATICS," RATHER THAN IN THE SWING ITSELF.

Play, Don't Practice, After Layoff

STARTING GOLF AGAIN AFTER A LONG LAYOFF?

DON'T GO OUT THE FIRST TIME AND BEAT A THOUSAND RANGE BALLS: YOUR MUSCLES AREN'T READY FOR IT AND THEY WILL DEFINITELY PUNISH YOU!

INSTEAD, DO WHAT YOU'VE BEEN DYING TO DO, WHICH IS **PLAY**, NOT PRACTICE. USE AN OUTING OR TWO ON THE COURSE TO REKINDLE YOUR ENTHUSIASM, AND ALSO TO TELL YOU WHAT AREAS OF YOUR SWING OR GAME PARTICULARLY NEED WORK. BY USING THIS EXPERIENCE TO CREATE A PRACTICE PLAN, YOU CAN THEN GO SERIOUSLY TO WORK WITH SOME **CLEAR** OBJECTIVES IN MIND.

Practice Regularly, Thoughtfully

KNOWING **HOW** TO PRACTICE IS AS IMPORTANT AS ACTUALLY DOING SO. FOR INSTANCE, FREQUENCY IS MORE IMPORTANT THAN QUANTITY, AND **THOUGHT** IS EQUALLY IMPORTANT AS PHYSICAL EFFORT IF YOU WANT TO GET MORE FROM PRACTICE THAN EXERCISE.

MOST AMATEURS HAVE A TENDENCY TO HIT TOO MANY SHOTS TOO FAST TOO HARD WHENEVER THEY GO TO THE DRIVING RANGE.

IF THAT'S YOU, PLACE YOUR PRACTICE BALLS THREE OR FOUR PACES AWAY FROM YOUR HITTING SPOT, SO THAT YOU ARE **FORCED** TO PAUSE AND THINK BETWEEN SWINGS.

Give Swing Changes Time to Work

IF YOU'VE RECENTLY HAD A LESSON, OR ARE WORKING ON SOMETHING YOU BELIEVE TO BE SOUND THAT YOU'VE FIGURED OUT FOR YOURSELF, THEN BE PATIENT — **GIVE IT TIME.**

REMEMBER THAT, EVEN FOR THE TOUR PROS, ANY SWING CHANGE, HOWEVER SLIGHT, TAKES WEEKS OF WORK BEFORE IT FEELS COMFORTABLE AND BECOMES "REPEATABLE."

MANY AMATEURS NEVER REACH ANYTHING LIKE THEIR FULL GOLFING POTENTIAL BECAUSE THEY ARE FOREVER TRYING SOMETHING DIFFERENT IN A SEARCH FOR INSTANT IMPROVEMENT. BELIEVE ME, THERE IS NO SUCH THING, JUST AS THERE ARE NO "SECRETS."

IF YOU WANT TO PLAY BETTER AT THIS GAME, THE ONLY ANSWERS ARE THE **FUNDAMENTALS + PERSEVERANCE + HARD WORK.**

Don't Over-Experiment

BIG DANGER WHEN A PRIDEFUL GOLFER DEVELOPS A PERSISTENT FLAW IN HIS GAME IS OVER-EXPERIMENTATION IN SEARCHING FOR A CURE.

SUCH A COURSE WILL OFTEN DESTROY YOUR GOOD MOVES FASTER THAN IT WILL RESOLVE YOUR INITIAL FAULT.

WHENEVER I'VE GOTTEN TO A POINT WHERE I COULDN'T RESOLVE A PROBLEM WITHIN MY BASIC SWING FUNDAMENTALS, I'VE ASKED JACK GROUT FOR HELP. BEFORE YOU'VE EXPERIMENTED YOURSELF INTO TOTAL CONFUSION, A VISIT TO A TEACHER WHO KNOWS YOUR GAME COULD SAVE YOU A LOT OF PAIN, TOO.

Make Friends with Long Irons

IF YOU'RE SCARED OF LONG IRONS, HERE'S A WAY TO GET FRIENDLY WITH THEM.

HIT A FEW EASY 9-IRONS TO FIND YOUR IDEAL TEMPO AND RHYTHM. THEN HIT A BATCH OF 4-IRONS USING EXACTLY THE SAME SWING.

DO THE SAME WITH THE 8-IRON/3-IRON, AND THE 7-IRON/2-IRON.

TWO OR THREE SESSIONS LIKE THAT AND YOU'LL LOSE YOUR FEAR — AND IMPROVE YOUR SCORE.

Work on Your Short Game, Too

PLAYING IN PRO-AMS, I SOMETIMES GET THE IMPRESSION THAT THE BETTER AN AMATEUR'S LONG GAME, THE WORSE HE'LL BE AT RECOVERY SHOTS.

IF THERE'S ANY TRUTH IN THIS, IT'S PROBABLY DUE TO AN IMBALANCE IN PRACTICE TIME.

GOOD FULL SWINGERS PROBABLY SPEND SO MUCH OF THEIR PRACTICE EFFORT WORKING ON THE BIG SHOTS THAT THEY LEAVE INSUFFICIENT TIME OR ENERGY FOR THE SHORT GAME.

THAT'S A COSTLY ERROR IF YOUR ULTIMATE CONCERN IS SCORE RATHER THAN SWING ESTHETICS.

34

Improving Your Attitude

Test Your Golfing Honesty

CONVINCED YOU ARE HITTING THE BALL AND PUTTING BETTER THAN YOU'RE SCORING?

WELL, THERE HAS TO BE A REASON, AND A LITTLE SELF-ANALYSIS MIGHT IDENTIFY IT.

TEST YOUR GOLFING HONESTY.

ASK YOURSELF HOW MANY SHOTS YOU WOULD HAVE SAVED IF YOU NEVER LOST YOUR TEMPER, NEVER GOT DOWN ON YOURSELF, ALWAYS DEVELOPED A STRATEGY BEFORE YOU HIT, ALWAYS PLAYED WITHIN YOUR OWN CAPABILITIES.

THE ANSWERS — IF YOU CAN BE TRULY HONEST WITH YOURSELF — MIGHT SOLVE MOST OF THOSE SCORING PROBLEMS.

Learn Golf's Terminology

MISUNDERSTANDING GOLF'S TERMINOLOGY CAN SLOW DOWN PROGRESS FOR THE BEGINNING PLAYER. SWING "PLANE" AND "ARC" FREQUENTLY SEEM TO BE CONFUSED — EVEN, SOMETIMES, BY EXPERIENCED GOLFERS.

YOUR SWING PLANE IS THE ANGLE AT WHICH YOUR ARMS AND THE CLUB SWING RELATIVE TO VERTICAL OR HORIZONTAL, AND THE CLOSER IT IS TO MIDWAY BETWEEN THE BETTER YOU'RE LIKELY TO PLAY.

YOUR SWING ARC IS THE PATH DESCRIBED BY THE CLUBHEAD WITHIN THAT PLANE — AND THE WIDER IT IS THE BETTER.

Precision Counts More Than Power

ANY MEN WOULD BE MUCH BETTER GOLFERS IF THEY COULD PLAY WITH A LITTLE LESS MACHO — IF THEY COULD EMOTIONALLY ACCEPT THE FACT THAT GOLF IS A GAME OF PRECISION RATHER THAN POWER.

LONG HITTING IN ITSELF HAS NEVER WON A TOURNAMENT THAT I KNOW ABOUT, BUT THE EFFORT TO HIT LONGER THAN NECESSARY TO SCORE WELL SURE HAS LOST AN AWFUL LOT DURING MY TIME IN THE GAME!

THAT'S WHY YOU'LL SO OFTEN SEE ME TEEING OFF WITH LESS THAN A DRIVER, ESPECIALLY ON TIGHT HOLES.

Focus on Remedies, Not Faults

AVOIDING FEAR OR ANGER AFTER A BAD MISHIT OR MISJUDGEMENT IS MAYBE GOLF'S SINGLE GREATEST CHALLENGE.

ONE TECHNIQUE I'VE FOUND SUCCESSFUL IS TO FORCE THE ERROR OUT OF MIND BY MAKING MYSELF IMMEDIATELY FOCUS VERY HARD ON THE NEXT SHOT IT REQUIRES ME TO PLAY.

IF A SWING FLAW RATHER THAN A JUDGEMENT CALL WAS THE PROBLEM, I DO MY BEST TO THINK POSITIVELY IN SEEKING A SOLUTION. FOR INSTANCE, IF TOO MUCH TENSION IN THE RIGHT ARM WOULD SEEM TO HAVE CAUSED THE MISHIT, I'LL TRY TO OFFSET IT WITH FIRMER LEFT-ARM OR LEFT-SIDE CONTROL ON THE UPCOMING SHOTS.

IN OTHER WORDS, I LIKE TO FOCUS ON REMEDIES, NOT ON FAULTS.

Take More Club More Often

WANT THE NEXT GOLF SEASON TO BE MORE FUN THAN THE LAST?

MAKE AND STICK TO A RESOLUTION TO TAKE ONE MORE CLUB THAN YOU FIRST THOUGHT OF ON EVERY TEE SHOT TO A PAR-THREE, AND EVERY APPROACH TO A PAR-FOUR, AND I PROMISE IT WILL BE.

I'LL ALSO PROMISE THAT YOU WILL GO OVER A LOT FEWER GREENS THIS SEASON THAN YOU WERE SHORT OF LAST YEAR. HOW CAN I BE SO SURE?

AS EVERY TOUR PRO WILL CONFIRM, THE SINGLE GREATEST FAULT OF ALL AMATEURS WORLDWIDE IS UNDER-CLUBBING.

JUST CURING THAT WOULD SAVE MOST GOLFERS A HATFUL OF STROKES IN EVERY ROUND.

Go to Woods for Safer Shots

I SEE A LOT OF GOLFERS IN PRO-AMS WHOSE PRIDE KEEPS THEM USING LONG-IRONS WHEN THEY WOULD CERTAINLY PLAY A LOT BETTER BY REPLACING THEM WITH WOODS.

IF THE 2, 3 AND 4 IRONS GET YOU INTO TROUBLE, CONSIDER EXCHANGING THEM FOR 4, 5 AND 6 WOODS. YOU'LL GET THE BALL IN THE AIR FASTER, HIT IT ABOUT THE SAME DISTANCE, AND BRING IT DOWN MORE SOFTLY. THE EASIER "LOOK" OF THESE WELL-LOFTED WOODS WILL ALSO BOOST YOUR CONFIDENCE OVER THE BALL.

Use Three-Wood to Avoid "Steering"

IN DOUBT AS TO WHETHER A FULL SWING WITH THE DRIVER MIGHT GET YOU IN TROUBLE FROM THE TEE?

ALWAYS GO TO THE THREE-WOOD IN SUCH CASES, RATHER THAN TRYING TO PLAY A LESS-THAN-FULL SHOT WITH THE DRIVER.

Reason?

LETTING UP WITH THE DRIVER ALMOST ALWAYS LEADS TO EITHER QUITTING ON THE SHOT OR AN INVOLUNTARY ATTEMPT TO "STEER" THE BALL INTO POSITION, EITHER OF WHICH CAN CAUSE BIG PROBLEMS.

SO TAKE LESS CLUB AND SWING FULLY AND FREELY.

Weigh Up All the Risks

SOMETIMES IT'S DIFFICULT IN ASSESSING A TIGHT TEE SHOT TO DECIDE WHETHER TO SACRIFICE DISTANCE FOR ACCURACY.

I'VE FOUND THE FOLLOWING QUESTION HELPFUL IN SUCH CIRCUMSTANCES.

"IS THE POSSIBLE REWARD FOR EXTRA YARDAGE WORTH THE POTENTIAL RISK?"

I USUALLY FIND THE ONLY TIME I ANSWER "YES" IS WHEN I **MUST** HIT A DRIVER OFF THE TEE TO HAVE ANY CHANCE OF REACHING THE GREEN IN REGULATION.

NO. 7
375 YDS
PAR 4

Don't Try to Be a Hero

HANDICAP GOLFERS FREQUENTLY PERFORM A LOT WORSE IN STROKE-PLAY EVENTS THAN AT MATCH-PLAY.

THE CHIEF REASON IS TRYING TO HIT "HERO" SHOTS, RATHER THAN WORKING ALWAYS ON KEEPING THE BALL IN PLAY.

IF PAR IS 72 AND YOUR HANDICAP IS SAY 14, THEN A GOOD SCORE FOR YOU IS 86. TRYING TO SHOOT 76 IS ALMOST ALWAYS GOING TO RESULT IN 96, BECAUSE YOU PUT YOURSELF UNDER PRESSURE THAT YOU CAN'T SUSTAIN. SO PLAY THE **ENTIRE COURSE** WITHIN YOUR CAPABILITIES – WHILE CONTINUALLY IMPROVING THEM VIA LESSONS AND PRACTICE.

Tee Ball Up on Par Threes

OCCASIONALLY YOU'LL SEE A GOLFER PLAYING A PAR-THREE SIMPLY THROW THE BALL ON THE GROUND AND HIT AWAY.

IN MY BOOK HE'S MAKING THE GAME MUCH TOUGHER THAN IT NEED BE.

I ALWAYS TEE THE BALL ON A PEG WHEN THE RULES ALLOW, FIRST BECAUSE IT IMPROVES MY CHANCE OF MAKING SOLID CONTACT, AND SECONDLY BECAUSE IT REDUCES THE RISK OF GRASS GETTING BETWEEN CLUBFACE AND BALL AT IMPACT, THEREBY REDUCING BACKSPIN.

YOU SHOULD DO THE SAME.

Be Ready When Your Turn Comes

SLOW PLAY IS A MAJOR PROBLEM IN GOLF TODAY, AND ONE THAT EVERY GOLFER SHOULD BE WORKING AT OUT OF CONSIDERATION FOR OTHERS, IF FOR NO OTHER REASON.

I TEND TO TAKE QUITE A WHILE OVER THE BALL, BUT FOR MANY YEARS I'VE TRIED TO MAKE UP FOR THAT BY WALKING TO IT AS FAST AS POSSIBLE, AND THEN BEING READY TO PLAY THE MOMENT MY TURN COMES.

MAKE BOTH OF THOSE THINGS A HABIT AND YOU'LL HAVE ALL THE TIME YOU NEED FOR SHOT EVALUATION AND PREPARATION WITHOUT BEING A SLOW COACH.

Know the Rules—They Can Help You

IT'S MY EXPERIENCE THAT VERY FEW GOLFERS WHO DON'T PLAY FOR EITHER A LIVING OR THE TOP AMATEUR TITLES KNOW MUCH ABOUT THE **RULES OF GOLF**.

AS A RESULT, THEY OFTEN INADVERTANTLY CHEAT AT THE GAME.

THIS CAN BE HIGHLY EMBARRASSING IF YOU ARE PAIRED WITH SOMEONE WHO **DOES** KNOW THE RULES, AND ALSO BELIEVES IN ENFORCING THEM. ALSO, AS THE RULES OFTEN WORK TO THE PLAYER'S ADVANTAGE, THE GOLFER WHO DOESN'T KNOW THEM OFTEN CHEATS HIMSELF.

Never Hit a Careless Shot

I HIT MY SHARE OF BAD SHOTS IN TOURNAMENT PLAY, BUT THIS IS RARELY THE RESULT OF CARELESSNESS.

I THINK THE REASON IS THAT I'VE TRIED ALL MY LIFE TO GIVE EVERY SHOT I HIT, IN PRACTICE OR IN PLAY, 100 PER CENT EFFORT.

MAN IS A CREATURE OF HABIT, THUS IF YOU HABITUALLY FAIL TO TRY YOUR HARDEST WHEN IT DOESN'T MATTER, THE CHANCES ARE YOU'LL ALSO GIVE LESS THAN YOUR BEST WHEN IT DOES.

TRYING 100 PER CENT ON **EVERY** SHOT IS FINE INSURANCE AGAINST THAT.

CHAPTER EIGHT

The Long Game

35

Preparing
to Swing

Pick a Target Before You Set-Up

DO YOU WAIT UNTIL YOU'RE ACTUALLY OVER THE BALL BEFORE DECIDING EXACTLY WHERE YOU'RE TRYING TO HIT IT?

MANY HIGH HANDICAPPERS DO — WHICH IS ONE REASON THEY STAY HIGH HANDICAPPERS.

YOU CAN'T AIM CORRECTLY UNLESS YOU IDENTIFY A SPECIFIC TARGET TO ALIGN YOURSELF ON, SO PICK ONE OUT **BEFORE** YOU BEGIN TO SET-UP TO THE BALL.

MAKE IT A POINT IN THE BACKGROUND OR A MARK ON THE GROUND IF YOU'RE NOT GOING FOR THE PIN, BUT WHATEVER YOU CHOOSE AIM SPECIFICALLY, NEVER VAGUELY.

Get the "Statics" Right

IF YOU HAVE NORMAL HEALTH AND STRENGTH, PLAY A COUPLE OF TIMES A WEEK OR MORE BUT CAN'T REGULARLY BREAK 90, YOUR PROBLEMS ALMOST CERTAINLY LIE IN YOUR GRIP AND SET-UP RATHER THAN IN THE WAY YOU SWING:

GETTING THESE "STATICS" RIGHT CAN BE UNCOMFORTABLE AND BORING COMPARED TO THE FUN OF WHACKING AT THE BALL. HOWEVER, UNLESS YOU DO SO, YOU'RE ALWAYS GOING TO TAKE A LOT MORE WHACKS THAN YOU'D LIKE. TO FIND OUT HOW, GO SEE A GOOD TEACHING PRO — AND WATCH GOOD GOLFERS WHENEVER YOU CAN.

Form Grip When Clubhead Is Square

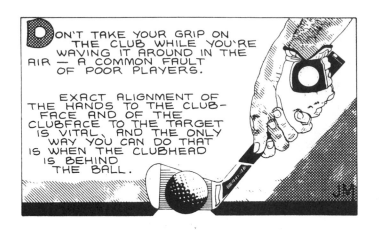

DON'T TAKE YOUR GRIP ON THE CLUB WHILE YOU'RE WAVING IT AROUND IN THE AIR — A COMMON FAULT OF POOR PLAYERS.

EXACT ALIGNMENT OF THE HANDS TO THE CLUBFACE AND OF THE CLUBFACE TO THE TARGET IS VITAL, AND THE ONLY WAY YOU CAN DO THAT IS WHEN THE CLUBHEAD IS BEHIND THE BALL.

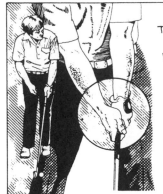

START BY SETTING THE CLUBFACE SQUARELY TO THE BALL AND THE TARGET WHILE HOLDING THE CLUB LIGHTLY IN YOUR LEFT HAND. NEXT ADJUST AND COMPLETE YOUR LEFT HAND PLACEMENT.

NOW ADD YOUR RIGHT HAND, SNUGGLING IT INTO POSITION WITHOUT CHANGING THE SQUARE ALIGNMENT OF THE CLUBFACE TO THE TARGET.

Make Your Hands a Single Unit

MANY BEGINNERS FIND IT DIFFICULT TO KEEP THEIR HANDS TOGETHER AND WORKING AS A SINGLE UNIT THROUGHOUT THE SWING.

LETTING THE HANDS SEPARATE OR WORK INDEPENDENTLY OF EACH OTHER IS ALSO RESPONSIBLE FOR MUCH POOR PLAY AMONG ESTABLISHED GOLFERS.

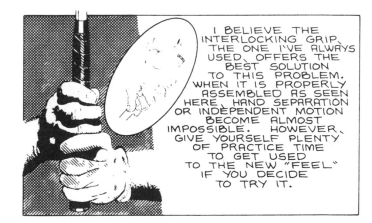

I BELIEVE THE INTERLOCKING GRIP, THE ONE I'VE ALWAYS USED, OFFERS THE BEST SOLUTION TO THIS PROBLEM. WHEN IT IS PROPERLY ASSEMBLED AS SEEN HERE, HAND SEPARATION OR INDEPENDENT MOTION BECOME ALMOST IMPOSSIBLE. HOWEVER, GIVE YOURSELF PLENTY OF PRACTICE TIME TO GET USED TO THE NEW "FEEL" IF YOU DECIDE TO TRY IT.

Grip with Left Hand First

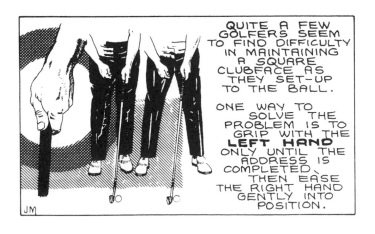

QUITE A FEW GOLFERS SEEM TO FIND DIFFICULTY IN MAINTAINING A SQUARE CLUBFACE AS THEY SET-UP TO THE BALL.

ONE WAY TO SOLVE THE PROBLEM IS TO GRIP WITH THE **LEFT HAND** ONLY UNTIL THE ADDRESS IS COMPLETED, THEN EASE THE RIGHT HAND GENTLY INTO POSITION.

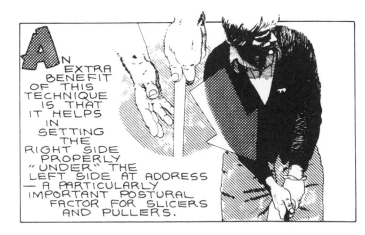

AN EXTRA BENEFIT OF THIS TECHNIQUE IS THAT IT HELPS IN SETTING THE RIGHT SIDE PROPERLY "UNDER" THE LEFT SIDE AT ADDRESS — A PARTICULARLY IMPORTANT POSTURAL FACTOR FOR SLICERS AND PULLERS.

Grip Lightly to Avoid Misalignment

LOT OF ERRANT SHOTS ARE THE RESULT OF INVOLUNTARILY MISALIGNING THE CLUBFACE RELATIVE TO THE TARGET, AT SOME POINT IN SETTING-UP TO THE BALL.

IT'S VERY EASY TO DO THIS WITH THE RIGHT HAND PARTICULARLY, AND ESPECIALLY IF YOU TEND TO "GRAB" THE CLUB WITH IT.

TO AVOID THIS SMALL BUT COSTLY FAULT, TRY HOLDING VERY LIGHTLY AS YOU SET-UP TO THE BALL, THEN FIRM UP YOUR GRIP TO THE CORRECT TAKEAWAY PRESSURE JUST BEFORE BEGINNING THE BACKSWING.

AND TRY TO SUSTAIN AN EVEN PRESSURE RIGHT ON UP TO THE TOP — DON'T "GRAB."

Try This for an Even Grip Pressure

O ENSURE AN EVENLY SECURE GRIP PRESSURE THROUGHOUT THE SWING, BEGIN BY HOLDING THE CLUB FAIRLY EASILY AS YOU COMPLETE YOUR ADDRESS POSITION, THEN FIRM UP YOUR HANDS TO YOUR IDEAL SWING PRESSURE JUST BEFORE STARTING BACK.

IF YOU HAVE PROBLEMS MAINTAINING THE FIRMNESS AT THE TOP, PRACTICE HITTING SHOTS WHILE CONSCIOUSLY SNUGGLING THE PAD OF YOUR RIGHT THUMB AGAINST THE TOP OF YOUR LEFT THUMB. PREVENT GAPS BETWEEN THESE TWO AREAS AND IT IS ALMOST IMPOSSIBLE TO LET GO OF THE CLUB.

"Grip-Press" for Smooth Takeaway

OST GOLFERS KNOW THE IMPORTANCE OF STARTING THE CLUB AWAY FROM THE BALL SMOOTHLY, BUT MANY HAVE TROUBLE DOING SO.

HERE'S A TIP THAT MIGHT HELP.

HOLD THE CLUB FAIRLY LIGHTLY AS YOU FINALIZE YOUR SET-UP TO THE BALL, THEN FIRM UP YOUR HANDS AS THE LAST ACTION BEFORE YOU START THE CLUBHEAD BACK.

I'VE USED THIS "**GRIP-PRESS**" FOR YEARS AS AN AID TO A SMOOTH TAKEAWAY, AND IT COULD HELP YOUR GAME TOO.

Check Grip Pressure After Impact

IF YOU'RE HITTING THE BALL SOLIDLY BUT NOT AS ACCURATELY AS USUAL, CHECK YOUR GRIP PRESSURE AFTER IMPACT.

LOOSENING THE HANDS THROUGH THE IMPACT AREA – OFTEN INVOLUNTARILY – IS A COMMON BUT LITTLE-RECOGNIZED CAUSE OF "SPRAYING."

I FIRM UP MY HANDS AS PART OF MY FORWARD-PRESS, THEN TRY TO MAINTAIN AN EVEN PRESSURE RIGHT THROUGH TO THE END OF THE FOLLOW-THROUGH.

CONSCIOUSLY BEING FIRM THROUGH IMPACT WILL OFTEN ADD BOTH CRISPNESS AND CONTROL TO YOUR SHOTS.

Check Lower Hand for Unified Action

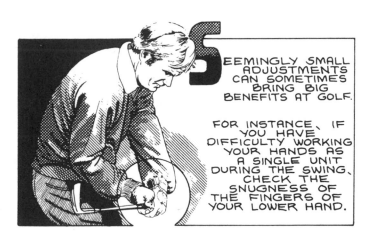

SEEMINGLY SMALL ADJUSTMENTS CAN SOMETIMES BRING BIG BENEFITS AT GOLF.

FOR INSTANCE, IF YOU HAVE DIFFICULTY WORKING YOUR HANDS AS A SINGLE UNIT DURING THE SWING, CHECK THE SNUGNESS OF THE FINGERS OF YOUR LOWER HAND.

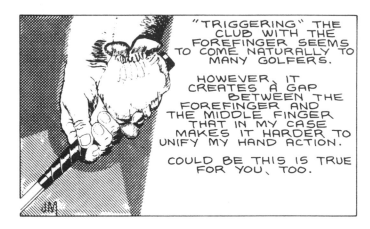

"TRIGGERING" THE CLUB WITH THE FOREFINGER SEEMS TO COME NATURALLY TO MANY GOLFERS.

HOWEVER, IT CREATES A GAP BETWEEN THE FOREFINGER AND THE MIDDLE FINGER THAT IN MY CASE MAKES IT HARDER TO UNIFY MY HAND ACTION.

COULD BE THIS IS TRUE FOR YOU, TOO.

Take a Natural Stance

WATCHING SOME HIGH HANDICAPPERS SET UP TO THE BALL MAKES ME WONDER HOW THEY DON'T DO THEMSELVES AN INJURY WHEN THEY SWING – THEIR POSTURE IS SO STRAINED AND STRESSFUL.

THE FOUR PRINCIPLES OF GOOD POSTURE ARE: BEND AT THE WAIST; KEEP THE BACK AS STRAIGHT AS COMFORTABLY POSSIBLE; LET THE ARMS HANG FREELY AND EASILY; AND SLIGHTLY FLEX THE KNEES. WITHIN THOSE SIMPLE GUIDELINES IT PAYS TO BE AS NATURAL AS POSSIBLE WHEN TAKING YOUR STANCE AT THE BALL.

Don't Contort Your Body at Address

FORCE SOME PART OF YOUR BODY INTO A CONTRIVED POSITION AT ADDRESS AND CHANCES ARE IT WILL REVERT TO NATURE ONCE YOU START MOVING, WITH NEGATIVE EFFECT ON YOUR SHOTS.

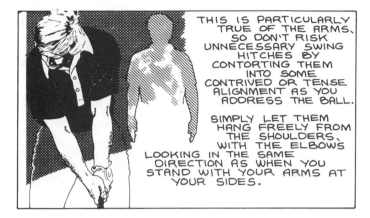

THIS IS PARTICULARLY TRUE OF THE ARMS, SO DON'T RISK UNNECESSARY SWING HITCHES BY CONTORTING THEM INTO SOME CONTRIVED OR TENSE ALIGNMENT AS YOU ADDRESS THE BALL.

SIMPLY LET THEM HANG FREELY FROM THE SHOULDERS, WITH THE ELBOWS LOOKING IN THE SAME DIRECTION AS WHEN YOU STAND WITH YOUR ARMS AT YOUR SIDES.

Never Start from Immobile Position

THE WORST WAY TO START YOUR GOLF SWING IS FROM A TOTALLY IMMOBILE POSITION, SO DEVELOP YOURSELF AN EFFECTIVE SWING "TRIGGER."

THIS COULD BE A FORWARD PRESS OF THE HANDS AND ARMS, OR A TARGETWARD SHIFT OF THE KNEES, OR ANY **SMALL** MOTION THAT ENABLES YOU TO START THE CLUB BACK FLUIDLY.

MY "TRIGGER" IS A FIRMING OF THE GRIP COMBINED WITH A SWIVELING OF THE CHIN AWAY FROM THE TARGET TO ALLOW THE FULLEST POSSIBLE COILING OF MY SHOULDERS GOING BACK. EXPERIMENT IN PRACTICE TO DETERMINE WHAT WORKS BEST FOR YOU, THEN "GROOVE" YOUR OWN PERSONAL TRIGGER UNTIL YOU DO IT SUBCONSCIOUSLY ON EVERY SHOT.

Begin the Swing Deliberately

MOST GOLFERS KNOW THAT THE PACE AT WHICH THEY START THE CLUB BACK FROM THE BALL IS CRITICAL TO THE SUCCESS OF THE SHOT, BUT MANY STILL HAVE TROUBLE ACHIEVING A CONSISTENTLY SMOOTH MOTION.

THE THOUGHT THAT HELPS ME MOST IN BEGINNING THE BACKSWING IS "DELIBERATENESS."

TO PICTURE THAT PACE, COMPARE IT TO GETTING A CAR ROLLING AS SMOOTHLY AS POSSIBLE, WITH A GENTLE STARTING MOTION FOLLOWED BY A GRADUAL BUILD-UP IN ACCELERATION.

CHECK YOUR BALL POSITION AT ADDRESS ANY TIME YOUR SHOTS START CURVING BADLY RIGHT OR LEFT.

SETTING THE BALL TOO FAR FORWARD OR BACK IN RELATION TO YOUR FEET COULD BE THE CAUSE OF THE PROBLEM.

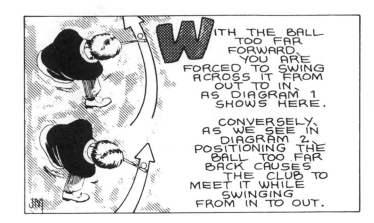

WITH THE BALL TOO FAR FORWARD, YOU ARE FORCED TO SWING ACROSS IT FROM OUT TO IN, AS DIAGRAM 1 SHOWS HERE.

CONVERSELY, AS WE SEE IN DIAGRAM 2, POSITIONING THE BALL TOO FAR BACK CAUSES THE CLUB TO MEET IT WHILE SWINGING FROM IN TO OUT.

36

Avoiding Head Movement

Make "Head Still" No. 1 Rule

WE'VE SAID IT BEFORE, BUT IT'S WORTH SAYING AGAIN: KEEPING THE **HEAD STILL** IS THE NO. 1 FUNDAMENTAL OF GOLF.

BECAUSE IT'S SO DIFFICULT TO SELF-DIAGNOSE, IT'S WORTH HAVING YOUR PRO OR A PAL CHECK YOU OUT PERIODICALLY.

ASK HIM OR HER TO WATCH FOR UP AND DOWN MOVEMENT AS WELL AS LATERAL MOTION.

AND REMEMBER THAT "KEEPING YOUR EYE ON THE BALL" AND KEEPING YOUR HEAD STEADY AREN'T NECESSARILY THE SAME THING — I CAN MOVE MY HEAD AT LEAST A FOOT AND STILL KEEP MY "EYE ON THE BALL."

Watch Shadow to Check Movement

PRONOUNCED HEAD MOVEMENT AT ANY POINT FROM TAKEAWAY TO IMPACT IS A SURE SHOT-WRECKER.

BEST WAY TO CHECK THAT YOURS IS STAYING STEADY IS WITH THE HELP OF YOUR PRO OR A GOLFING FRIEND.

WHEN THAT'S IMPRACTICAL, YOU CAN GET A PRETTY GOOD READING SIMPLY BY PRACTICE SWINGING WITH THE SUN DIRECTLY BEHIND YOU.

HIT AT A TEE PEG OR A WEED, WATCHING YOUR SHADOW CAREFULLY WHILE DOING SO.

Try Checking Head Sway This Way

MANY GOLFERS WHO MOVE THEIR HEADS DURING THE SWING DON'T BELIEVE THEY

ARE DOING SO BECAUSE THEY CAN'T ACTUALLY FEEL OR SENSE IT HAPPENING.

IF YOU'D LIKE TO TAKE THE ULTIMATE TEST REGARDING HEAD MOVEMENT, HAVE SOMEONE GRAB YOUR HAIR WHILE STANDING IN FRONT OF YOU AS YOU SWING WITH A SHORT OR MEDIUM IRON.

THE FEELING IN YOUR SCALP WILL GIVE YOU A VERY CONCLUSIVE ANSWER!

Beware Up-and-Down Movement, Too

A STEADY HEAD IS THE SINGLE MOST IMPORTANT FACTOR IN GOLF — AN **ABSOLUTE MUST**.

MOST GOLFERS KNOW AND TRY TO AVOID THE DESTRUCTIVE EFFECTS OF SIDE-TO-SIDE MOVEMENT.

WHAT MANY OVERLOOK ARE THE EQUALLY RUINOUS RESULTS OF UP-AND-DOWN MOVEMENT.

LIFT OR LOWER YOUR HEAD AT ANY POINT IN THE SWING AND YOU CHANGE IT'S ARC.

SO IF YOU TEND EITHER TO TOP SHOTS OR HIT A LOT OF THEM "FAT," HAVE SOMEONE CHECK OUT HOW YOUR HEAD IS BEHAVING.

IF IT'S WOBBLING IN ANY DIRECTION, MAKE KEEPING IT STEADY YOUR NO. 1 CONSCIOUS SWING THOUGHT FOR THE MONTH.

Keep Feet Grounded to Steady Head

HERE'S A TIP TO HELP YOU LEARN TO KEEP YOUR HEAD STEADY THROUGHOUT THE SWING — AN ABSOLUTE "MUST" FOR PLAYING UP TO YOUR FULL POTENTIAL.

IT WILL ALSO, INCIDENTALLY, IMPROVE YOUR FOOTWORK.

ON THE PRACTICE TEE, HIT FULL SHOTS WITH A MEDIUM-IRON.. SAY A NO. 5.. WHILE KEEPING BOTH FEET FIRMLY GROUNDED, THUS MINIMIZING ANY TENDENCY TO SWAY YOUR UPPER BODY.

KEY TO THE ACTION IS ROLLING THE ANKLES — THE LEFT INWARD GOING BACK AND THE RIGHT INWARD COMING DOWN.

Think "Head Still"!

keep your head still IS AN AGE-OLD GOLFING MAXIM, BUT THE FACT IS IT RARELY HAPPENS EVEN IN THE FINEST SWINGS. PHOTOGRAPHY PROVES THAT GOOD PLAYERS' HEADS USUALLY MOVE A LITTLE BACK AND DOWN AS THEY HIT THROUGH THE BALL.

NEVERTHELESS, I BELIEVE THE **THOUGHT** OF KEEPING THE HEAD AS **STEADY** AS POSSIBLE THROUGHOUT THE SWING IS SOLID COUNSEL, BECAUSE IT HELPS PREVENT SWAYING THE ENTIRE BODY EITHER GOING BACK OR COMING DOWN. BOTH THOSE MOTIONS WILL GET YOU IN DEEP TROUBLE UNLESS YOU CAN COMPENSATE FOR THEM EVERY TIME.

37

Improving Your Tempo

Don't Let ''Grabbing'' Wreck Your Rhythm

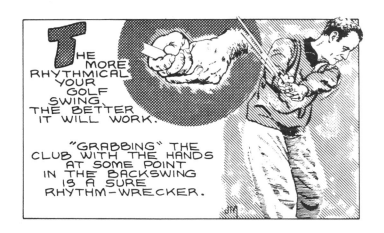

THE MORE RHYTHMICAL YOUR GOLF SWING, THE BETTER IT WILL WORK.

"GRABBING" THE CLUB WITH THE HANDS AT SOME POINT IN THE BACKSWING IS A SURE RHYTHM-WRECKER.

OFTEN THIS ACTION IS INVOLUNTARY. IF YOU SUSPECT YOU ARE DOING IT, TRY MAKING A **CONSCIOUS** EFFORT ON EVERY SWING TO HOLD THE CLUB FIRMLY BUT NOT TIGHTLY AT ADDRESS, THEN MAINTAIN THE EXACT SAME PRESSURE FROM THERE ON THROUGH. IF YOUR SWING BEGINS TO FEEL SMOOTHER, YOU CAN BE SURE YOU'VE BEEN A 'GRABBER.'

Use Big Muscles to Smooth Tempo

GOT TIMING PROBLEMS??

THE BIGGER THE MUSCLE-GROUPS YOU USE IN EVERYDAY ACTIONS, THE MORE DELIBERATELY AND THUS THE MORE SMOOTHLY YOU'LL TEND TO MOVE.

SAME IN GOLF.

TO IMPROVE YOUR TEMPO AND RHYTHM, TRY MOTIVATING THE CLUB MORE WITH YOUR BODY AND LESS WITH YOUR HANDS, WRISTS AND ARMS.

WORK PARTICULARLY ON A FULL UPPER TORSO TURN GOING BACK, AND FULL HIP CLEARANCE ON THE WAY TO AND THROUGH THE BALL.

Swing in "Slow Motion" to Improve Form

IF YOU'VE TRIED EVERYTHING ELSE TO ELIMINATE A SWING FLAW AND HAVEN'T SUCCEEDED, TRY SLOWING DOWN YOUR TEMPO. ON SECOND THOUGHTS, TRY THIS FIRST BECAUSE IT MIGHT SAVE YOU A GREAT DEAL OF TIME AND EFFORT.

BY PLAYING IN EFFECT IN SLOW MOTION, YOU GIVE YOURSELF TIME TO REALLY **FEEL** WHAT YOU ARE DOING AS YOU EXECUTE THE SWING. VERY OFTEN THAT ALONE WILL TELL YOU HOW TO GO ABOUT CORRECTING IT — PLUS GIVING YOU THE TIME TO DO SO.

SLOW TEMPO

Lengthen Swing to Slow It Down

IF YOU THINK YOU'D PLAY BETTER WITH A SLOWER TEMPO, TRY LENGTHENING YOUR SWING BY INCREASING YOUR SHOULDER TURN AND ARM EXTENSION.

THE FULLER THE SWING, THE LONGER IT TAKES TO EXECUTE — WHICH WILL AUTOMATICALLY SLOW DOWN YOUR OVERALL TEMPO.

KEY IS TO **COIL** AND **EXTEND** MORE, RATHER THAN SIMPLY BENDING YOUR LEFT ARM OR RELAXING YOUR GRIP TO LET THE CLUB GO BACK FARTHER.

Keep the Pace the Same

PROPERLY TIMING THE TRANSITION FROM BACKSWING TO THROUGH-SWING IS ONE OF GOLF'S TOUGHEST CHALLENGES.

MOST GOLFERS TEND TO RUSH THE CHANGEOVER CAUSING THEM TO SWING "OVER AND OUT" WITH THEIR SHOULDERS.

TO PREVENT THIS, PRACTICE ONE OF MY KEY SWING THOUGHTS, WHICH IS:

"SWING THE HANDS AND ARMS DOWN AT THE SAME **DELIBERATE** PACE YOU SWUNG THEM STARTING BACK."

THE MOVEMENT WILL ACTUALLY BE FASTER THAN YOUR STARTING-BACK MOTION, BUT THE **THOUGHT** OF BEING EQUALLY DELIBERATE WILL DEFINITELY HELP YOU ACHIEVE PROPER TIMING.

Try This Drill for Better Timing

TIMING YOUR SHOTS POORLY?

OUT OF BALANCE AT IMPACT?

HIT SOME SHOTS WITH YOUR FEET **TOGETHER** —

ACTUALLY TOUCHING AT THE HEELS.

USE A FIVE- OR SIX-IRON, AND BUILD UP GRADUALLY FROM A HALF- TO A THREE-QUARTER SWING.

REGULAR PRACTICE LIKE THIS WILL DO WONDERS FOR YOUR TEMPO AND BALANCE — AND TEACH YOU GOOD HAND ACTION AS WELL.

38

Building a Better Swing

Check These Fundamentals

BEWARE OF OVER-EXPERIMENTING ANY TIME YOUR GAME GOES SOUR.

GIMMICKS MAY WORK FOR SHORT PERIODS, BUT IN THE LONG RUN THERE IS NO SUBSTITUTE FOR FUNDAMENTALS.

JM

IF YOU'RE PLAYING CONSISTENTLY POORLY, CHECK IN ORDER - PREFERABLY WITH THE HELP OF A TEACHING PROFESSIONAL - YOUR GRIP, YOUR AIM, YOUR ALIGNMENT, AND YOUR POSTURE. USUALLY THE FAULT WILL LIE, AT **ROOT**, IN ONE OF THOSE AREAS. ONLY AFTER YOU'VE SATISFIED YOURSELF THAT IT DOESN'T SHOULD YOU CONSIDER ACTUAL SWING CHANGES.

Develop One Basic Swing

BEGINNERS AND SELF-TAUGHT GOLFERS OFTEN SEEM TO THINK THAT, BECAUSE THEIR GOLF CLUBS VARY IN LENGTH AND HEAD CONFIGURATION, EACH OF THEM MUST BE SWUNG DIFFERENTLY. THAT'S 100% THE WRONG APPROACH.

JM

DEVELOP ONE BASIC, FUNDAMENTALLY SOUND SWING PATTERN AND IT WILL WORK EQUALLY WELL WITH ALL THE CLUBS. THE ONLY VARIATION IS THAT YOU STAND NEARER TO THE BALL THE SHORTER THE CLUB, BUT THAT HAPPENS INSTINCTIVELY — AS DOES THE SHORTENING OF THE SWING ARC AS THE SHAFT LENGTH DECREASES.

Cock Chin for a Complete Backswing

COMING "OVER" OR "OFF" THE BALL IN THE DOWNSWING??

THOSE ARE VERY COMMON FAULTS, AND FREQUENTLY THEIR CAUSE IS NOTHING MORE COMPLICATED THAN AN INCOMPLETE BODY TURN ON THE BACKSWING.

HERE'S A TIP THAT WILL HELP ANYONE WHO TENDS TO START DOWN BEFORE THEY'VE FINISHED GOING BACK.

AS YOU BEGIN THE BACKSWING, SIMPLY TURN YOUR CHIN A FEW DEGREES TO THE RIGHT.

YOU'LL FIND THIS ACTION, COMMON TO MANY TOUR PLAYERS, INCLUDING ME, ALLOWS YOU A LOT MORE ROOM TO FULLY WIND UP THOSE SHOULDERS AND HIPS.

Stay "Soft" in Your Trailing Hand

GOLF IS A TWO-HANDED GAME, BUT UNTIL A GOLFER'S MUSCLES ARE FULLY TRAINED THERE'S A GREAT DANGER HIS STRONGER HAND AND ARM WILL OVERPOWER HIS WEAKER SIDE.

WAY TO OVERCOME THIS IS TO ESTABLISH A SENSATION OF "SOFTNESS" IN THE TRAILING HAND AND ARM AT ADDRESS, THEN CONSCIOUSLY TRY TO KEEP THEM PASSIVE THROUGHOUT THE SWING. LET THEM JUST "GO ALONG FOR THE RIDE" MOST OF THE TIME, AND THEY'LL AUTOMATICALLY DO THEIR JOB IN THE HITTING AREA IN RESPONSE TO CENTRIFUGAL FORCE.

Don't Let the Clubhead Lag

ALL KINDS OF MISHITS CAN RESULT FROM ALLOWING THE CLUBHEAD TO **LAG** BEHIND THE HANDS STARTING BACK, BREAKING THE IDEAL STRAIGHT LEFT ARM/CLUBSHAFT TAKEAWAY RELATIONSHIP.

OVERLY RELAXED WRISTS CAN CAUSE THIS FAULT, SO BE SURE YOU'RE FIRM HERE AS THE BACKSWING MOTION BEGINS.

CHECK HOW YOU GROUND THE CLUB, ALSO, BECAUSE STUBBING THE CLUB THROUGH PRESSING DOWN TOO FIRMLY AT ADDRESS CAN ALSO CAUSE A SHOT-WRECKING LAG.

Keep Hands Passive for Fuller Turn

HAVE PROBLEMS MAKING A GOOD UPPER BODY TURN?

KEEPING YOUR HANDS AND WRISTS PASSIVE UNTIL THE CLUB HAS SWUNG BEYOND HIP HEIGHT GOING BACK WILL HELP YOU TO EXTEND YOUR ARMS AND COIL YOUR SHOULDERS FULLY.

TRY TO START EVERYTHING AWAY FROM THE BALL IN ONE PIECE, WITH NO BREAKING OF THE WRISTS UNTIL THE MOMENTUM OF THE CLUBHEAD PULLS THEM INTO A COCKED POSITION AS YOU APPROACH COMPLETION OF THE BACKSWING.

REMEMBER THAT THE EARLIER YOU COCK YOUR WRISTS, THE LESS FULLY YOU ARE LIKELY TO COIL YOUR SHOULDERS.

Keep Left Arm Firmly Extended

ONE OF THE BIGGEST FAULTS OF BEGINNERS AND POOR PLAYERS IS BENDING THE LEFT ARM DURING THE BACKSWING, CAUSING LOSS OF BOTH CONTROL AND POWER.

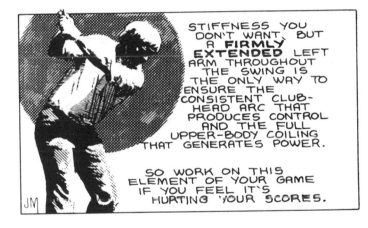

STIFFNESS YOU DON'T WANT, BUT A **FIRMLY EXTENDED** LEFT ARM THROUGHOUT THE SWING IS THE ONLY WAY TO ENSURE THE CONSISTENT CLUBHEAD ARC THAT PRODUCES CONTROL AND THE FULL UPPER-BODY COILING THAT GENERATES POWER.

SO WORK ON THIS ELEMENT OF YOUR GAME IF YOU FEEL IT'S HURTING YOUR SCORES.

Keep Your Right Knee Flexed

ANY TIME YOUR RIGHT KNEE STRAIGHTENS ON THE BACKSWING, YOU DIMINISH DISTANCE-PRODUCING TORQUE AND RISK SWINGING "OVER THE TOP."

INCLINING MY RIGHT KNEE SLIGHTLY IN TOWARDS THE TARGET AT ADDRESS HELPS ME TO KEEP IT FLEXED, AND MY WEIGHT PROPERLY ON THE INSIDE OF THE FOOT GOING BACK.

STARTING DOWN I'M THEN IN IDEAL SHAPE TO USE MY LEGS CORRECTLY.

Check Your Backswing Hip Turn

"SPINNING OUT?"

COMING "OVER THE BALL?"

CHECK HOW YOUR HIPS ARE WORKING IN THE BACKSWING --- ESPECIALLY IF YOUR LEGS AREN'T PARTICULARLY STRONG OR WELL-CONDITIONED.

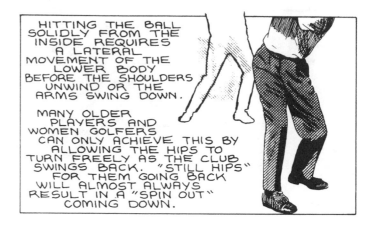

HITTING THE BALL SOLIDLY FROM THE INSIDE REQUIRES A LATERAL MOVEMENT OF THE LOWER BODY BEFORE THE SHOULDERS UNWIND OR THE ARMS SWING DOWN.

MANY OLDER PLAYERS AND WOMEN GOLFERS CAN ONLY ACHIEVE THIS BY ALLOWING THE HIPS TO TURN FREELY AS THE CLUB SWINGS BACK. "STILL HIPS" FOR THEM GOING BACK WILL ALMOST ALWAYS RESULT IN A "SPIN OUT" COMING DOWN.

Try "Long Left Thumb" for Over-Wristiness

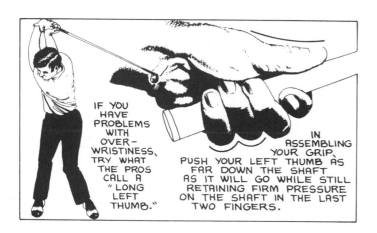

IF YOU HAVE PROBLEMS WITH OVER-WRISTINESS, TRY WHAT THE PROS CALL A "LONG LEFT THUMB."

IN ASSEMBLING YOUR GRIP, PUSH YOUR LEFT THUMB AS FAR DOWN THE SHAFT AS IT WILL GO WHILE STILL RETAINING FIRM PRESSURE ON THE SHAFT IN THE LAST TWO FINGERS.

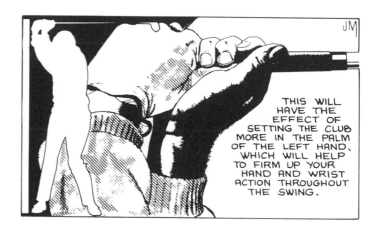

THIS WILL HAVE THE EFFECT OF SETTING THE CLUB MORE IN THE PALM OF THE LEFT HAND, WHICH WILL HELP TO FIRM UP YOUR HAND AND WRIST ACTION THROUGHOUT THE SWING.

Cultivate Feeling of "Coiled Strength"

BACKSWING HIP ACTION SEEMS TO TROUBLE A LOT OF WEEKEND PLAYERS.

FEELING TO STRIVE FOR IS THAT THE RIGHT SIDE IS NEITHER LOCKED TIGHT NOR LOOSELY RELAXED AS THE BACKSWING IS COMPLETED.

LEFT HIP FOR A LEFTY

A SENSATION OF **COILED STRENGTH** IS MY OBJECTIVE.

THE SENSATION IS NOT OF TENSION BUT OF SPRINGINESS — GIVING ME THE CAPABILITY TO MOVE MY LEGS AND HIPS QUICKLY BUT SMOOTHLY INTO THE DOWNSWING.

Learn to Stay Behind the Ball

MOVE YOUR BODY FORWARD OF ITS ADDRESS POSITION DURING THE SWING AND YOU CAN HIT EVERY TYPE OF CROOKED SHOT IN THE BOOK.

AN OVER-VIOLENT EFFORT TO SHIFT THE WEIGHT TO THE LEFT SIDE CAN CAUSE THE ENTIRE BODY TO MOVE FORWARD. SO CAN TOO MUCH LATERAL HIP SLIDE COMING DOWN AND THROUGH, AS OPPOSED TO A SLIDE-AND-TURN HIP ACTION.

SIMPLE WAY TO BE SURE OF STAYING BEHIND THE BALL, HOWEVER, IS TO KEEP YOUR HEAD STEADY. DO THAT AND IT'S IMPOSSIBLE TO MOVE YOUR UPPER HALF FORWARD ALONG WITH YOUR LOWER HALF.

Trust Your Centrifugal Force

SOME GOLFERS FAIL TO INITIATE AND LEAD THE DOWNSWING WITH THEIR LEGS AND HIPS BECAUSE OF FEAR THAT THEIR HANDS AND WRISTS WON'T GET THE CLUBHEAD TO THE BALL IN TIME TO MAKE FLUSH CONTACT.

DON'T FALL INTO THAT TRAP. CORRECT LOWER-BODY ACTION COMING DOWN BUILDS UP SUCH MASSIVE CENTRIFUGAL FORCE IN THE CLUBHEAD THAT YOUR HANDS AND WRISTS WILL REACT TO IT REFLEXIVELY.

IN FACT, THE "LATER" YOU CAN MAKE THE RELEASE THE BETTER — SO LONG AS YOU DO RELEASE FULLY WHEN THE TIME COMES.

Angle Left Foot for Easier Unwinding

HAVE TROUBLE BEGINNING THE DOWNSWING WITH YOUR LEGS AND HIPS??

CHECK YOUR LEFT FOOT POSITIONING AT ADDRESS, BECAUSE A SLIGHT CHANGE HERE COULD SOLVE THE PROBLEM.

FOR MOST GOLFERS, THE MORE TOWARDS THE TARGET THE LEFT FOOT IS ANGLED AT ADDRESS, THE EASIER IT BECOMES TO UNWIND THE LOWER BODY THROUGHOUT THE DOWNSWING.

TRY THIS ON THE PRACTICE TEE, ESPECIALLY IF YOU'VE HABITUALLY SET UP WITH YOUR LEAD FOOT SET PRETTY MUCH SQUARE.

Use Legs Properly Coming Down

MOST HANDICAP GOLFERS **UNDER-USE** THEIR LEGS ON THE DOWNSWING, THROWING THE CLUB AT THE BALL WITH THEIR HANDS, ARMS AND SHOULDERS BEFORE THEIR FEET AND KNEES HAVE SHIFTED TARGETWARDS.

THE RESULT IS USUALLY A SLICE, PULL, OR PULL-HOOK.

HOWEVER, IT'S ALSO POSSIBLE TO **OVER-USE** THE LEGS, MOVING THE LOWER HALF OF THE BODY SO FAR AND SO VIOLENTLY TARGETWARDS THAT THERE IS NO TIME TO UNWIND THE HIPS TO MAKE ROOM FOR THE HANDS AND ARMS TO SWING FREELY THROUGH ALONG THE TARGET LINE.

HOOKING, PUSHING AND PUSH-SLICING ARE SIGNS OF THIS FAULT.

Feel Firm in Your Left Side

BOTH ACCURACY AND POWER ARE LOST BY CRUMPLING OR COLLAPSING THE LEFT SIDE THROUGH IMPACT — A COMMON EVENT IN HIGH-HANDICAP PLAY.

COMING INTO THE BALL I HAVE THE FEELING OF EXTENDING AND FIRMING MY ENTIRE LEFT SIDE WITH THE EXCEPTION OF THE KNEE, WHICH REMAINS SLIGHTLY FLEXED.

THAT WAY I HAVE SOMETHING SOLID TO SWING MY ARMS AND THE CLUB PAST, WHILE ENSURING THAT MY RIGHT SIDE MOVES DOWN AND UNDER, NOT OUT AND AROUND.

Never Fully Straighten Left Knee

"HIT AGAINST A FIRM LEFT SIDE," GOLFERS ARE FREQUENTLY TOLD. UNFORTUNATELY, MANY INTERPRET THIS ADVICE TO MEAN HITTING AGAINST A STRAIGHT, STIFF, BRACED LEFT LEG. THIS CAUSES THE HIPS TO STOP TURNING AND THE CLUB TO BE THROWN OUT AND OVER THE BALL.

BY ALL MEANS STRETCH AND EXTEND YOUR LEFT SIDE THROUGH THE BALL, BUT DO IT WITH A SLIGHT **FLEX** IN THE LEFT KNEE.

THAT WAY YOUR HIPS CAN KEEP TURNING THROUGH THE SHOT, WHICH ALLOWS YOUR RIGHT SHOULDER TO SWING DOWN AND UNDER, NOT OUT AND AROUND.

Clear Hips on Through-Swing

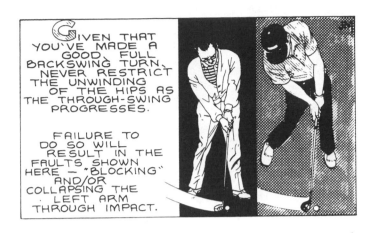

GIVEN THAT YOU'VE MADE A GOOD, FULL BACKSWING TURN, NEVER RESTRICT THE UNWINDING OF THE HIPS AS THE THROUGH-SWING PROGRESSES.

FAILURE TO DO SO WILL RESULT IN THE FAULTS SHOWN HERE — "BLOCKING" AND/OR COLLAPSING THE LEFT ARM THROUGH IMPACT.

CLEARING THE HIPS COMING DOWN IS THE ONLY WAY TO MAKE ROOM FOR YOUR ARMS TO SWING FREELY PAST YOUR BODY AND ON OUT TOWARDS THE TARGET.

SO WIND UP FULLY ON THE BACKSWING, THEN LET THOSE HIPS UNWIND AS YOUR LEGS MOVE YOU INTO THE BALL.

Practice ''Staying Down''

ANXIETY CAUSES MANY GOLFERS TO RAISE UP TOO QUICKLY AS THEY HIT THE BALL. SO DOES POOR SWING FORM. ONE ANTIDOTE TO BOTH IS TO PRACTICE DELIBERATELY "STAYING DOWN" LONGER THROUGH THE IMPACT AREA.

EASIEST WAY I KNOW TO ACHIEVE THIS IS TO TRY TO KEEP THE FOLLOW-THROUGH AS LOW AS POSSIBLE FOR AS LONG AS POSSIBLE. A FEELING OF EXTENDING THE ARMS AS FAR AS THEY'LL GO AFTER THE HIT IS ALSO HELPFUL.

SO IS KEEPING THE LEFT KNEE SLIGHTLY FLEXED THROUGH IMPACT.

Try This for Truer Swinging Motion

MANY HIGH-HANDICAPPERS WOULD IMPROVE ENORMOUSLY SIMPLY BY CONSCIOUSLY THINKING ON EVERY SHOT OF SWINGING THROUGH RATHER THAN TO THE BALL.

ONE USEFUL MENTAL PICTURE IS SIMPLY OF THE BALL ACCIDENTALLY HAPPENING TO BE ON THE CLUBHEAD PATH.

ANOTHER IS THINKING OF SWEEPING THE CLUB AS SMOOTHLY AS POSSIBLE THROUGH AN ARC FROM THREE OR FOUR FEET BEHIND THE BALL TO THREE OR FOUR FEET BEYOND IT.

Beware Letting Go of Club

LETTING GO OF THE CLUB AT SOME POINT IN THE SWING IS A COMMON CAUSE OF MISHITTING THE BALL AMONG LESS SKILLED GOLFERS.

YOU SHOULD STOP SHORT OF A VICE-LIKE GRIP, BUT THE CLUB MUST BE HELD SECURELY IF YOU HOPE TO DEVELOP ANY KIND OF SWING CONSISTENCY.

CHECK ESPECIALLY THAT YOU'RE HANGING ON FIRMLY WITH THE LITTLE FINGER OF YOUR LEFT HAND.

IN FACT, TO CONVINCE YOURSELF OF THE IMPORTANCE OF THIS FINGER IN WEDGING THE CLUB SECURELY AGAINST THE BUTT OF THE HAND, TRY HITTING SHOTS WITH IT OFF THE SHAFT.

YOU'LL GET THE MESSAGE VERY FAST, I PROMISE.

Let Hands Work Reflexively

OVER-ACTIVE HANDS CAUSE MANY OF THE OFF-SHOTS THAT PLAGUE HIGH-HANDICAPPERS.

OBVIOUSLY THE HANDS MUST DO A JOB IN THE GOLF SWING, BUT THEIR ROLE SHOULD BE AS **FOLLOWERS**, NOT LEADERS — THEY SHOULD WORK **REFLEXIVELY**, NOT AS CONTROLLERS OF THE ACTION.

TO "FEEL" THE PROPER ROLE OF THE HANDS, CONSCIOUSLY TRY TO MAKE THEM PASSIVE IN RELATION TO YOUR ARM, BODY AND LEG ACTION WHILE HITTING EASILY WITH A SHORT-IRON.

THINKING OF THE HANDS SIMPLY AS A HINGE OR CONNECTING LINK BETWEEN YOUR ARMS AND THE CLUB WILL HELP YOU DEVELOP THE PROPER **REFLEXIVE** HAND ACTION.

Beat "Throwing" Tendency This Way

THROWING THE CLUBHEAD AT THE BALL WITH THE HANDS AND WRISTS FROM THE TOP OF THE BACKSWING IS PROBABLY THE MOST COMMON SHOT-WRECKER IN GOLF. THE ONLY EFFECTIVE WAY TO PREVENT THIS ACTION IS TO BEGIN THE DOWNSWING WITH THE LEGS AND HIPS, AND HERE'S ONE WAY TO ACHIEVE THAT.

WORK ON THE FEELING OF TURNING THE SHOULDERS FULLY, THEN KEEPING THEM **FULLY COILED** AS LONG AS YOU POSSIBLY CAN WHILE YOUR KNEES MOVE TARGETWARDS AND YOUR HIPS UNWIND.

IT WILL TAKE EFFORT AND PRACTICE IF YOU ARE A HABITUAL "THROWER," BUT THE BENEFITS WILL BE IMMENSE.

Don't Let the Years Limit Your Swing

INCREASING YEARS MAKE IT TOUGHER TO SUSTAIN A FULL TURN AND GOOD ARM/CLUB EXTENSION, BUT DON'T GIVE UP TOO EASILY ON THESE BASICS OF AUTHORITATIVE SHOT-MAKING.

RATHER THAN RELYING ON SIMPLY YOUR HANDS AND ARMS TO SWING THE CLUB, IF YOU'RE A SENIOR TRY LETTING YOUR **HIPS TURN** MORE FULLY ALONG WITH YOUR SHOULDERS GOING BACK.

REMEMBER, SO LONG AS YOU DON'T SWAY YOUR BODY OR LOOSEN YOUR GRIP YOU WON'T LOSE CONTROL OVER THE CLUB — AND YOU MAY WELL REGAIN SOME VERY USEFUL DISTANCE.

Tuck Right Elbow for Later Hit

IF YOU TEND TO HIT "EARLY" WITH YOUR HANDS AND WRISTS, CHECK YOUR RIGHT ARM AND SHOULDER DOWNSWING ACTION.

IF THE RIGHT ELBOW FLIES FORWARD, OR THE SHOULDER RIDES TOO HIGH — OR BOTH — YOU'RE ALMOST BOUND TO "HIT FROM THE TOP."

PRACTICE KEEPING YOUR RIGHT ELBOW TUCKED IN RIGHT UP UNTIL IMPACT. THE CLOSER YOU CAN KEEP IT TO YOUR BODY COMING DOWN, THE MORE YOU'LL BE ABLE TO SWING YOUR RIGHT SHOULDER "UNDER" YOUR HEAD — AND THE LATER THAT WILL ALLOW YOU TO RELEASE YOUR WRISTS.

Don't "Poke" with Your Irons

HIT YOUR WOODS BETTER THAN YOUR IRONS MUCH OF THE TIME?

COULD BE YOU ARE SUFFERING FROM THAT COMMON WEEKENDER'S DISEASE, "ACCURACY-ANXIETY."

IN OTHER WORDS, YOU'RE POKING AT THE BALL WITH THE IRONS BECAUSE YOU'RE OVERLY DIRECTION-CONSCIOUS.

CURE IS TO THINK OF **SWINGING** THE CLUB **THROUGH** THE BALL TO THE TARGET, INSTEAD OF TRYING TO "PLACE" THE BALL ON A PARTICULAR SPOT BY HITTING AT IT. AIM AND ALIGN YOURSELF PROPERLY, THEN LET IT ALL GO AS FREELY AS YOU DO WITH THE WOODS.

YOU MAY STILL MISS A FEW TARGETS, BUT NOT AS MANY AS BY TRYING TO STEER THE BALL TO THEM.

Beware Swinging Too Flat

A VERY COMMON FAULT AMONG HIGH HANDICAPPERS IS A FLAT OR HORIZONTAL SHOULDER TURN AWAY FROM THE BALL. THIS CAUSES THE LEFT ELBOW TO FLY FORWARD - TOWARDS THE BALL - AND THE CLUB TO BE PICKED UP WITH THE HANDS AND ARMS AND "LAID OFF" AT THE TOP.

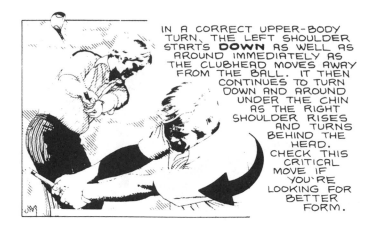

IN A CORRECT UPPER-BODY TURN, THE LEFT SHOULDER STARTS **DOWN** AS WELL AS AROUND IMMEDIATELY AS THE CLUBHEAD MOVES AWAY FROM THE BALL. IT THEN CONTINUES TO TURN DOWN AND AROUND UNDER THE CHIN AS THE RIGHT SHOULDER RISES AND TURNS BEHIND THE HEAD. CHECK THIS CRITICAL MOVE IF YOU'RE LOOKING FOR BETTER FORM.

Don't Be an Outward Looper

QUITE A NUMBER OF GOOD GOLFERS LOOP THE CLUB **INWARD** AT SOME POINT IN THE SWING.

ONLY POOR GOLFERS LOOP IT **OUTWARD**, ALWAYS WITH PAINFUL RESULTS.

COMMON CAUSE OF OUTWARD LOOPING OR "THROWING" IS SWAYING RATHER THAN TURNING THE HIPS GOING BACK. THIS CAUSES SPINNING AROUND THE RIGHT HIP STARTING DOWN, WHICH FORCES THE CLUB FORWARD BEYOND ITS CORRECT ARC.

CURE LIES IN <u>TURNING</u> THE HIPS GOING BACK, THEN <u>SLIDE-TURNING</u> THEM GOING DOWN AND THROUGH.

Aim Club at Target at Top of Swing

"LAY OFF" THE CLUB AT THE TOP OF THE BACKSWING AND YOU ENCOURAGE AN OUTSIDE-IN CLUBHEAD PATH AT IMPACT.

CONVERSELY, "CROSS THE LINE" AT THE TOP AND YOU RISK AN <u>INSIDE-OUT</u> ATTACK ON THE BALL.

IDEAL CLUB POSITION AT THE TOP IS POINTING DIRECTLY AT THE TARGET.

THUS ALIGNED, NO SWING COMPENSATION OR CLUB MANIPULATION IS NECESSARY TO DELIVER THE CLUBHEAD TO THE BALL TRAVELING <u>ALONG</u> RATHER THAN ACROSS, THE TARGET LINE AT IMPACT.

Firm Wrists to Prevent Over-Swing

SWINGING TOO FAR BACK CAN CAUSE CLUBHEAD DECELERATION BEFORE IMPACT UNLESS A GOLFER IS VERY SUPPLE OR WELL COORDINATED.

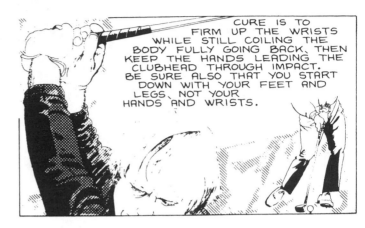

CURE IS TO FIRM UP THE WRISTS WHILE STILL COILING THE BODY FULLY GOING BACK. THEN KEEP THE HANDS LEADING THE CLUBHEAD THROUGH IMPACT. BE SURE ALSO THAT YOU START DOWN WITH YOUR FEET AND LEGS, NOT YOUR HANDS AND WRISTS.

39

Hitting Farther

Relax More Before Big Drive

TRY THIS APPROACH WHEN YOU NEED AN EXTRA BIG DRIVE.

FIRST, **RELAX** — LET YOUR MUSCLES GO AS LOOSE AND EASY AS POSSIBLE AS YOU WALK TO THE TEE. NEXT, AVOID ANY BUILD UP OF TENSION BY BEGINNING THE SWING AS SOON AS YOU FEEL COMFORTABLY SET UP TO THE BALL.

FINALLY, TRY TO SWING THE CLUB AWAY FROM THE BALL AS **LEISURELY** AND **DELIBERATELY** AS POSSIBLE.

I THINK YOU'LL FIND THIS "EASY" APPROACH ADDS USEFUL EXTRA YARDAGE -- BUT KEEP THE BIG ONES FOR WHEN ACCURACY ISN'T A KEY FACTOR.

EASY does it

Tee the Ball Higher

TIME AND AGAIN I SEE PRO-AM PARTNERS GIVING UP YARDS ON DRIVES SIMPLY BY TEEING THE BALL TOO **LOW**.

THE PICTURE TELLS WHY: THE LOWER YOU TEE THE BALL, THE MORE **DOWNWARD** RATHER THAN DIRECTLY FORWARD YOU'LL APPLY THE FORCE OF THE CLUBHEAD.

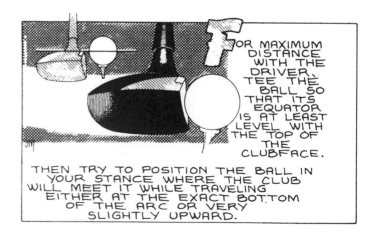

FOR MAXIMUM DISTANCE WITH THE DRIVER, TEE THE BALL SO THAT ITS EQUATOR IS AT LEAST LEVEL WITH THE TOP OF THE CLUBFACE.

THEN TRY TO POSITION THE BALL IN YOUR STANCE WHERE THE CLUB WILL MEET IT WHILE TRAVELING EITHER AT THE EXACT BOTTOM OF THE ARC OR VERY SLIGHTLY UPWARD.

Adjust Your Stance

TRY A SMALL STANCE ADJUSTMENT ANY TIME YOU NEED AN EXTRA BIG HIT. SIMPLY ANGLE YOUR LEFT FOOT A LITTLE MORE TOWARDS THE TARGET - SAY AT 45 DEGREES.

POSITIONING THE LEAD FOOT THUS HAS THE EFFECT OF ACCELERATING THE LOWER BODY UNCOILING DURING THE DOWN-SWING, WHICH INCREASES LEVERAGE AND THEREBY CLUBHEAD SPEED.

BUT BE SURE TO KEEP YOUR UPPER BODY WELL BEHIND THE BALL AS YOUR LOWER HALF GOES TO WORK.

Hit Through, Not to, the Ball

HITTING AT, NOT THROUGH, THE GOLF BALL IS ONE OF THE MOST COSTLY FAULTS YOU CAN COMMIT IN TERMS OF BOTH LOST DISTANCE AND OFF-LINE TRAJECTORY.

IT SEEMS PARTICULARLY PREVALENT AMONG AMATEURS WITH THE WOODS AND LONG IRONS.

TO BEAT THIS TENDENCY, FOCUS IN PRACTICE ON GENERATING MAXIMUM CLUB-HEAD SPEED THROUGHOUT THE **ENTIRE IMPACT ZONE**, NOT JUST AT THE BALL. IN OTHER WORDS, TRY TO AGGRESSIVELY HIT THROUGH AN AREA SAY A COUPLE OF FEET BEHIND AND A COUPLE OF FEET BEYOND THE BALL, RATHER THAN JUST AT THAT LITTLE OBJECT ITSELF.

Seek a More Solid Strike

HOW FAR YOU CAN HIT THE BALL IS DETERMINED BY HOW FAST YOU CAN SWING THE CLUBHEAD **SQUARELY** THROUGH IT.

THROUGH PRACTICE, A FEW GOLFERS COULD DEVELOP MORE CLUBHEAD SPEED AND STILL HIT SQUARELY. BUT MOST LONG HANDICAPPERS WOULD GET MORE DISTANCE BY SACRIFICING A LITTLE CLUBHEAD SPEED FOR A MORE SOLID CLUBFACE DELIVERY.

2-2

Increase Your Swing Arc

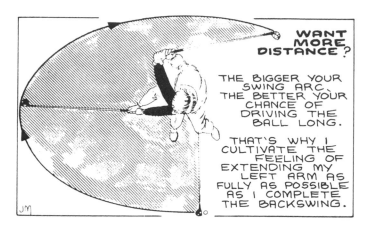

WANT MORE DISTANCE?

THE BIGGER YOUR SWING ARC, THE BETTER YOUR CHANCE OF DRIVING THE BALL LONG.

THAT'S WHY I CULTIVATE THE FEELING OF EXTENDING MY LEFT ARM AS FULLY AS POSSIBLE AS I COMPLETE THE BACKSWING.

MANY GOLFERS CRAMP THEMSELVES BY TRYING TO OVER-CONTROL THE SWING.

AS LONG AS YOU DON'T SWAY OR RAISE YOUR HEAD AND UPPER BODY, OR LOOSEN YOUR GRIP, "**REACHING FOR THE SKY**" SHOULD ADD POWER TO YOUR SHOTS WITHOUT LOSS OF ACCURACY.

Work on a Full Upper-Body Coil

WANT TO HIT FARTHER?

HERE'S MY FORMULA: **DISTANCE** COMES FROM CLUBHEAD SPEED SQUARELY APPLIED, CLUBHEAD SPEED COMES FROM LEVERAGE, AND LEVERAGE COMES FROM TORSION OR TORQUE.

THEREFORE, THE FARTHER AND TIGHTER YOU CAN WIND THE UPPER PART OF YOUR BODY AGAINST THE RESISTANCE OF YOUR LOWER HALF, THE BETTER THE CHAIN REACTION AND THE GREATER THE CLUBHEAD SPEED YOU'LL CREATE.

SO WORK ON COILING YOURSELF FULLY GOING BACK.

Go Back Before You Start Down

SOMETIMES BOTH GREAT ACCURACY **AND** MAXIMUM DISTANCE ARE ESSENTIAL ON A DRIVE. IN THOSE CIRCUMSTANCES MY PRIMARY CONCERN IS TO START THE CLUB BACK FROM THE BALL AS SLOWLY AND SMOOTHLY AS I POSSIBLY CAN.

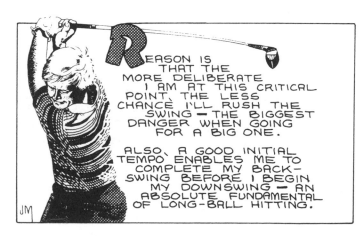

REASON IS THAT THE MORE DELIBERATE I AM AT THIS CRITICAL POINT, THE LESS CHANCE I'LL RUSH THE SWING — THE BIGGEST DANGER WHEN GOING FOR A BIG ONE.

ALSO, A GOOD INITIAL TEMPO ENABLES ME TO COMPLETE MY BACKSWING BEFORE I BEGIN MY DOWNSWING — AN ABSOLUTE FUNDAMENTAL OF LONG-BALL HITTING.

"Draw" Shots to Beat the Years

LOSING DISTANCE AS TIME MARCHES ON?

IF YOU'VE ALWAYS TENDED TO SLICE OR FADE THE BALL THERE'S A SURE WAY TO DELAY THAT PROCESS, BUT IT WILL PROBABLY REQUIRE BOTH WORK AND PATIENCE.

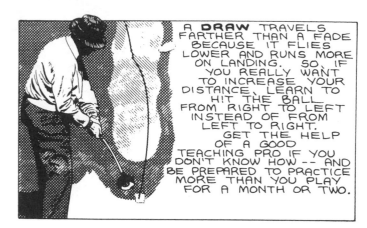

A DRAW TRAVELS FARTHER THAN A FADE BECAUSE IT FLIES LOWER AND RUNS MORE ON LANDING. SO, IF YOU REALLY WANT TO INCREASE YOUR DISTANCE, LEARN TO HIT THE BALL FROM RIGHT TO LEFT INSTEAD OF FROM LEFT TO RIGHT. GET THE HELP OF A GOOD TEACHING PRO IF YOU DON'T KNOW HOW -- AND BE PREPARED TO PRACTICE MORE THAN YOU PLAY FOR A MONTH OR TWO.

40

Slicing and Hooking, Pulling and Pushing

Match Clubface Aim and Clubhead Path . . .

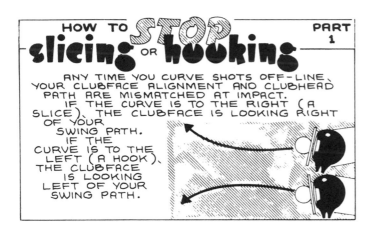

HOW TO STOP
slicing OR hooking
PART 1

ANY TIME YOU CURVE SHOTS OFF-LINE, YOUR CLUBFACE ALIGNMENT AND CLUBHEAD PATH ARE MISMATCHED AT IMPACT.
IF THE CURVE IS TO THE RIGHT (A SLICE), THE CLUBFACE IS LOOKING RIGHT OF YOUR SWING PATH.
IF THE CURVE IS TO THE LEFT (A HOOK), THE CLUBFACE IS LOOKING LEFT OF YOUR SWING PATH.

USUALLY THIS MISMATCHING IS THE RESULT OF A FAULTY GRIP. IF YOU SLICE, MOVE BOTH HANDS GRADUALLY MORE TO THE **RIGHT** UNTIL THE BALL FLIES STRAIGHT IN THE SAME DIRECTION AS IT STARTS, WHICH WILL BE TO THE LEFT OF TARGET. REVERSE THAT PROCESS — MOVE YOUR HANDS GRADUALLY **LEFT** — IF YOU PREDOMINANTLY HOOK SHOTS.

. . . Then Adjust Your Body Set-Up

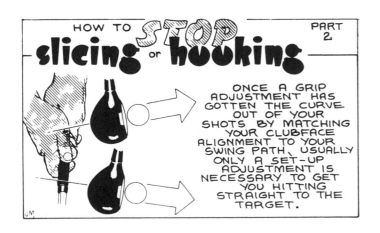

HOW TO STOP
slicing OR hooking
PART 2

ONCE A GRIP ADJUSTMENT HAS GOTTEN THE CURVE OUT OF YOUR SHOTS BY MATCHING YOUR CLUBFACE ALIGNMENT TO YOUR SWING PATH, USUALLY ONLY A SET-UP ADJUSTMENT IS NECESSARY TO GET YOU HITTING STRAIGHT TO THE TARGET.

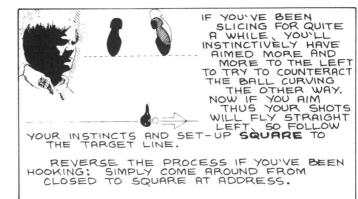

IF YOU'VE BEEN SLICING FOR QUITE A WHILE, YOU'LL INSTINCTIVELY HAVE AIMED MORE AND MORE TO THE LEFT TO TRY TO COUNTERACT THE BALL CURVING THE OTHER WAY. NOW IF YOU AIM THUS YOUR SHOTS WILL FLY STRAIGHT LEFT. SO FOLLOW YOUR INSTINCTS AND SET-UP **SQUARE** TO THE TARGET LINE.

REVERSE THE PROCESS IF YOU'VE BEEN HOOKING: SIMPLY COME AROUND FROM CLOSED TO SQUARE AT ADDRESS.

Always Double-Check Address Alignment

FIRST THING TO CHECK WHENEVER YOU BEGIN SLICING OR HOOKING THE BALL BADLY IS THAT YOU ARE SQUARELY ALIGNED AT ADDRESS — THAT YOUR FEET, HIPS AND SHOULDERS **PARALLEL** YOUR TARGET LINE.

IF YOU'VE BEEN ALIGNED LEFT IN SQUARING UP, YOU'LL INSTINCTIVELY WANT TO MOVE THE BALL FARTHER BACK IN YOUR STANCE — OR FARTHER FORWARD IF YOU'VE BEEN AIMING RIGHT.

LETTING THAT HAPPEN IS THE ESSENTIAL SECOND STEP IN IMPROVING YOUR SWING PATH.

Keep Your Upper Body "Quieter"

GOLFERS WHO SLICE MANY SHOTS AND ALSO SHANK OCCASIONALLY WITH THE IRONS CAN BE SURE THE PROBLEM LIES IN THEIR UPPER-BODY ACTION STARTING THE DOWNSWING. "CASTING" WITH THE HANDS, AND HITTING WITH THE SHOULDERS FROM THE TOP, THROWS THE CLUB OUTWARD AND ACROSS THE TARGET LINE FROM OUT-TO-IN. WHEN THE OUTWARD MOVEMENT IS PARTICULARLY SEVERE, CONTACT IS ON THE HOSEL RATHER THAN THE CLUB'S BLADE.

THE CURE TO BOTH PROBLEMS LIES IN KEEPING THE UPPER BODY QUIETER OR MORE PASSIVE, AND USING THE LEGS AND HIPS TO **PULL** THE CLUB DOWN, RATHER THAN THROWING IT OUTWARD AT THE BALL.

WATCH THE TOUR PROS TO GET THE FEEL OF THIS VITAL GOLFING MOVE.

Try This "Band-Aid" if You Must

EVER BEEN SUDDENLY STRUCK WITH A CRIPPLING **SLICE** — BAD ENOUGH TO MAKE YOU WONDER IF YOU'LL HAVE ENOUGH BALLS TO COMPLETE THE ROUND??

HERE'S A "BAND-AID" TO AT LEAST GET YOU AS FAR AS THE PRO SHOP TO MAKE A DATE FOR A LESSON.

SIMPLY MOVE THE BALL BACK AT ADDRESS AS FAR AS YOU CAN MAKE YOURSELF. THIS WILL HAVE THE EFFECT OF SQUARING UP YOUR SHOULDERS SOMEWHAT, AND THEREBY GREATLY INCREASE YOUR CHANCE OF MAKING CONTACT BEFORE THE CLUB SWINGS BEYOND THE TARGET LINE.

BUT **DO** STILL GO TO WORK WITH THE PRO LATER.

Consider Making Fade Work for You

"Palm" Club More to Reduce Hook

Check Your Ball Position

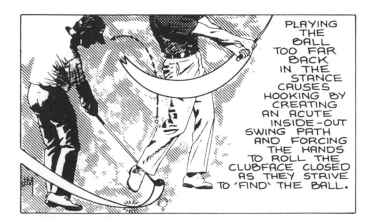

Start to Swing Straight Back

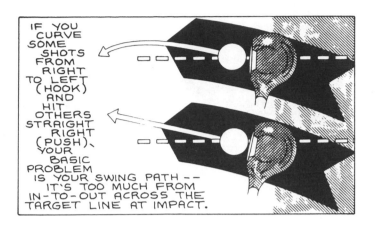

IF YOU CURVE SOME SHOTS FROM RIGHT TO LEFT (HOOK) AND HIT OTHERS STRAIGHT RIGHT (PUSH), YOUR BASIC PROBLEM IS YOUR SWING PATH -- IT'S TOO MUCH FROM IN-TO-OUT ACROSS THE TARGET LINE AT IMPACT.

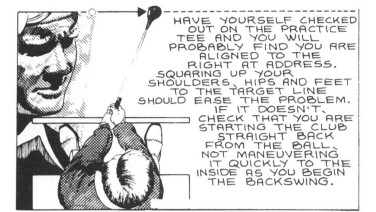

HAVE YOURSELF CHECKED OUT ON THE PRACTICE TEE AND YOU WILL PROBABLY FIND YOU ARE ALIGNED TO THE RIGHT AT ADDRESS. SQUARING UP YOUR SHOULDERS, HIPS AND FEET TO THE TARGET LINE SHOULD EASE THE PROBLEM. IF IT DOESN'T, CHECK THAT YOU ARE STARTING THE CLUB STRAIGHT BACK FROM THE BALL, NOT MANEUVERING IT QUICKLY TO THE INSIDE AS YOU BEGIN THE BACKSWING.

Check Your Left Wrist Action

GOT A SUDDEN CASE OF THE **HOOKS**??

IF YOU FEEL YOU ARE BASICALLY SWINGING WELL BUT THE BALL KEEPS CURVING TO THE LEFT, CHECK YOUR LEFT WRIST ACTION THROUGH IMPACT.

NO

YES

TOO RELAXED OR "SOFT" A LEFT WRIST AS YOU'RE HITTING THROUGH THE BALL ALLOWS THE HARD-HITTING RIGHT HAND TO ROLL OVER THE LEFT TOO QUICKLY, CLOSING THE CLUBFACE AND SPINNING THE BALL TO THE LEFT. SIMPLY FIRMING UP THE LEFT WRIST MIGHT BE THE ONLY "MEDICINE" YOU NEED.

Improve Your Lower-Body Motion

HERE ARE A NUMBER OF CAUSES OF HOOKING, BUT ONE OF THE MOST PREVALENT IS INSUFFICIENT OR IMPROPER LOWER-BODY ACTION ON THE DOWNSWING.

TO PUT IT ANOTHER WAY, MANY GOLFERS HOOK SHOTS SIMPLY BY "GETTING IN THEIR OWN WAY."

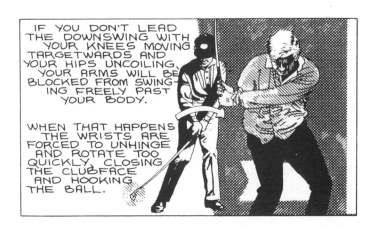

IF YOU DON'T LEAD THE DOWNSWING WITH YOUR KNEES MOVING TARGETWARDS AND YOUR HIPS UNCOILING, YOUR ARMS WILL BE BLOCKED FROM SWINGING FREELY PAST YOUR BODY.

WHEN THAT HAPPENS THE WRISTS ARE FORCED TO UNHINGE AND ROTATE TOO QUICKLY, CLOSING THE CLUBFACE AND HOOKING THE BALL.

Beware Trying to "Kill" the Ball

A DUCK-HOOK IS A SHOT WHERE THE BALL DIVES QUICKLY LEFT AND EARTHWARD AFTER TRAVELING ONLY SOME 50 TO 100 YARDS.

MAJOR CAUSE OF THIS HIGHLY DESTRUCTIVE SHOT IS WHIRLING THE BODY AROUND FROM THE TOP OF THE BACKSWING, OFTEN AS THE RESULT OF TRYING TO HIT HARDER.

CURE IS BETTER DOWNSWING-INITIATING LEG ACTION, COMBINED WITH MORE PASSIVE SHOULDERS AND HANDS UNTIL CENTRIFUGAL FORCE NATURALLY CAUSES THE CLUBHEAD TO BE RELEASED.

Focus on the Swing Path

IF YOU ARE MISDIRECTING THE BALL BADLY — PARTICULARLY PULLING OR PUSHING IT STRAIGHT LEFT OR RIGHT — HERE'S A TIP THAT MIGHT HELP YOU.

SET UP SQUARE AND MAKE A COUPLE OF PRACTICE SWINGS MENTALLY VISUALIZING THE PATH THE CLUBHEAD FOLLOWS ON ITS FIRST FEW FEET BACK FROM THE BALL.

THEN, ON THE SHOT PROPER, FOCUS YOUR MIND SOLELY ON TRYING TO MAKE THE CLUBHEAD RETURN INTO THE BALL ALONG THE **SAME PATH.**

Move Your Weight Faster

PULLING SHOTS STRAIGHT LEFT IS A PROBLEM EVEN TOP PLAYERS ENCOUNTER PERIODICALLY.

BASIC CAUSE IS SWINGING THE CLUBHEAD ACROSS THE TARGET LINE FROM OUT TO IN THROUGH IMPACT.

FREQUENT CAUSE OF THAT FAULT IS TOO LATE A WEIGHT TRANSFER TO THE LEFT SIDE DURING THE DOWNSWING.

CURE IS TO CONCENTRATE ON SHIFTING YOUR WEIGHT SMARTLY BUT SMOOTHLY TO YOUR LEFT, WHILE SWINGING YOUR RIGHT SHOULDER DOWN AND UNDER A STEADY HEAD.

Make Sure You Coil Fully

INSUFFICIENT SHOULDER TURN IS THE CHIEF CAUSE OF A PULL OR PULL-HOOK.

WHEN THEY'RE INSUFFICIENTLY TURNED GOING BACK, YOUR SHOULDERS UNWIND TOO FAR TOO FAST IN THE DOWNSWING, CAUSING AN OUT-TO-IN SWING PATH AT IMPACT.

IN ADDITION TO MAKING A FULL BACKSWING TURN, IT'S IMPORTANT FOR THE PULLER OR PULL-HOOKER TO WORK AT MAKING THE SHOULDERS LAG MOMENTARILY BEHIND THE LEG ACTION STARTING DOWN.

SEEK THE FEELING THAT THE LOWER BODY IS PULLING THE UPPER BODY ALONG AFTER IT, NOT THE OTHER WAY AROUND.

Check Ball Position if You're Pushing

IF YOU PUSH OR PUSH-SLICE A LOT OF SHOTS TO THE RIGHT, CHECK YOUR BALL POSITION AT ADDRESS. COULD BE SITUATING THE BALL TOO FAR BACK IN YOUR STANCE IS CAUSING YOU TO HIT IT WHILE THE CLUB IS STILL TRAVELING TO THE RIGHT OF — RATHER THAN STRAIGHT ALONG — THE TARGET LINE.

CONVERSELY, IF YOU PULL OR PULL-HOOK A LOT OF SHOTS, COULD BE THE BALL IS TOO FAR FORWARD, CAUSING THE CLUB TO STRIKE IT AFTER IT'S STARTED BACK TO THE LEFT OF THE TARGET LINE.

FINDING THE BALL POSITION THAT COINCIDES WITH YOUR CLUBHEAD PATH MOMENTARILY PARALLELING YOUR TARGET LINE CAN SOLVE A TON OF DIRECTIONAL PROBLEMS.

Don't "Get in Your Own Way"

"BLOCKING" SHOTS TO THE RIGHT, WITH OCCASIONAL DUCK HOOKS THROWN IN?

COULD BE YOU'RE NOT GETTING OUT OF YOUR OWN WAY AS YOU SWING THROUGH THE BALL.

IF YOUR HIPS DON'T UNCOIL TARGETWARDS AS YOUR KNEES LEAD THE DOWNSWING, YOU'LL MAKE INSUFFICIENT ROOM FOR YOUR ARMS TO SWING FREELY PAST YOUR BODY.

RESULT GENERALLY IS EITHER A SHOT PUSHED RIGHT IF YOUR WRISTS DON'T ROLL OVER THROUGH IMPACT, OR A FAST HOOK TO THE LEFT IF THEY DO.

41

Other Mis-hits

Check Your Weight Distribution

HITTING A LOT OF WOOD SHOTS OUT OF THE HEEL??

SHANKING IRON SHOTS OCCASIONALLY?

CHECK YOUR WEIGHT DISTRIBUTION BOTH AT ADDRESS AND DURING THE SWING.

SWINGING WITH YOUR WEIGHT TOO FAR FORWARD — TOO MUCH TOWARDS YOUR TOES — CAN CAUSE YOU TO FALL FORWARD THROUGH IMPACT.

TRY SETTING YOUR WEIGHT BACK MORE TOWARDS YOUR HEELS AT ADDRESS, AND THEN KEEPING IT THERE THROUGHOUT THE SWING.

JM

Don't Rise Up Coming Down

COMING OFF THE BALL?

THE SYMPTOMS ARE TOPPING, SLICING AND PULLING — ALTHOUGH ANY KIND OF MIS-HIT CAN RESULT.

JM

MAIN CAUSE OF THIS COSTLY FAULT IS RAISING UP DURING THE DOWNSWING — ESPECIALLY THE HEAD. ANTIDOTE IS TO PRACTICE WITH YOUR HEAD "FIXED" INTO POSITION, AND YOUR EYES GLUED TO THE ORIGINAL BALL POSITION FOR AS LONG AS POSSIBLE. ALSO, KEEP A LITTLE FLEX IN YOUR KNEES WELL INTO THE FOLLOW-THROUGH.

Understand What Causes a Shank

ANY GOLFER WHO SHANKS THE BALL MORE THAN VERY OCCASIONALLY NEEDS PROFESSIONAL HELP, BECAUSE HE DEFINITELY POSSESSES SOME MAJOR SWING FLAWS.

BASIC CAUSE OF SHANKING IS MOVING THE PLANE OF THE SWING **OUTWARD** COMING DOWN.

STANDING TOO CLOSE TO THE BALL CAN PRODUCE THIS SOUL-DESTROYING SHOT, IN THAT IT FORCES THE ARMS OUTWARD IN ORDER TO SWING PAST THE BODY.

SO CAN STANDING TOO FAR FROM THE BALL, BY CAUSING THE GOLFER TO "THROW" THE CLUBHEAD FROM THE TOP, OR TO TOPPLE FORWARD DURING THE DOWNSWING, OR BOTH.

To Stop Shanking, Look to Your Head . . .

A **SHANK** IS CAUSED BY THE HOSEL RATHER THAN THE FACE OF THE CLUB CONTACTING THE BALL.

IT'S BY FAR THE WORST SHOT IN GOLF — IN FACT, IF IT BECOMES HABITUAL, IT MAKES THE GAME VIRTUALLY IMPOSSIBLE.

A LOT OF SWING FACTORS CAN CAUSE OR CONTRIBUTE TO A SHANK. HOWEVER, THE UNDERLYING FACTOR IN MOST CASES I'VE SEEN IS HEAD MOTION. LINE UP AT A REASONABLE DISTANCE FROM THE BALL — NEITHER REACHING NOR CROWDING — AND KEEP YOUR HEAD STEADY THROUGHOUT THE SWING, AND YOU WILL VERY RARELY SHANK A SHOT.

. . . Then Try This

MY LIFELONG TEACHER, JACK GROUT, HAD AN EFFECTIVE WAY OF CURING SHANKING.

FIRST, HE'D ASK THE SUFFERER TO ADDRESS THE BALL OPPOSITE THE TOE OF THE CLUB AND THEN TRY TO HIT IT THERE.

NEXT, IF THIS ALONE DIDN'T FIX THE PROBLEM, HE WOULD ASK THE PUPIL TO FIRM UP HIS WRIST ACTION DURING THE SWING.

THIS GENERALLY DID THE TRICK, IN THAT EXCESSIVE WRIST ACTION OFTEN CAUSES THE CLUB TO BE THROWN OUTWARD ON THE DOWNSWING, THUS CAUSING THE HOSEL RATHER THAN THE BLADE TO MAKE CONTACT WITH THE BALL.

FLOPPY

Sweep Club Back Low to Stop "Skying"

"SKIED" OR "BALLOONED" SHOTS ARE THE RESULT OF HITTING DOWN INTO THE BALL TOO STEEPLY.

THIS IS CAUSED IN NUMEROUS WAYS, ONE OF THE MOST COMMON BEING A TOO-EARLY COCKING OF THE WRISTS IN THE BACKSWING.

THIS CREATES A VERY ABRUPT ARC BOTH AWAY FROM AND BACK TO THE BALL THAT CAN RESULT IN ALL SORTS OF IMPACT FAULTS, AS WELL AS "SKYING."

CURE IS TO START THE CLUB BACK LOW TO THE GROUND IN A ONE-PIECE HANDS/ARM/SHOULDERS SWEEPING MOTION. TRY TO ALLOW YOUR WRISTS TO COCK ONLY IN RESPONSE TO THE SWINGING MOMENTUM OF THE CLUBHEAD.

Move Ball and Head Back to Quit "Thinking"

HITTING A LOT OF SHOTS "THIN," WITH AN OCCASIONAL FULL-BLOODED TOP? TRY MOVING BOTH THE **BALL** AND YOUR **HEAD** A LITTLE FARTHER BACK (AWAY FROM THE TARGET) AT ADDRESS.

AND **KEEP** YOUR HEAD BACK THERE AS YOU SWING DOWN AND THROUGH.

IF THAT DOESN'T WORK, CHECK THAT YOU'RE RELEASING FULLY ENOUGH COMING INTO IMPACT TO SWING THE CLUBHEAD INTO THE BACK OF THE BALL AT GROUND LEVEL.

IN OTHER WORDS, DON'T HOLD BACK WITH YOUR HANDS AND WRISTS ONCE YOUR LEGS HAVE GONE TO WORK.

Keep Fixed Axis to Stop Hitting "Fat"

LOOK FOR AWAY-FROM-THE-TARGET HEAD AND BODY SWAY GOING BACK WHENEVER YOU CATCH THE GROUND BEHIND THE BALL.

ANY UPPER BODY MOVEMENT AWAY FROM THE TARGET DURING THE BACKSWING OBVIOUSLY MOVES THE ENTIRE ARC OF THE SWING BACKWARDS ALSO.

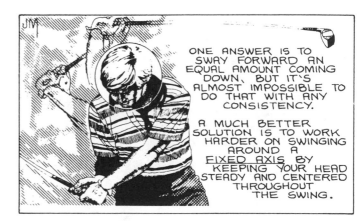

ONE ANSWER IS TO SWAY FORWARD AN EQUAL AMOUNT COMING DOWN, BUT IT'S ALMOST IMPOSSIBLE TO DO THAT WITH ANY CONSISTENCY.

A MUCH BETTER SOLUTION IS TO WORK HARDER ON SWINGING AROUND A FIXED AXIS BY KEEPING YOUR HEAD STEADY AND CENTERED THROUGHOUT THE SWING.

Eliminate Reverse Weight Shift

TOPPED SHOTS — AND A LOT OF OTHER FAULTS — ARE OFTEN CAUSED BY THE REVERSE WEIGHT SHIFT SHOWN HERE ... THE "FIRE AND FALL BACK," AS IT'S OFTEN CALLED. LESSONS FROM A PROFESSIONAL ARE GENERALLY THE BEST ANSWER TO THIS KIND OF ACTION.

JM

HOWEVER, IF YOU WANT TO TRY SOME SELF-HELP, THEN WORK ON GETTING YOUR WEIGHT ALMOST ENTIRELY OVER ONTO YOUR **LEFT** SIDE BEFORE THE CLUB MEETS THE BALL.

(LETTING YOUR WEIGHT MOVE FULLY TO THE RIGHT SIDE GOING BACK WILL HELP YOU MAKE THAT ESSENTIAL DOWNSWING SHIFT.)

Lead Clubhead with Hands at Impact

HITTING "**FAT**"?? **TOPPING** SHOTS??

BOTH THESE PROBLEMS CAN COME FROM ALLOWING THE CLUBHEAD TO GET AHEAD OF THE HANDS PRIOR TO IMPACT, AS IN THE ILLUSTRATION. OFTEN THE BASIC FAULT LIES AT ADDRESS.

SET-UP TO THE BALL WITH THE CLUBHEAD AHEAD OF THE HANDS AND INSTINCTIVELY YOU'LL DELIVER IT THAT WAY AT IMPACT.

TO CURE THE FAULT, ADDRESS THE BALL AS I DO WITH THE LEFT ARM AND CLUBSHAFT IN A STRAIGHT LINE, WHICH AUTOMATICALLY SETS THE HANDS WHERE THEY SHOULD BE AT IMPACT — A LITTLE AHEAD OF THE BALL.

Be Sure to Release in Time

VARIOUS SWING FAULTS CAN CAUSE **TOPPING** — HITTING THE BALL ABOVE ITS EQUATOR — BUT ONE OF THE MOST COMMON AMONG GOOD GOLFERS IS TRYING TO **KILL** SHOTS!!

IT'S NATURAL WHEN REALLY GOING FOR A BIG ONE TO ACCELERATE THE LEG AND HIP ACTION ON THE DOWNSWING, BUT THIS CAN EASILY OVERDELAY THE RELEASE OF THE CLUBHEAD, CAUSING WHAT YOU SEE HERE.

SO BE SURE TO RELEASE SOON ENOUGH WITH YOUR HANDS AND WRISTS WHEN YOU'RE SEEKING EXTRA DISTANCE.

JM

42

Difficult Lies and Different Flights

Consider All the Options

SOMETIMES A DROP CLEAR AND AN UNPLAYABLE-LIE PENALTY IS THE ONLY WAY OUT OF A TROUBLE SITUATION.

BUT DON'T MAKE THAT DECISION BEFORE YOU'VE FULLY CONSIDERED ALL THE OPTIONS.

I'VE SAVED SHOTS MANY TIMES IN MY CAREER BY:

— PLAYING LEFT-HANDED.

— BOUNCING THE BALL BACK INTO PLAY OFF A WALL OR OTHER OBSTACLE.

— BUNTING THE BALL CLEAR WITH A PUTTER.

Adjust Thus for Ball Below Feet

HERE'S THE ROUTINE TO FOLLOW WHEN THE BALL IS BELOW THE LEVEL OF YOUR FEET.

1) BEND MORE AT THE KNEES AND WAIST, AND GRIP THE CLUB AS CLOSE TO ITS END AS POSSIBLE, TO ENABLE YOU TO GET WELL "DOWN" TO THE SHOT.

2) SET MOST OF YOUR WEIGHT ON YOUR HEELS TO HELP YOU STAY BALANCED.

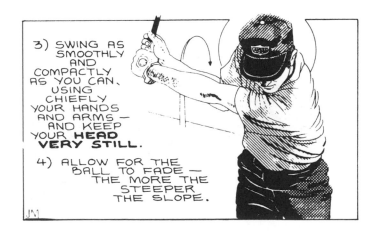

3) SWING AS SMOOTHLY AND COMPACTLY AS YOU CAN, USING CHIEFLY YOUR HANDS AND ARMS — AND KEEP YOUR **HEAD VERY STILL.**

4) ALLOW FOR THE BALL TO FADE — THE MORE THE STEEPER THE SLOPE.

And Like This for Ball Above Feet

HERE'S A CHECKLIST OF THE CHIEF ADJUSTMENTS TO MAKE WHEN THE BALL IS ABOVE THE LEVEL OF YOUR FEET.

1) STAND MORE ERECT THAN USUAL AND CHOKE DOWN ON THE CLUB TO IMPROVE YOUR BALANCE.

2) SET YOUR WEIGHT MORE TOWARD YOUR TOES TO FURTHER IMPROVE YOUR BALANCE.

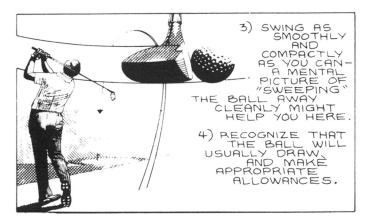

3) SWING AS SMOOTHLY AND COMPACTLY AS YOU CAN—A MENTAL PICTURE OF "SWEEPING" THE BALL AWAY CLEANLY MIGHT HELP YOU HERE.

4) RECOGNIZE THAT THE BALL WILL USUALLY DRAW, AND MAKE APPROPRIATE ALLOWANCES.

Strive for Balance on Downhill Lie

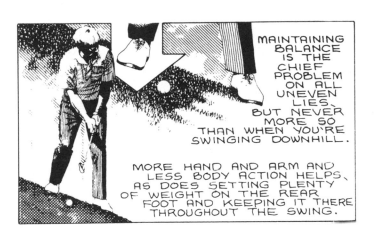

MAINTAINING BALANCE IS THE CHIEF PROBLEM ON ALL UNEVEN LIES, BUT NEVER MORE SO THAN WHEN YOU'RE SWINGING DOWNHILL.

MORE HAND AND ARM AND LESS BODY ACTION HELPS, AS DOES SETTING PLENTY OF WEIGHT ON THE REAR FOOT AND KEEPING IT THERE THROUGHOUT THE SWING.

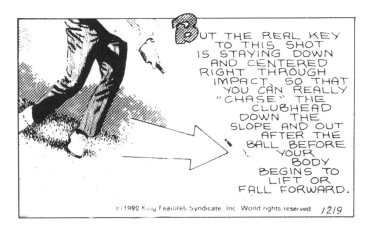

BUT THE REAL KEY TO THIS SHOT IS STAYING DOWN AND CENTERED RIGHT THROUGH IMPACT, SO THAT YOU CAN REALLY "CHASE" THE CLUBHEAD DOWN THE SLOPE AND OUT AFTER THE BALL BEFORE YOUR BODY BEGINS TO LIFT OR FALL FORWARD.

1219

And Avoid Body Sway on Uphill Lie

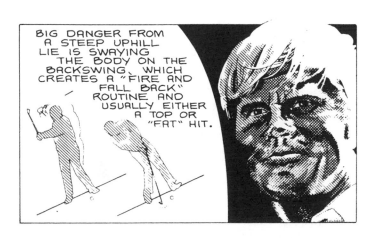

BIG DANGER FROM A STEEP UPHILL LIE IS SWAYING THE BODY ON THE BACKSWING, WHICH CREATES A "FIRE AND FALL BACK" ROUTINE AND USUALLY EITHER A TOP OR "FAT" HIT.

ON THIS SHOT I LIKE TO SET MYSELF WELL BEHIND THE BALL WITH THE LEFT LEG FLEXED AS MUCH AS NECESSARY TO MAINTAIN BALANCE. THEN I TRY TO REDUCE THE TENDENCY TO SWAY BY MINIMIZING MY BODY ACTION AND SWINGING PRIMARILY WITH MY HANDS AND ARMS. IT HELPS, TOO, TO LET THE CLUB FOLLOW THE GENERAL CONTOUR OF THE SLOPE BOTH BACK AND THROUGH.

9-23

Play Cut Shot from Hardpan

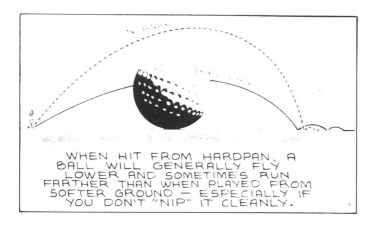

WHEN HIT FROM HARDPAN, A BALL WILL GENERALLY FLY LOWER AND SOMETIMES RUN FARTHER THAN WHEN PLAYED FROM SOFTER GROUND — ESPECIALLY IF YOU DON'T "NIP" IT CLEANLY.

TO OVERCOME THIS I WILL OFTEN TAKE ONE CLUB MORE THAN NORMAL, CHOKE DOWN A LITTLE, OPEN THE CLUBFACE, AIM LEFT, AND PLAY AN INTENTIONAL CUT SHOT.

PRACTICING THIS TECHNIQUE WILL PAY OFF IF YOU PLAY A LOT ON DRY COURSES.

BUT BE SURE NOT TO TRY TO "SWEEP" THE BALL AWAY — HIT SLIGHTLY DOWN AND FIRMLY THROUGH.

Try Bunker Technique from Loose Material

So LONG AS THE LIE IS CLEAN, A BALL SITTING ON TWIGS, LEAVES, PINE NEEDLES OR OTHER LOOSE MATERIAL WILL USUALLY BEHAVE MUCH AS IT DOES FROM THE FAIRWAY ON FULL SHOTS, SO SWING NORMALLY.

Around THE GREEN, LOOSE MATERIALS REACT PRETTY MUCH LIKE SOFT SAND WHEN THE BALL IS HIT WITH ANYTHING LESS THAN FULL FORCE, SO CONSIDER PLAYING A BUNKER-TYPE SHOT.

IN BOTH CASES, YOU WILL MINIMIZE THE RISK OF INCURRING A PENALTY FOR MOVING THE BALL IF YOU AVOID GROUNDING THE CLUB AT ADDRESS.

Punch Ball from Divot Mark

FIRST THINGS **NOT** TO DO WHEN CONFRONTED WITH A BALL IN A DIVOT MARK ARE FUME OR PANIC.

NEITHER ONE IS CONDUCIVE TO A GOOD RECOVERY STROKE.

SAFEST APPROACH TO THIS "RUB OF THE GREEN" IS A **PUNCH** SHOT. GO DOWN AT LEAST ONE AND POSSIBLY TWO CLUBS (7 TO A 6 OR 5, FOR EXAMPLE); PLAY THE BALL BACK MORE TOWARDS THE RIGHT FOOT; USE A THREE-QUARTER SWING PICKING THE CLUB UP SHARPLY STARTING BACK; AND SWING SHARPLY DOWN INTO THE BALL WITHOUT LETTING YOUR WRISTS ROLL OVER UNTIL WELL AFTER IMPACT.

ALLOW FOR A LOW TRAJECTORY AND LOTS OF RUN.

"Feel" Swing Length When Restricted

KEY TO PLAYING ANY SHOT WITH A RESTRICTED BACKSWING IS TO MAKE PLENTY OF "MEASURING" PRACTICE SWINGS TO GET THE FEEL OF THE ABBREVIATED STROKE.

ONCE YOU'VE GOT A SENSE OF HOW FAR YOU CAN LET THE CLUB SWING BACK, FORGET THE OBSTACLE THAT'S RESTRICTING YOU AND CONCENTRATE ON WATCHING THE BALL CLOSELY AND STRIKING IT CLEANLY.

Make It Easier for Yourself

IT'S TRUE THAT THE PROS CAN SOMETIMES BEST CONTROL RECOVERY SHOTS FROM LIGHT OR MEDIUM ROUGH WITH THE LONGER IRONS, ESPECIALLY THOSE PLAYERS WHO NATURALLY SWING ON A FAIRLY UPRIGHT PLANE.

FOR AVERAGE GOLFERS, HOWEVER, THE BEST BETS FROM ALMOST ANY TYPE OF ROUGH ARE THE WELL-LOFTED WOODEN CLUBS, SIMPLY BECAUSE THEIR ROUNDED SOLES CUT THROUGH LONG GRASS A LOT MORE EASILY THAN THE STRAIGHT LEADING EDGES OF LONG IRONS.

Get Distance from Rough Like This . . .

FORCED TO GO FOR MAXIMUM DISTANCE FROM A TOUGH LIE IN THE ROUGH?

YOU'LL ALWAYS BE GAMBLING HEAVILY ON SUCH A SHOT, BUT IF YOU'RE IN A **DO-OR-DIE** SITUATION THEN TRY THIS TECHNIQUE.

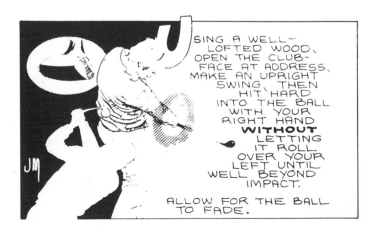

USING A WELL-LOFTED WOOD, OPEN THE CLUB-FACE AT ADDRESS, MAKE AN UPRIGHT SWING, THEN HIT HARD INTO THE BALL WITH YOUR RIGHT HAND **WITHOUT** LETTING IT ROLL OVER YOUR LEFT UNTIL WELL BEYOND IMPACT.

ALLOW FOR THE BALL TO FADE.

. . . or Like This

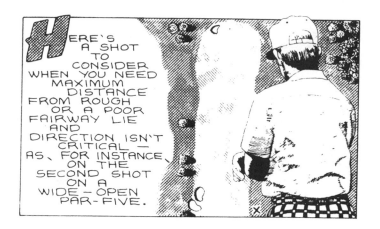

HERE'S A SHOT TO CONSIDER WHEN YOU NEED MAXIMUM DISTANCE FROM ROUGH OR A POOR FAIRWAY LIE AND DIRECTION ISN'T CRITICAL — AS, FOR INSTANCE, ON THE SECOND SHOT ON A WIDE-OPEN PAR-FIVE.

TRY **PUNCHING** THE BALL INSTEAD OF SWEEPING IT AWAY. HIT SHARPLY DOWN ON IT HARD WITH YOUR **RIGHT HAND**, AND WATCH IT SQUIRT FORWARD LOW AND FAST AND RUN A MILE ON LANDING.

THIS IS NOT AN ELEGANT STROKE, BUT IT CAN BE A VERY USEFUL ONE AT TIMES.

Don't Panic Over a Sandy Lie

DON'T PANIC ANY TIME YOU ENCOUNTER A SANDY LIE IN THE ROUGH, EVEN THOUGH THE LIE MAY LOOK FRIGHTENINGLY TIGHT.

TRY THE FOLLOWING TECHNIQUE, ESPECIALLY WHEN THE SAND IS FIRM.

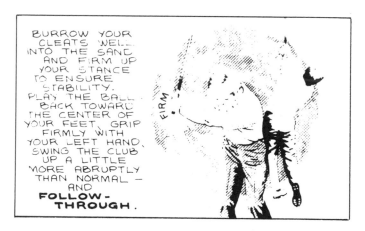

BURROW YOUR CLEATS WELL INTO THE SAND AND FIRM UP YOUR STANCE TO ENSURE STABILITY. PLAY THE BALL BACK TOWARD THE CENTER OF YOUR FEET, GRIP FIRMLY WITH YOUR LEFT HAND, SWING THE CLUB UP A LITTLE MORE ABRUPTLY THAN NORMAL — AND **FOLLOW-THROUGH**.

Take Less Club from a "Flier" Lie

BE AWARE OF WHAT WILL HAPPEN TO THE BALL ANY TIME YOU HIT IT FROM THICK VEGETATION — CLOVER PARTICULARLY AFFECTS A SHOT BECAUSE OF ITS SPIN-REDUCING "GREASINESS."

CONFRONTED WITH A "FLIER" LIE, TAKE ONE LESS CLUB TO COMPENSATE FOR LOWER FLIGHT AND ADDITIONAL RUN. THEN, IN SWINGING, TRY TO HIT **DOWN** MORE WITH YOUR HANDS TO ENSURE YOU GET THE CLUBFACE AS FULLY ONTO THE BACK OF THE BALL AS POSSIBLE.

MOST OF ALL, DON'T EXPECT MIRACLES — PLAY THE SAFE SHOT.

Play Lob Shot for Extra "Stop"

STOPPING THE BALL QUICKLY BY APPLYING HEAVY BACKSPIN FROM ROUGH IS ALWAYS DIFFICULT, AND SOME-TIMES IMPOSSIBLE. GIVEN A LIE WHERE THE BALL SITS FAIRLY WELL ATOP A CUSHION OF GRASS, I DON'T TRY.

INSTEAD, I PLAY A LOB-TYPE SHOT, POSITIONING THE BALL FARTHER FORWARD IN MY STANCE, THEN RELEASING THE CLUBHEAD EARLY FOR A MORE SWEEPING CONTACT WITH THE LOWER BACK PART OF THE BALL. PROPERLY EXECUTED, THE RESULT IS A HIGH, "FLOATING" TYPE SHOT THAT SETTLES QUICKLY EVEN THOUGH IT CARRIES LITTLE BACKSPIN.

Consider Direction of Grass Growth

DIRECTION OF GRASS GROWTH CAN BE A BIG FACTOR IN SHOTS FROM ROUGH.

WHEN THE GRAIN IS LYING AGAINST YOU, TRY TO HIT "UNDER" THE BALL AS MUCH AS POSSIBLE — LIKE YOU WOULD FOR A HIGH SHOT.

USE ONE OR TWO CLUBS MORE THAN NORMAL TO COUNTERACT THE DISTANCE YOU'LL LOSE.

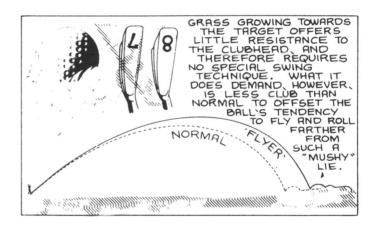

GRASS GROWING TOWARDS THE TARGET OFFERS LITTLE RESISTANCE TO THE CLUBHEAD, AND THEREFORE REQUIRES NO SPECIAL SWING TECHNIQUE. WHAT IT DOES DEMAND, HOWEVER, IS LESS CLUB THAN NORMAL TO OFFSET THE BALL'S TENDENCY TO FLY AND ROLL FARTHER FROM SUCH A "MUSHY" LIE.

NORMAL

"FLYER"

Tee the Ball Higher

YOU'LL FREQUENTLY ENCOUNTER THE NEED FOR EXTRA HEIGHT ON AN IRON SHOT ON A PAR-THREE HOLE — AS, FOR INSTANCE, IN THE SITUATION SHOWN HERE, WHERE THE BALL MUST BE STOPPED VERY QUICKLY.

TEEING THE BALL A LITTLE HIGHER THAN NORMAL CAN HELP YOU GET ADDITIONAL HEIGHT BY PROMOTING A MORE **SWEEPING** ACTION THROUGH IMPACT — ESPECIALLY WITH THE MEDIUM AND LONG IRONS. TRY IT ON THE PRACTICE TEE TO FAMILIARIZE YOURSELF WITH THE EFFECT.

Adjust Thus to Fly High

ONE OF MY GREATEST ASSETS THROUGHOUT MY CAREER HAS BEEN THE ABILITY TO HIT THE BALL HIGH WITH ALL THE CLUBS. THIS IS PARTICULARLY HELPFUL ON LONG APPROACH SHOTS, WHERE BOTH DISTANCE AND STOPPING POWER ARE REQUIRED.

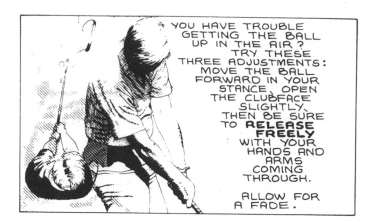

YOU HAVE TROUBLE GETTING THE BALL UP IN THE AIR? TRY THESE THREE ADJUSTMENTS: MOVE THE BALL FORWARD IN YOUR STANCE, OPEN THE CLUBFACE SLIGHTLY, THEN BE SURE TO **RELEASE FREELY** WITH YOUR HANDS AND ARMS COMING THROUGH.

ALLOW FOR A FADE.

Check Your Body Action

HITTING THE BALL TOO LOW WITH YOUR LONG CLUBS?

CHECK FIRST THAT YOUR RIGHT SHOULDER IS DRIVING <u>DOWN AND UNDER</u> YOUR CHIN AS YOU HIT THROUGH, NOT OUT AND AROUND YOUR HEAD.

IF THIS DOESN'T ADD HEIGHT AND CARRY, HAVE SOMEONE CHECK YOUR HEAD AND UPPER BODY MOTION THROUGH THE HITTING AREA.

ANY FORWARD MOVEMENT OF YOUR TOP HALF COMING DOWN AND THROUGH WILL PROMOTE A DELOFTING OF THE CLUBFACE — NOT TO MENTION A HOST OF OTHER FAULTS.

Hit the Ball Lower Like This

TO KEEP THE BALL LOW, I SIMPLY MOVE IT BACK IN RELATION TO MY FEET AT ADDRESS, THEN KEEP MY HANDS LEADING THE CLUBFACE A LITTLE LONGER THAN NORMAL THROUGH IMPACT.

TENDENCY IN PLAYING THIS SHOT IS TO HOOK OR DRAW THE BALL, ESPECIALLY WITH THE STRAIGHTER-FACED CLUBS. SO THE BEST POLICY IS TO ALLOW FOR A LITTLE RIGHT-TO-LEFT CURVE.

43

Combating
Bad Weather

Be Realistic!

MOST GOLFERS RECOGNIZE THAT REALLY BAD WEATHER REQUIRES MODIFICATIONS IN TECHNIQUE, AND TRY TO MAKE THEM TO THE BEST OF THEIR ABILITY.

WHAT MANY DON'T MAKE, HOWEVER, IS A PROPER MENTAL ADJUSTMENT TO THE REALITIES OF SCORING UNDER ROUGH CONDITIONS.

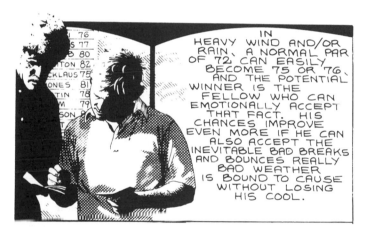

IN HEAVY WIND AND/OR RAIN, A NORMAL PAR OF 72, CAN EASILY BECOME 75 OR 76, AND THE POTENTIAL WINNER IS THE FELLOW WHO CAN EMOTIONALLY ACCEPT THAT FACT. HIS CHANCES IMPROVE EVEN MORE IF HE CAN ALSO ACCEPT THE INEVITABLE BAD BREAKS AND BOUNCES REALLY BAD WEATHER IS BOUND TO CAUSE WITHOUT LOSING HIS COOL.

Match Flight to Wind Conditions . . .

WHENEVER YOU NEED MAXIMUM DISTANCE HITTING INTO A HEADWIND, TRY TO MOVE THE BALL FROM RIGHT TO LEFT...

NO 15
457 YDS
PAR 4

... IN OTHER WORDS, SET UP AND SWING FOR A DRAW RATHER THAN A STRAIGHT SHOT OR A FADE.

WHY?

ONE REASON IS THAT YOU'LL GET MAXIMUM ROLL FROM THIS TYPE OF FLIGHT.

AN EVEN BETTER REASON IS THAT THE COUNTERCLOCKWISE SIDESPIN YOU IMPART TO THE BALL CAUSES IT TO FLY LOWER, AND THUS MORE "UNDER" THE WIND THAN A STRAIGHT OR FADED SHOT.

. . . and Take Ample Club

IN A BIG WIND THERE'S A NATURAL TENDENCY TO WIDEN THE STANCE TO ESTABLISH FIRMER FOOTING AND BETTER BALANCE. PROBLEM IS THAT THIS REDUCES BODY TURN AND SHORTENS THE BACK-SWING, THUS REDUCING DISTANCE.

THE EASIEST SOLUTION IS SIMPLY TO TAKE ENOUGH CLUB TO OFFSET THE EFFECT OF THE MORE COMPACT SWING. THIS HAS THE ADDITIONAL ADVANTAGE OF KEEPING THE BALL LOW AND THUS LESS AFFECTED BY THE WIND.

Consider Driver from Fairway

WITH A HARD WIND AGAINST OR ACROSS ME, I'LL OFTEN CONSIDER HITTING A DRIVER FROM THE FAIRWAY INSTEAD OF A THREE-WOOD, TO REDUCE THE CHANCE OF THE BALL "BALLOONING" AND SO BEING HELD SHORT AND BLOWN OFF LINE.

A GOOD LIE IS ESSENTIAL, HOWEVER.

THIS IS NEVER AN EASY SHOT, BUT YOU'LL FIND IT CONSIDERABLY LESS DIFFICULT IF YOU CHOKE WELL DOWN ON THE DRIVER GRIP, THEREBY INCREASING YOUR CONTROL AND AT THE SAME TIME ENSURING A LOW AND BORING FLIGHT.

ALSO, SWING **SMOOTHLY** — AND NEVER TRY TO FORCE THE SHOT.

Play Straight in Wet Conditions

THE WETTER THE CONDITIONS, THE TOUGHER IT IS TO DRAW OR FADE SHOTS.

THIS IS DUE TO THE REDUCED AMOUNT OF SIDESPIN THAT CAN BE IMPARTED TO A GOLF BALL WHEN WATER INTERVENES BETWEEN IT AND THE CLUBFACE AT IMPACT.

PROS CALL SHOTS THAT ARE INTENDED TO CURVE INTO THE TARGET BUT DON'T DO SO "SLIDERS" AND THEY CAN BECOME REAL SCORE-WRECKERS IF YOU TRY TO GET TOO FANCY IN WET WEATHER.

BEST STRATEGY IS TO TRY TO HIT THE BALL AS STRAIGHT AS POSSIBLE WITH EVERY CLUB.

Check Your Footing in Mud . . .

AY CAREFUL ATTENTION TO YOUR FOOTING WHEN PLAYING IN WET OR MUDDY CONDITIONS, BECAUSE THE SLIGHTEST SLIP COULD PUT A VERY LARGE NUMBER ON YOUR SCORECARD.

ALWAYS ENSURE, FOR EXAMPLE, THAT YOUR SPIKES ARE CLEAN BEFORE STEPPING UP TO A SHOT.

IN REALLY SLOPPY CONDITIONS IT MIGHT EVEN PAY TO PLAY FROM A MORE FLAT-FOOTED STANCE THAN NORMAL, ESPECIALLY IF YOU ARE A "DANCER." HOWEVER, THIS WILL REDUCE YOUR BODY ACTION AND THUS YOUR DISTANCE, SO BE SURE TO TAKE PLENTY OF EXTRA CLUB.

. . . and Try to ''Pick'' Ball Cleanly

HE MORE CLEANLY YOU CAN "PICK" THE BALL FROM SODDEN OR MUDDY GROUND, THE BETTER YOU WILL PLAY — ESPECIALLY WITH THE LONG AND MEDIUM IRONS.

CHOKING DOWN ON THE CLUB SLIGHTLY WILL PROMOTE A CLEANER STRIKE.

IN REALLY SWAMPY CONDITIONS, IT'S POSSIBLE YOU MIGHT EVEN SINK A LITTLE AS YOU ADDRESS THE BALL, GIVING YOU THE EFFECT OF A SLIGHT SIDEHILL LIE.

CHOKING DOWN ALSO HELPS TO OFFSET THIS VARIATION.

Hit from Water Like a Buried Sand Lie

HE MORE DEEPLY SUBMERGED THE BALL, THE WORSE YOUR CHANCE OF HITTING IT OUT OF THE WATER.

HOWEVER, IF YOU WANT TO TAKE YOUR CHANCE AND DON'T MIND GETTING WET (AND PROBABLY DIRTY), HERE IS THE TECHNIQUE TO TRY.

PLAY THE STROKE LIKE A BURIED SAND LIE USING A 9-IRON OR A PITCHING WEDGE. IN OTHER WORDS, SET THE CLUBFACE SQUARE OR SLIGHTLY CLOSED AT ADDRESS, WITH YOUR HANDS WELL AHEAD OF THE BALL . . . MAKE AN ABRUPT BACKSWING, AND HIT HARD INTO THE WATER TWO OR THREE INCHES BEHIND THE BALL.

CHAPTER NINE

The Short Game

44

Pitching the Ball

Never Scoop!

TRYING TO GET THE BALL AIRBORNE BY SCOOPING UP AT IT WITH THE CLUBHEAD IS A COMMON FAULT OF NOVICE GOLFERS.

IT'S PARTICULARLY EVIDENT — AND DISASTROUS — ON SHORT PITCH AND CHIP SHOTS.

A GOLF BALL MUST BE STRUCK <u>DOWN</u> TO FLY **UP**. ONE SIMPLE WAY TO ENSURE THIS ON SHORT SHOTS IS TO SET THE HANDS AHEAD OF THE CLUBFACE AT <u>ADDRESS</u>, THEN <u>KEEP</u> <u>THEM</u> <u>THERE</u> THROUGHOUT THE STROKE. IF YOUR HANDS NEVER PASS YOUR CLUBFACE UNTIL AFTER IMPACT, IT'S ALMOST IMPOSSIBLE TO SCOOP AT THE BALL.

SO TRY <u>CONSCIOUSLY</u> LEADING WITH YOUR HANDS IF YOU'RE MIS-HITTING A LOT OF SHORT SHOTS.

Beware of Forcing Wedge Shots

WEEKEND PLAYERS MISS A LOT OF WEDGE SHOTS BY TRYING TO FORCE THE CLUB. THE WEDGE IS NOT A DISTANCE WEAPON — IT'S BUILT FOR FINESSING THE BALL.

IF YOU CAN'T GET HOME WITHOUT SWINGING IT FLAT-OUT, TAKE A BIGGER CLUB.

I RARELY TRY TO HIT A WEDGE MORE THAN 100 YARDS, AND NEITHER SHOULD YOU.

SWING THE CLUB **SMOOTHLY** AND WELL WITHIN YOURSELF, CONCENTRATING PARTICULARLY ON FIRM HAND ACTION THROUGH IMPACT.

FIRM

Swing the Club More Crisply

A LOT OF WEDGE SHOTS ARE MISSED AS A RESULT OF OVER-SWINGING GOING BACK, THEN SLOWING DOWN COMING THROUGH THE BALL. THIS IS PARTICULARLY EASY TO DO ON 'PART' SHOTS - ANYTHING REQUIRING LESS THAN YOUR FULL SWING ARC AND FORCE.

ONE WAY TO STRENGTHEN THIS AREA OF YOUR GAME IS TO DEVELOP A CRISPER STROKE BASED ON EXTRA WRIST ACTION. HOLD THE CLUB FIRMLY, KEEP THE BACKSWING AS SHORT AS POSSIBLE, THEN APPLY WHATEVER DEGREE OF EXTRA PUNCH IS REQUIRED WITH YOUR WRIST RELEASE THROUGH IMPACT. PRACTICE THIS 'FEEL' SHOT BEFORE YOU TAKE IT TO THE COURSE.

Set Weight More to the Left

IF YOU HAVE PROBLEMS WITH YOUR WEDGE PLAY, TRY SETTING MORE OF YOUR WEIGHT ON YOUR LEFT FOOT AT ADDRESS AND LEAVING IT THERE DURING THE BACKSWING.

THIS WILL HELP TO FIRM UP YOUR STRIKING ACTION BY CUTTING DOWN ON YOUR BODY MOTION.

EQUALLY IF NOT MORE IMPORTANT, IT WILL ENSURE THAT YOU SWING THE CLUB ON THE ABRUPT ARC NECESSARY TO HIT CRISPLY DOWN AND THROUGH THE BALL.

"Sweep" More from Uphill Lies

PLAYED CORRECTLY, A SHORT PITCH FROM AN UPHILL LIE - A COMMON SHOT ON COURSES WITH ELEVATED GREENS - ISN'T AS TOUGH AS IT LOOKS.

KEY IS TO SET YOURSELF AND SWING SO THAT THE CLUB FOLLOWS THE ANGLE OF THE SLOPE BACK AND THROUGH.

USE A SWEEPING RATHER THAN A PUNCHING ACTION AND THE BALL WILL CLIMB OUT SOFT AND HIGH AND STOP QUICKLY.

HIT A LITTLE HARDER THAN NORMAL TO COMPENSATE FOR THE HIGHER TRAJECTORY.

Use Sand-Wedge from Tough Grass

HIGHER HANDICAP GOLFERS OFTEN HAVE A TENDENCY TO HIT "FAT" ON SHORT PITCH SHOTS, ESPECIALLY FROM TOUGH GRASSES LIKE BERMUDA WHERE IT'S EASY TO "STICK THE CLUB IN THE GROUND."

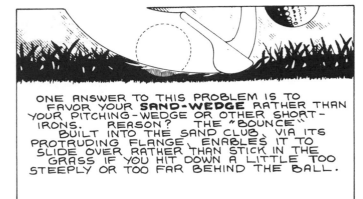

ONE ANSWER TO THIS PROBLEM IS TO FAVOR YOUR **SAND-WEDGE** RATHER THAN YOUR PITCHING-WEDGE OR OTHER SHORT-IRONS. REASON? THE "BOUNCE" BUILT INTO THE SAND CLUB, VIA ITS PROTRUDING FLANGE, ENABLES IT TO SLIDE OVER RATHER THAN STICK IN THE GRASS IF YOU HIT DOWN A LITTLE TOO STEEPLY OR TOO FAR BEHIND THE BALL.

Try These Methods for Half Wedge

HITTING FORCE IS HARD TO JUDGE ON ANY LESS-THAN-FULL SHOT, BUT NEVER MORE SO THAN ON A HALF WEDGE PITCH OF BETWEEN 30 AND 50 YARDS.

YOU CAN PLAY THESE SHOTS BY SWINGING EITHER 1) SHORT AND FIRM, OR 2) FULL AND EASY. TRY BOTH IN PRACTICE TO DETERMINE WHICH TECHNIQUE WORKS BEST FOR YOU.

THE REALLY IMPORTANT THING, ONCE A PREFERRED TECHNIQUE EMERGES, IS TO STICK WITH IT. CONSTANTLY VARYING THE "HOW" MAKES IT DIFFICULT TO GROOVE THE "FEEL" NECESSARY TO HIT THE BALL SPECIFIC DISTANCES WITH LESS THAN A FULL SWING.

45

Bunker Play

First, Get the Ball Out!

IN THIS OR SIMILARLY PROBLEM-ATICAL SAND SITUATIONS, FIX YOUR MIND ON THE FIRST RULE OF BUNKER PLAY BEFORE YOU DRAW THE CLUB BACK: **FIRST, GET THE BALL OUT!**

DECIDE WHICH IS BETTER: BEING FORCED TO ATTEMPT MUCH THE SAME SHOT AGAIN, OR STANDING OVER A LONGISH PUTT AFTER HAVING TAKEN A LESS DIRECT BUT SAFER ROUTE. I CERTAINLY KNOW WHICH I'D PREFER!

Lose Your "Ball Fixation"

MANY HIGH-HANDICAPPERS SUFFER IN SAND TRAPS BECAUSE OF "BALL FIXATION"— THEY CAN'T MAKE THEM-SELVES FOCUS BOTH MIND AND EYE ON HITTING INTO AND THROUGH THE SAND, RATHER THAN AT THE BALL ITSELF.

HERE'S A TIP THAT WILL HELP. ENVISION AN AREA OF SAND ABOUT THREE INCHES WIDE AND EIGHT INCHES LONG OF WHICH THE BALL IS PART. THEN, IN SETTING UP AND PLAYING THE SHOT, FOCUS MENTALLY ON REMOVING THE **ENTIRE OBLONG** OF SAND YOU ARE PICTURING. ACHIEVE THAT AND THERE'S NO WAY THE BALL CAN STAY IN THE BUNKER!

Set Up Slicing Action This Way

HERE'S A TIP THAT MIGHT TAKE MUCH OF THE TERROR OUT OF BUNKER SHOTS EXPERIENCED BY SO MANY BEGINNERS AND "RABBITS."

AT LEAST IT SHOULD ENSURE THAT YOU GET THE BALL OUT OF THE SAND IN ONE SHOT.

AT ADDRESS, SET-UP OPEN (AIMED LEFT) OF WHERE YOU WANT THE BALL TO FINISH. THEN OPEN THE CLUBFACE - ALIGN IT TO THE RIGHT OF THE TARGET AN EQUIVALENT AMOUNT.

YOU'VE NOW ESTABLISHED A SLICING ACTION OF THE CLUBHEAD THAT WILL EASILY REMOVE THE BALL IF YOU SIMPLY SWING NORMALLY AND HIT **SMOOTHLY** THROUGH THE SAND **BEHIND** IT.

Execute Sand Shots Purposefully

BUNKERED BESIDE THE GREEN?

USE YOUR SAND WEDGE, OPEN THE CLUBFACE, AIM A LITTLE LEFT OF TARGET, COCK YOUR WRISTS QUICKLY GOING BACK, THEN HIT FIRMLY THROUGH THE SAND UNDER THE BALL WITH YOUR RIGHT HAND.

DO THOSE FIVE THINGS GUARANTEE A SUCCESSFUL RECOVERY SHOT?

THE ANSWER IS YES, **ONLY** IF YOU HAVE SUFFICIENTLY OVERCOME ANY INHERENT FEAR OF SAND. YOU MAY HAVE TO EXECUTE THEM **PURPOSEFULLY**. FOR MOST GOLFERS THAT WILL REQUIRE ACTUALLY PRACTICING THESE TECHNIQUES FOR A WHILE.

Think and Act in Slow Motion

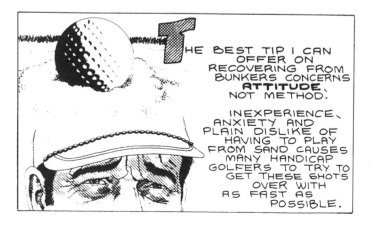

THE BEST TIP I CAN OFFER ON RECOVERING FROM BUNKERS CONCERNS **ATTITUDE**, NOT METHOD.

INEXPERIENCE, ANXIETY AND PLAIN DISLIKE OF HAVING TO PLAY FROM SAND CAUSES MANY HANDICAP GOLFERS TO TRY TO GET THESE SHOTS OVER WITH AS FAST AS POSSIBLE.

THE RESULT IS THAT, IN RUSHING THE SHOT, THEY OFTEN COMPOUND THE ERROR BY LEAVING THE BALL IN THE BUNKER OR SKULLING IT OVER THE GREEN. IF THAT'S YOU, **SLOW DOWN**. STUDY THE LIE OF THE BALL AND THE GREEN, AND TAKE THE TIME TO FIGURE OUT WHAT YOU CAN REALISTICALLY HOPE TO ACHIEVE IN TERMS OF A RECOVERY. THEN **TAKE YOUR TIME** IN GETTING SET AND SWINGING. TRY TO THINK AND ACT ALMOST IN SLOW MOTION.

Use Different Arcs for Different Lies

HE VERY ABRUPT ARC YOU SEE HERE IS USEFUL WHEN YOU HAVE TO "KNIFE" THE CLUB DOWN HARD UNDER A BALL BURIED IN SAND. COMBINE IT WITH A SQUARE CLUBFACE AND A VERY FIRM HIT.

HOWEVER, FOR A NORMAL EXPLOSION SHOT FROM A GOOD LIE, I PREFER THE MORE FLAT-BOTTOMED ARC THAT COMES FROM A NORMAL SWING, FIRST TO AVOID HITTING TOO CLOSE TO THE BALL, AND SECOND TO INSURE AGAINST TAKING TOO MUCH SAND.

KEEP THE CLUBFACE OPEN THROUGH IMPACT AND SWING SMOOTHLY.

Try for Distance Like This

LONG SHOTS FROM BUNKERS ARE ALWAYS TOUGH. HERE ARE THREE TIPS THAT WILL MAKE THEM EASIER.

FIRST, CHOKE DOWN ON WHATEVER CLUB YOU SELECT TO COMPENSATE FOR STANDING NEARER TO THE BALL AS A RESULT OF DIGGING YOUR FEET INTO THE SAND.

SECOND, TAKE A FULL PRACTICE SWING TO MAKE SURE THAT YOUR FEET REALLY ARE FIRMLY PLANTED.

THIRD, REDUCE THE CHANCE OF MEETING SAND BEFORE BALL BY LOOKING AND AIMING AT THE TOP RATHER THAN THE BACK OF THE BALL.

46

On the Green

Work Thus to Improve Your Putting

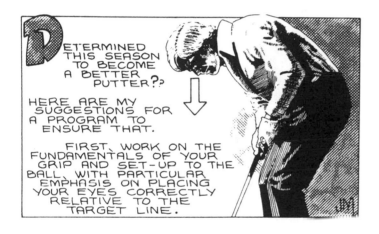

DETERMINED THIS SEASON TO BECOME A BETTER PUTTER??

HERE ARE MY SUGGESTIONS FOR A PROGRAM TO ENSURE THAT.

FIRST, WORK ON THE FUNDAMENTALS OF YOUR GRIP AND SET-UP TO THE BALL, WITH PARTICULAR EMPHASIS ON PLACING YOUR EYES CORRECTLY RELATIVE TO THE TARGET LINE.

NEXT, WORK ON THE STROKE ITSELF, CONCENTRATING ON SMOOTHNESS AND ON MEETING THE BALL CONSISTENTLY ON THE PUTTER'S SWEET SPOT. FINALLY, WORK ON JUDGING SPEED AND BREAK BY PRACTICING REGULARLY AND ON AS MANY DIFFERENT TYPES OF GREENS AS POSSIBLE.

Take Time for a Proper Survey

THE WAY MANY AMATEURS STEP UP AND HIT LONG PUTTS AFTER ONLY A CURSORY GLANCE AT THE LINE SOMETIMES MAKES YOU THINK THEY ENJOY THREE-PUTTING!

WET AND DRY SPOTS, CHANGING GRAIN DIRECTION AND SLOPE, VARYING GRASS THICKNESS — ALL WILL AFFECT THE BALL'S COURSE AND SPEED.

SO TAKE A FEW MOMENTS TO TAKE A GOOD LOOK AROUND — PREFERABLY WHILE YOUR PLAYING COMPANIONS ARE DOING THEIR OWN SURVEYING.

Check Your Eye Alignment

PERHAPS THE MOST IMPORTANT SINGLE FACTOR IN PUTTING FOR MOST GOLFERS IS THEIR EYE-LINE IN RELATION TO THE BALL.

IF YOUR EYES ARE OUT BEYOND THE BALL, YOU'LL TEND TO PULL PUTTS TO THE LEFT, AND IF THEY'RE INSIDE THE LINE YOU'LL TEND TO PUSH PUTTS TO THE RIGHT.

SO IT'S WORTH PERIODICALLY CHECKING YOUR EYE ALIGNMENT.

TO DO SO, ASSUME YOUR USUAL PUTTING SET-UP WHILE HOLDING A SPARE BALL IN YOUR TEETH, THEN TAKE ONE HAND FROM THE CLUB AND WITH IT DROP THE SPARE BALL STRAIGHT DOWN FROM THE BRIDGE OF YOUR NOSE. ADJUST YOUR EYE-LINE ACCORDING TO WHERE THE BALL LANDS.

Tuck Right Elbow at Address

VERY SMALL THINGS CAN MAKE VERY LARGE DIFFERENCES IN PUTTING, AND A CASE IN POINT IN MY GAME IS THE RIGHT **ELBOW**.

IF IT CREEPS AWAY FROM MY SIDE, I'LL TEND TO CLOSE THE FACE OF THE PUTTER AND ALSO SWING ACROSS THE TARGET LINE FROM OUTSIDE-TO-IN.

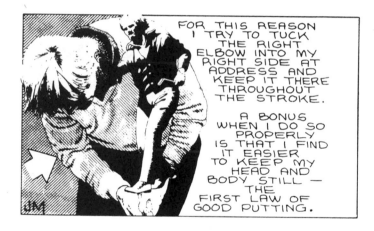

FOR THIS REASON I TRY TO TUCK THE RIGHT ELBOW INTO MY RIGHT SIDE AT ADDRESS AND KEEP IT THERE THROUGHOUT THE STROKE.

A BONUS WHEN I DO SO PROPERLY IS THAT I FIND IT EASIER TO KEEP MY HEAD AND BODY STILL — THE FIRST LAW OF GOOD PUTTING.

And Look to Left Elbow, Also

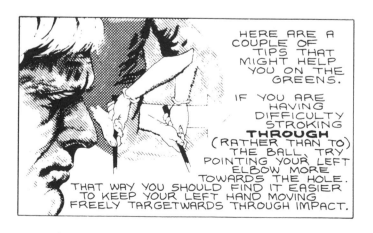

HERE ARE A COUPLE OF TIPS THAT MIGHT HELP YOU ON THE GREENS.

IF YOU ARE HAVING DIFFICULTY STROKING **THROUGH** (RATHER THAN TO) THE BALL, TRY POINTING YOUR LEFT ELBOW MORE TOWARDS THE HOLE. THAT WAY YOU SHOULD FIND IT EASIER TO KEEP YOUR LEFT HAND MOVING FREELY TARGETWARDS THROUGH IMPACT.

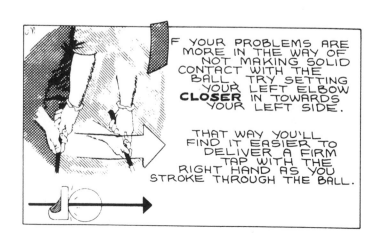

IF YOUR PROBLEMS ARE MORE IN THE WAY OF NOT MAKING SOLID CONTACT WITH THE BALL, TRY SETTING YOUR LEFT ELBOW **CLOSER** IN TOWARDS YOUR LEFT SIDE.

THAT WAY YOU'LL FIND IT EASIER TO DELIVER A FIRM TAP WITH THE RIGHT HAND AS YOU STROKE THROUGH THE BALL.

Check Putter Alignment at Address

ANYTIME THE BALL ISN'T ROLLING SMOOTHLY OFF THE PUTTER BLADE, CHECK THE ALIGNMENT OF YOUR PUTTER AT ADDRESS.

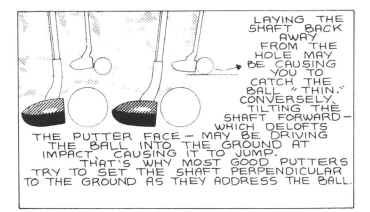

LAYING THE SHAFT BACK AWAY FROM THE HOLE MAY BE CAUSING YOU TO CATCH THE BALL "THIN." CONVERSELY, TILTING THE SHAFT FORWARD — WHICH DELOFTS THE PUTTER FACE — MAY BE DRIVING THE BALL INTO THE GROUND AT IMPACT, CAUSING IT TO JUMP.
THAT'S WHY MOST GOOD PUTTERS TRY TO SET THE SHAFT PERPENDICULAR TO THE GROUND AS THEY ADDRESS THE BALL.

Start Backswing off Forward Press

HAVE DIFFICULTY STARTING THE PUTTERHEAD AWAY FROM THE BALL SMOOTHLY? TENSION IS OFTEN THE PROBLEM, AND ONE WAY TO BREAK IT DOWN IS TO INITIATE THE BACKSWING OFF A SLIGHT FORWARD PRESS.

SIMPLY EASE YOUR WRISTS TOWARDS THE HOLE SLIGHTLY, THEN GO RIGHT INTO THE BACKSWING OFF THIS ACTION.

BUT DON'T OVER-DO THE FORWARD PRESSING MOTION OR YOU'LL OPEN THE FACE OF THE PUTTER.

Accelerate Through the Ball

THERE ARE SCORES OF WAYS TO MISS PUTTS, BUT IN MY BOOK THE MOST FREQUENT ONE IS **DECELERATING** THE CLUBHEAD THROUGH IMPACT. FALLING SHORT IS ONE RESULT, AND MISDIRECTING THE PUTT IS ANOTHER AS A RESULT OF THE PUTTERFACE DEFLECTING FROM SQUARE AS IT SLOWS DOWN.

SO DON'T BE TENTATIVE.

MAKE A FIRM, SMOOTH, CONTROLLED BACKSWING, THEN **ACCELERATE** RIGHT **THROUGH** THE BALL. A GOOD PRACTICE EXERCISE IS TO MAKE SURE THE CLUBHEAD FOLLOWS THROUGH AT LEAST A FOOT ON PUTTS OF SIX FEET OR LESS.

Work on Stroke to Master Speed

GOT THE PUTTING BLUES?

MOST THREE-PUTTS ARE THE RESULT OF LEAVING THE BALL SHORT OR HITTING IT TOO FAR, NOT OF KNOCKING IT WAY WIDE OF THE HOLE.

SO FIRST WORK ON **SPEED**, RATHER THAN ON LINE.

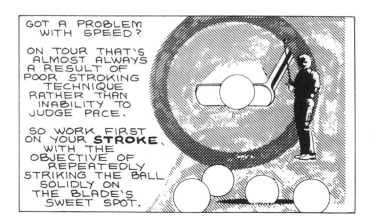

GOT A PROBLEM WITH SPEED?

ON TOUR THAT'S ALMOST ALWAYS A RESULT OF POOR STROKING TECHNIQUE RATHER THAN INABILITY TO JUDGE PACE.

SO WORK FIRST ON YOUR **STROKE**, WITH THE OBJECTIVE OF REPEATEDLY STRIKING THE BALL SOLIDLY ON THE BLADE'S SWEET SPOT.

Go with Your Instincts

GIVEN THE CHOICE, SHOULD YOU PUTT THE BALL OR CHIP IT FROM JUST OFF THE GREEN?

MY ADVICE WOULD BE TO GO WITH YOUR INSTINCTS, BECAUSE THEY PROBABLY REFLECT YOUR CONFIDENCE LEVEL IN THE TWO OPTIONS.

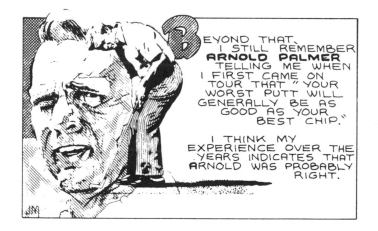

BEYOND THAT, I STILL REMEMBER **ARNOLD PALMER** TELLING ME WHEN I FIRST CAME ON TOUR THAT "YOUR WORST PUTT WILL GENERALLY BE AS GOOD AS YOUR BEST CHIP."

I THINK MY EXPERIENCE OVER THE YEARS INDICATES THAT ARNOLD WAS PROBABLY RIGHT.

Don't Be Too Bold on Downhill Putts

BEWARE OVER-BOLDNESS ON SHORT, BREAKING, DOWNHILL PUTTS.

BY BEING LOWER THAN THE FRONT, THE REAR OF THE CUP OFFERS LESS OF A BACKSTOP THAN ON A LEVEL OR UPHILL PUTT.

MY STRATEGY ON SUCH TESTERS IS USUALLY TO TRY TO 'DIE' THE BALL INTO THE FRONT OF THE HOLE WITH A GENTLE STROKE. GENERALLY I'LL ALLOW FOR A LITTLE MORE BREAK, TOO, TO MATCH THE SLOWER ROLL OF THE BALL.

Learn to "Feel" Speed on Long Putts

A VERY LONG PUTT IS ONE OF GOLF'S TOUGHEST SHOTS.

HOW WELL YOU PLAY IT DEPENDS CHIEFLY ON HOW WELL YOU CAN MENTALLY "FEEL" THE SPEED YOU NEED TO IMPART TO THE BALL.

I'VE FOUND THAT STANDING A LITTLE TALLER OR MORE UPRIGHT OVER THE BALL AT ADDRESS HELPS ME IN SENSING SPEED, PROBABLY BY GIVING ME A BETTER VIEW OF THE DISTANCE TO BE COVERED.

ALSO, STANDING TALLER PROMOTES A FREER AND MORE FLUID STROKE.

Putt to More Than Cup Itself

DON'T BE TOO "HOLE-CONSCIOUS" ON VERY LONG PUTTS.

YOU MIGHT OCCASIONALLY MAKE A 40- OR 50-FOOTER, BUT ACTUALLY TRYING TO DO SO ALL THE TIME IS UNREALISTIC — AND CAN DEFINITELY LEAD TO THREE-PUTTING.

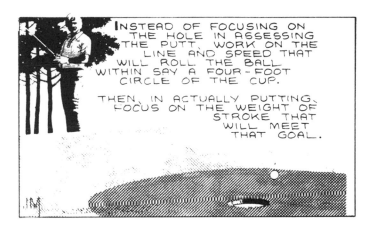

INSTEAD OF FOCUSING ON THE HOLE IN ASSESSING THE PUTT, WORK ON THE LINE AND SPEED THAT WILL ROLL THE BALL WITHIN SAY A FOUR-FOOT CIRCLE OF THE CUP.

THEN, IN ACTUALLY PUTTING, FOCUS ON THE WEIGHT OF STROKE THAT WILL MEET THAT GOAL.

Check Grass Around Hole Late in Day

THE LATER IN THE DAY YOU PLAY, ESPECIALLY IN CONDITIONS WHEN GRASS GROWTH IS SLOW, THE MORE CLOSELY YOU SHOULD EXAMINE THE AREA AROUND THE HOLE ON ALL LONG PUTTS.

HEAVY WEAR WILL USUALLY CAUSE THE BALL TO TRAVEL FASTER AND BREAK MORE AT THE END OF ITS JOURNEY, SO MAKE SPECIAL ALLOWANCES FOR THAT — PARTICULARLY ON DOWNHILLERS.

I'D RATHER PUTT FROM SIX FEET **UPHILL** THAN FROM THREE FEET **DOWNHILL** OR **SIDEHILL** ON VERY WORN AND SLICK GREENS.